MORE

ILLUSTRATED BY B. S. BIRO, FSIA

MORE
COUNTRY
TALK

J. H. B. Peel

ROBERT HALE · LONDON

© J. H. B. Peel 1973

First published in Great Britain 1973

ISBN 0 7091 4176 9

Robert Hale & Company
63 Old Brompton Road
London SW 7

Printed in Great Britain by
Willmer Brothers Limited, Birkenhead

Contents

Poetry lifts the veil from the hidden beauties
of the world, and makes familiar objects
to be as if they were not familiar . . .

Shelley

I

A Room with a View

I have always lived in a room with a view. As a small child I looked to the northern fells, and at bedtime was enchanted by the sight of the Scots expresses that sped like glowing castles through the night. As a boy I gazed at Bow Brickhill, a modest height in Buckinghamshire, which to me seemed mountainous. For thirty-five years I lived on a Chiltern hilltop, whence I gazed across a valley to another summit, crowned with beech trees left and right, proffering what James Thomson called "a gaily-chequered, heart-expanding view". Nowadays my desk overlooks one of the steepest combes in Devon, dappled with sheep, palisaded now with leafless trees, at all times serenaded by water music from a stream. Beyond, the arcs of Exmoor glow purple or green according to the season and the weather; and below them shines the Severn Sta.

To some people a room with a view is a luxury; to others, a necessity. If you have lived most of your life among hills, you are never wholly at ease in a flat country. Nothing lower than six hundred feet contents you. When the summits reach a thousand feet, you begin to feel at home. If your everyday view both opens and expands the eye, you become myopic when sitting in a room that is bounded by a garden wall or a row of houses. The ideal vista is not so extensive that its details can never seem familiar, nor so enclosed that a curve in the lane or a gap through the hills cannot stir the imagination to remember what lies beyond. Though it would take the better part of an hour to walk there, you can visualise every bend in the footpath through the woods. When time or the weather dissuade you from venturing out of doors, you need only sit by the window, and allow memory to take you for a stroll. Such a view strikes the happiest balance, perfected by old acquaintance. Siegfried Sassoon achieved it in Kent: "Looked at from our lawn," he wrote, "the Weald was as good a view as anyone could wish to live with. You could run your eyes along more than twenty miles of a low-hilled horizon never more than ten or twelve miles away. The farthest distance had the advantage of being near enough for its details to be, as it were, within recognisable reach." John Ruskin preferred a loftier outlook, for on the hill—or brow, as they call it—at Kirkby Lonsdale in Westmorland, you will find a brass plaque, recording his belief that the view therefrom—across the Lune and thence to Barbon Fell—is among the most beautiful in the kingdom.

Bath Abbey was dubbed "the lantern of England" because of the size and number of its windows. The whole of Britain is lit by windows which in Wordsworth's phrase "add sunshine to daylight by making the happy happier". I remember staying at John o'Groat's, in a room overlooking the last few yards of the northernmost corner of this island. The sky that day burned blue; the Pentland Firth sparkled; and beyond it the island of Stroma was "wearing white for Eastertide", snow having fallen during the night. This was *ultima thule* indeed; the end of our island world. I remember, too, another kind of frontier, near the hamlet of Lingen in Herefordshire, where the old coach road—a steep and narrow lane—toiled uphill and down to Presteigne in Wales. Pausing to rest on the summit, I entered a meadow, and found there an empty farmhouse with a view of Herefordshire and the Hay Bluff, carved like an inland cliff. I wished I could buy that house, and set my desk at one of its wide-eyed windows.

As in some other matters, the biggest is not always the best. Although hill-dwellers will demand a long-range prospect, even a constricted outlook may achieve the variety that never cloys. At Great Missenden, for instance, there is a brick-and-flint cottage whose narrow outlook can seem as cosmic as Blake's grain of sand. The cottage stands behind and a little above the High Street, and is reached by passing under the beams of a venerable archway which joins two houses in the street itself. During September and October the view from that cottage becomes dazzling because its horizon is half-hidden by dahlias and chrysanthemums. Above them you can just glimpse the brick-and-flint backsides of other houses in the street; and since they, too, are flamboyant, the effect resembles an autumnal rainbow.

It was said of the mediaeval Cliffords that they could ride through a large part of Yorkshire and Westmorland without straying from their own land. Landor felt a similar, though less lordly, pride when he surveyed his estate at Llanthony, which he had transformed from barrenness to fertility. Indeed, his handiwork so impressed him that, in a letter to Leigh Hunt, he transcended mere prose:

> Homeward I turn: o'er Hateril's rocks
> I see my trees, I hear my flocks.
> Where alders mourn'd their fruitless bed,
> Ten thousand cedars raise their head . . .

Another literary landscape was enjoyed by Gilbert White, the parson at Selborne in Hampshire, whose parlour overlooked a lawn that ended among trees and flowers, and was dominated by the Hanger. White's outer garden, covering seven acres, was arranged as a series of grass walks, divided by high hedges. In May his favourite path reaped a red harvest from the west: "the sun at setting," he reported, "shines up my great walk."

Some views are so impressive that the beholder claims them *de facto*. Housman, for example, came from Worcestershire, and spent most of his life in London and Cambridge, yet posterity acclaims him as a lad from Shropshire's

> hanging woods and hamlets
> That gaze through orchards down
> On many a windmill turning
> And far-discovered town . . .

Replying to a reader who asked why he had called his book *A Shropshire Lad*, Housman confessed: "I had a sentimental feeling for Shropshire because its hills were our western boundary." Another poet, Elizabeth Barrett Browning, was only four years old when she went to live at Hope End in Herefordshire, yet the view from the mansion so delighted her that in later years she remembered the exact number of trees:

> And five apple trees stand, dropping
> Separate shadows toward the Vale . . .

An intangible bond unites all those many sorts of countryfolk —farmers, housewives, shepherds, artists, fishermen—for whom Sir Arthur Quiller-Couch spoke when he sat at his desk overlooking Fowey harbour in Cornwall: 'My calling ties me to no office, makes me no man's slave, compels me to no action which my soul condemns. It sets me free from town life, which I loathe; and allows me to breathe clean air, to exercise limbs as well as brain, and to wake up each morning to that wide prospect which to my eyes is the dearest on earth."

Teacup in a Storm

You could detest the weather, but to despise it was impossible because the day was too imperious, so twisted and torn that the gale seemed to shriek Edmund Spenser's question: "And is there care in Heaven?" Heaven itself had disappeared. In its place came a whirlwind of clouds which, when they met a hilltop, parted like the waters of the Jordan, and then came together again, and continued their stampede, but not unscathed, for they left behind them their wounded wisps, greyer than Old Man's Beard.

A clump of six oaks on the cliff were as shrill as the sea, and the illusion was heightened when two of them became so entangled that their upper branches creaked like the timbers of a ship. This was winter, scooping-up the relics of autumn—the fallen leaves— whirling them aloft, ten feet above the lane, to scurry like clowns in russet pantaloons and then again like frightened sheep, not holding a straight course but swerving right and left without apparent reason. Crows took-off like overladen aircraft scarcely able to reach the end of a furrow's runway. When at last they did rise they careened, trying every conceivable tack, sometimes toiling into the wind, sometimes sliding away from it, never making much headway. One crow gave up the struggle, and was content to walk home. The clouds meanwhile relieved themselves incontinently, so that the rain seemed not so much to fall as to be driven sideways in bars of horizontal steel, barbed and abrasive on the face. And everything was loud. Telephone wires screeched as though the world were sending news of its own imminent ending. Tarpaulins writhed on hayricks, slapping like a schooner coming into the wind. Segments of corrugated roof banged a tattoo, idiotic as Macbeth's tale, "full of sound and fury, signifying nothing." Somewhere a dustbin lid was bowled hooplike along the lane, pandemonium run amok.

Down by the sea the gusts drowned the waves. When it struck the cliff, each breaker became a waterspout climbing the rungs of an invisible ladder. Falling back, the spray met other waves, and was hurled upward again. Far as the eye could see, black troughs foamed at the mouth, rearing like a herd of stallions. Once or twice a wave was beheaded by the wind. Baulks of timber, too heavy for a man to lift, were being tossed about, lighter than twigs. On the jetty beetleback oilskins flapped against seaboots while fishermen moved warily, gripping an iron rail for lifeline; sometimes running a few paces, sometimes ducking in order to dodge a wave. Every flag flew taut, except for its tip, which quivered. Although she lay under the lee of the jetty, a drifter rose and fell pistonwise, her fenders chaffing the sea wall. Through a chink in the after-hatch a cabin table was visible, and on it a cup of tea that had overspilled in a brown pool. Muffled voices told the story.

"Who the hell put this damned cup . . ."

"I told 'ee five minutes ago, 'tis getting cold."

"Then why the devil . . ."

"And five minutes afore that, I said, if you want any sugar in it you'll have to nip ashore 'cause we've run out."

Everywhere the dinghies tug at their mooring, vicious as mules against a halter. Ominous yet full of faith, the lifeboat, too, flops up and down. Even in harbour she looks small; she will look smaller still if the rockets go up, summoning her to ride that heaving skyline. On days like this the men of few words become even more frugal, for none knows when nor whence distress may call. Anchored in the bay, a Fishery Protection vessel mimes a rocking-horse, her ensign a weathervane pointing nor'ard; her bows a breakwater, smothered in spray. With hands clasped behind his back, the First Lieutenant paces the bridge, now and again taking a sighting to ensure that the anchors have not dragged. "Force Nine," he mutters . . . a reference to the scale of twelve wind-forces that was devised in 1805 by Captain Sir Francis Beaufort, RN, who classified Force Nine as a Strong Gale (the sort which reduces visibility at sea, and removes chimney-pots ashore). John Masefield weathered such storms, climbing aloft while wind whipped the rigging, and

> many a ship,
> Saved by her lucky oil-bags's steady drip,
> Came limping into harbour all forlorn,
> Her boats in matchwood and her bulwarks torn . . .

Village women stoop into the storm, their shawls outstretched behind. If they venture father than next door or the nearest shop, they fling an oilskin over their head, exclaiming: "My dear soul, did 'ee ever know anything like it?" The question is rhetorical because all souls thereabouts know something like it every winter. Shop-doors are slammed by the gale. Grey pavements grow red with earth from the hills. Puddles enter uninvited under the mat . . . cats, also, weary of being rubbed up the wrong way by wind and rain. Sometimes a faint tinkle announces the fall of a window that was insecurely latched. Smoke from chimneys is flattened before it can rise; and away it goes, zig-zagging like lightning. In the quayside shelter a mariner empties his seaboots: "Tis what I do call an indoors day." On the cliff a tractor plies its own lawful occasions, the ploughman swathed in sacking, from which the tail of his dog protrudes. But no gulls haunt the plough today. They have sought calmer pastures inland, where cattle meet the storm stern-first, scrounging shelter from naked hedgerows.

The onset of twilight seems no more than a deepening of day-long gloom. One by one the cottage windows shine like blurred glow-worms, and buoys in the fairway are emeralds and rubies. Through the last of the light you glimpse the yellow oilskin of a mechanic rowing out to check the lifeboat's engine. Grasping the painter, he leaps aboard as his dinghy rises parallel with the gunwhale. Six deft turns, and the rope is secured. Then the masthead lamp goes on, port to starboard, pitch and roll. Remembering a snatch from the Prayer Book, even a mechanised mariner knows that his engines are not a power "at whose commands the winds blow, and lift up the waves of the sea, and who stillest the rage thereof . . ."

Drawing their curtains, the sailors' womenfolk hope for the best as they turn to chuck another log on the fire.

Crossing the Border

I was in two places at once, with one foot in Wales and the other in England. To be precise, I stood astride the border which bisects a bridge over the River Lugg at Presteigne in Radnorshire. And while I stood there I reflected that, despite passports and Customs posts, the national frontiers have become less conspicuous because millions of people now cross them in an aircraft, neither knowing nor caring that a split second has spanned thousands of years of history.

As I never travel by air, I retain an old-fashioned fondness for frontiers, and can find more adventure from crossing a parish boundary than some people find from crossing the equator. Nor is that fondness a fantasy, because the bridge at Presteigne recalls the rise of the Saxons and the fall of the Celts whom they conquered; a conflict which Housman summarised:

> The flag of morn in conqueror's state
> Enters at the English gate;
> The vanquished eve, as night prevails,
> Bleeds upon the road to Wales.

The crossing of that border did not lead me into a morass of memories. On the contrary, it held me where I stood, with both feet planted firmly on the ground of present circumstances. For example, east of the river an English farmer had directed me through a steep field which he called "a stiffish bank"; but east of the river a Welsh botanist was addressing five students in his native language, which to me sounded incomprehensible.

No doubt it is a stirring thing to pass from Russia into China, though for me not more memorable than to cross the Border fence dividing Scotland from England on a wild moor in the Cheviots. There, as at Presteigne, a poet set the old wars to song, mourning the death of many warriors: "The Flowers of the Forest are a' wede away." There, too, the past has bequeathed a present indicative, for on one side of the border an old Northumbrian shepherd remarks wryly on the speed of his collie: "Gurt bitch rins fast an' I rin slaw." On the other side, in accents unmistakably different, a young Roxburghshire forester remarks

B

wryly on last night's celebration: "Yestreen I'd a wee dram, an' I'm no' yet mesel'."

An Englishman marvels that the Stars and Stripes should unite many nationalities, yet his own island contains hundreds of thousands of natives who daily speak what is to him a foreign tongue, the Gaelic and the Welsh. Moreover, while the grandson of a German emigré in New York tends to discard his ancestry, the men of Merionethshire and the Hebrides cherish their national identity. Some, alas, cherish it with arrogant rancour, as though bilingual signposts could erase centuries of political and economic history; others dismiss it with careless ignorance; but a true *modus vivendi* demands mutual tolerance and esteem. Arrogance debases its national anthem into a war cry; courtesy shares Sir Walter Scott's love song:

> Breathes there a man with soul so dead,
> Who never to himself hath said,
> This is my own, my native land.

A generation which flies above national frontiers is unlikely to feel impressed by county borders; yet they, also, have their significance. Gazing at Penrith across the River Eden, a Westmorlander will exclaim: "There's nobbut two counties in't north, and the second on 'em is Cumberland." Sometimes a village street separates two counties, and sometimes the counties observe different licensing laws, so that the taverns on one side of the street close at 10 p.m. while those on the other remain open until 10.30. At about 10.10 you will hear the pitter-patter of large and not always steady feet crossing the road into the next county and another half-hour of mild-and-bitter.

Even the parish boundaries have something to say for themselves. Indeed, they used to seem more important than national frontiers, at least to a wandering beggar, because all parishes were required to support the vagrant within their bounds ... an obligation that was sometimes shirked by chasing him beyond those bounds. In order to make quite certain that a knowledge of its territorial privileges and obligations was handed down from generation to generation, the parish led some of its boys along the boundary, and imprinted landmarks on their memory by imprinting birchmarks on their backside. We still speak of "beating the bounds". In the Scottish lowlands they beat them on horseback, consuming an immense quantity of whisky before, during, and after the ride. Many parish boundaries follow the *agger* of a Roman road. You will find examples along the Watling Street from Dover or *Dubrae* to Wroxeter or *Viroconium*. One Oxfordshire boundary used to bisect a kitchen oven, into which a bound-beating boy was thrust headfirst, the better to remind him if, as an old man, he should be asked to define the boundary. A farmwife in Buckinghamshire once told me that she was delivered of her firstborn in a bedroom which marked the boundary between Prestwood and Great Hampden. Fortunately, the boundary did not cross the bed itself, so there was no doubt as to the parish in which her son had been born. It remains to be seen for how much longer our religious or ecclesiastical parishes will survive. At present, most villagers retain their parish pride, even although few of them even enter their parish church, unless to be baptised, or married, or buried. If, however, more and more countryfolk dislike surrendering their local jurisdiction to distant and pre-dominantly urban councils, then the parish boundary may regain something of its ancient significance, if only as a symbol of self-identity in an anonymous hive.

The parish boundary nearest my own home is as pleasant as any in England. I reach it by descending a 1-in-3 lane to a bridge across a stream. The parish itself has neither shop nor inn, and is so sparsely populated that a farm and two cottages near the bridge create a sociable scene, enhanced by flowers and shrubs beside the water, planted by one of the cottagers. It is restful to lean against the bridge, watching the eddies, hearing the gurgles, sharing the flowers. Gazing up at the hills, a stranger would detect little differences between the two parishes, but a native knows better, for whereas the next parish is intensively farmed, this one is commonly regarded as moorland. Indeed, it was from one of our rectors—his own grandfather—that R. D. Blackmore first learned about the Doones of Exmoor.

Even the longest life is but a brief lesson, and we must close the book while we are still learning to read; yet if a man acquaints himself with his local boundaries he will go some way toward heeding Sir Thomas Browne's advice: "Be not an alien in thine own land."

At the End of the Day

An east wind mocked them while they laid the ashes in the churchyard. The cry of the seagulls mocked them, too, and became all the harder to bear because they knew that it was not mockery—nor even indifference—but sheer ignorance of their grief. When the last rite had been performed, and the final word spoken, the priest stood awhile in the church porch, his cassock flapping on the wind. Then, one by one, the mourners went their ways; some of them still weeping; all oppressed by mystery and sadness.

Nowadays we feel free to discuss many facts of life which our grandparents regarded as unmentionable; but fear and fashion have set a taboo on death. "Don't," we say, "be so depressing." Then, like Canute's counsellors, we bid the waves recede. Nevertheless, the most important fact of life is death. In the presence of mystery all dogmatism is certainly presumptuous and probably fallacious. Neither our reason nor our imagination can produce a satisfactory definition of immortality. The Prayer Book's "communion of saints" is a beautiful concept memorably expressed, but who shall say precisely what it means? Clearly it contradicts A. N. Whitehead's belief that immortality is a matter of no importance ("an irrelevancy", as he put it). "God," declared Dostoievsky, "creates nothing but riddles." The riddle of death has engaged the keenest intellects, and still their verdict is divided. Some primitive people furnish the dead with food and finery; so strong is their conviction that Paradise must be a Heaven on Earth. Many sophisticated people take the opposite view, assuming that Heaven is a delusion. In the country, however, most people believe that the truth may lie between those two extremes. Villagers hold fast to a hope which John Masefield shared with the girl whom he married:

> And may we find, when ended is the page,
> Death but a tavern on our pilgrimage.

What we call a State funeral tends to smother its sorrow beneath a pall of pomp. At its worst it confirms Seneca's belief that the rites of death can seem more distressing than death itself. But when two or three are gathered together in a country church, intimacy consoles sadness, and simplicity draws something of the sting. Faith cannot escape the storms of life, but it does meet them hopefully, and may enable a believer not to create them by his own actions.

It is very moving to observe the fidelity with which some graves are tended. Throughout the year the grass is trimmed, the headstone cleaned; each anniversary brings a posy of remembrance. Death does indeed overwhelm some mourners, as Emily Bronte knew:

> All my life's bliss is in the grave with thee.

Irremediable desolation, however, is exceptional. When Sir Walter Raleigh wrote to console Sir Robert Cecil on the death of his wife, he ended with some words of manly common sense: "Sorrows draw not the dead to life, but the living to death." Like plants, we possess remarkable powers of resilience. Even the oldest widow may have much to live for, since there are many who need her own good example. Is there in all Britain a single village without some mourner who has regained the gifts of humour and courage, and the hope that "God shall wipe away all tears from their eyes"? Lacking that hope—no matter what the Humanists may say—the struggle availeth nought, and is seen to avail nought, and is therefore a callous mockery.

Confronted by death, the salt of the earth often find sweetness in their own good humour, especially when the end was swift and gentle. "Went as he'd wished," says the farmhand, flicking a crumb of sandwich from his black tie. "Just came back from a stroll, sat in his chair, and woke up wherever he is now. Th'old girl's took it hard, though." Then follows the wink that never offends. "But I know Bessy. She's not the one to mope. Come the spring, she'll be in circulation again." True solace practices its own preaching. During the early days of bereavement the village women will keep a kindly eye on any widow or widower who has been left to fend alone. The deeper the country, the greater the response. There are still some families who would stint themselves rather than allow their old folk to die among strangers.

Time, they say, will heal the wound; but that is misleading because bereavement is not a wound; it is an amputation; and the void remains unfilled. Some relatives feel troubled when the face and the voice so soon grow dim; yet their self-rebuke is often unjustified. We were born to live as well as to die; and life itself implants in us an activity whereby life goes on, so that love mellows with our own maturing, and may at last learn to encompass all things.

Whenever I pass a country funeral, I am reminded of a portrait that was famous in its day, though now fallen from favour. It shows an elderly cottager, seated at a table, shortly after the death of his wife. Before him lies an open Bible, and on his face a look of serenity, similar to that which is sometimes seen on the face of the dead. Few people now attain such peace of mind; yet, if they find nothing absurd in that portrait, they have at least accepted the doubt without dismissing the possibility. Moreover, the fact that they do hope for something, is not necessarily a proof that the hope will never be fulfilled. At the end of the day, however—when friends and relatives have rendered all that love can offer—still the cottager must go to his room, alone at last and for the first time in half a century. In that room he must confront what Mary Webb called "the blank wall which rises between the last tremor and the eternal stillness on the beloved's face". He will lack the intellectual's salves and drugs . . . St Augustine's *crede ut intelligas,* Nicholas of Cusa's merging contraries, the iconoclasm of anti-metaphysics. A couple of aspirins may be the only palliative while his tired old brain wrestles to make meaning of mystery. At best he will murmur: "Help thou mine unbelief."

Bereavement occurs every day, every hour; and never so noticeably as in a village, where all are known, and many remembered. Like the elderly cottager, we continue to rack our brains even while we acknowledge that faith is a gift, not a syllogism; perhaps a genetic gift, not an *ad hoc* dispensation. Nevertheless, when the blow does fall, some people find comfort and courage in the most tremendous prophecy ever heard by men: "Be ye faithful unto death, and I will give you a crown of life."

From Father to Son

He is the sort of man to whom you take an instant liking, regardless of who he is or what he is. His voice—leisurely yet confident—causes you to listen for a north country accent, but without ever quite persuading yourself that you have detected it. He is forthright, humorous, and so evidently kindhearted that a stranger may ask how on earth he became managing director. Only lately did I discover that he walks four of the eight miles from his house to his factory. The rest of the journey is completed by a car which meets him at some cross-roads. Nothing except deep snow or domestic drama is allowed to curtail his daily exercise. That, no doubt, is why, at the age of fifty-six, he coaches the works football team, and plays much tennis at his home, the Grange, which he acquired from a family who, having lived in it for three centuries, found themselves taxed out of it, or at any rate out of their ability to employ a gardener and two domestics. The grounds cover twelve acres, and include a swimming pool.

The managing director's father—a robust eighty-two, and still chairman of the board—has his own quarters at the Grange, which have been converted into a self-contained flat. Unlike his son, the father speaks pure West Riding, and is apt to call the vicar "Sir", which makes everyone feel even fonder of him. He takes salt with his porridge, a kipper afterwards, and tea in place of coffee. The Spanish maid-of-all-things has endeared herself to him by the skill with which she makes beef dripping. During his grandchildren's nursery days he would sometimes remind their father: "Thou wast same at that age. Let 'em have another if they want it. 'Tis only a bit o' spongecake." The hall of the Grange contains an embrowned photograph of the chairman's father, taken at the door of the shed wherein he founded the firm. Bearded and bowlered and minus a neck-tie, he is seen displaying a machine whose design and manufacture he conceived, executed, and ultimately exported to many parts of the world.

No matter how you define national greatness, those were the men who fed it, clothed it, transported it, and therefore in part created it. Their achievement forms a long chapter of English history . . . the mediaeval de la Poles, for example, who within three generations climbed from the counting house to a dukedom; then the Newfoundlanders and the East Indiamen; and after them the industrial revolutionaries, the Arkwrights, Telfords, Wedgwoods, Brunels, Nuffields. It is not enough simply to arraign the "dark Satanic mills", judging one era by the yardstick of another. Justice is done only when we have acknowledged the boon as well as the bane. But our tenses are becoming muddled. Let us therefore set the paradigm in true perspective.

The bearded bowler one day had an idea so good that he attended night classes in order not to spoil it. After ten hours' work as foreman he cycled three times each week into a town six miles away, and there he learned whatever he needed to know. He was then forty-two years old, with a wife and five children (the sixth having succumbed to typhus and malnutrition). In due course he put his patent on the market, and soon afterwards leased a derelict factory. Forty years later he died of old age and contentment; and the Methodists buried him. His son (he of the self-contained flat) inherited a villa within half-a-mile of the factory, which by that time was employing thirty men. Having been educated at a grammar school, the son married a policeman's daughter, and sent his own firstborn, the present managing director, to a minor public school in the south. At the time of his wife's death the factory supported three hundred workpeople.

Life at the Grange is graced by the managing director's wife whom he met when, as a Commander's daughter, she was serving with the WRNS in 1939. For several years after their marriage she was joint master of the beagles, and is now unpaid chief of the local Girl Guides, unpaid hospital chauffeur, unpaid church organist, unpaid adviser to the firm's canteen, and—in an equally honorary capacity—president of the Old Folks' Club. The younger of her two boys went to Dartmouth, and is now a Lieutenant-Commander. The elder (a half-Blue) became his father's sales manager. And whenever any member of the family enters or leaves the Grange, they pass beneath that symbol of gratitude and family pride, the photograph of their foreman-founder.

There is no need to paint colours which do not exist. Blackening and whitewashing may be left to propagandists. The historian feels satisfied if he can depict a more or less accurate grey, which is the colour of most human beings and institutions. The managing director and his firm have prospered because four generations of canny and industrious men gave most of their energy to the task of making money. So also did Chaucer's businessman, cantering to Canterbury:

> A merchant was there with a forked beard . . .
> Always reckoning the increase of his winnings.

Four centuries later our literature created another moneymaker, Sir Andrew Freeport, who acquired both a fortune and a knighthood; being, as Steele remarked, "a Merchant of great Eminence in the City of London. A person of indefatigable Industry, strong Reason, and great Experience . . . and will tell you that it is a stupid and barbarous Way to extend Dominions by Arms; for true Power is to be got by Arts and Industry."

Businessmen are by definition professional moneymakers. Some of them never become any else; but not so the people at the Grange, for they have a proper care toward their employees. They move with the times, and are therefore abreast of any event or any attitude which they feel obliged to resist. Veteran members of their staff admit to an oldfashioned loyalty. The firm certainly has an oldfashioned way of dealing with troublemakers. It sacks them. And most of their mates bid good riddance: "No damned steward's going to close this shop. If I've a grouse, I take it straight t'Owd Man. I said to him once, 'There's no need to call a spade a bloody shovel.' So he looked at bowl of his pipe, and then at me, and he said, 'Aye . . . and there's no need to call a bloody shovel a spade.' You can talk with t'Owd Man. Happen you can talk wi' young Mr William, too. They're all reet at t'Grange. Plain speaking, fair dealing, and nowt up their sleeve."

By any standard the managing director is very comfortably off, even although his hard work and anxiety are penalised on behalf of those who prefer nightcaps to night classes. One thing is certain; had he not bought it, the Grange would have run to seed or— worse still—to Allied Developments Ltd (Projects Division). As it is, the previous family has been supplanted by a new one that seems likely to remain there until it grows old.

One of these days the sales manager's son will go to Eton or to Harrow or to Winchester; and *his* son may become a subaltern in the Blues. Yet I like to think that there will still be a Sir Charles or a Mr William presiding with authority over the old-established family business.

With Map and Compass

King Charles II, a travelled monarch, preferred the British climate because (he said) it allows a man to take outdoor exercise on all save five days of the year. Shepherds and other Spartans, however, must defy those inclement exceptions, venturing far afield while the more sheltered villager acknowledges that January really does shorten his journeys, and may make some of them unnecessary. Instead of striding out with John Clare,

> tramping 'neath winter sky
> O'er snow-track paths and rimy stiles,

he follows William Cowper's snug example:

> Now stir the fire, and close the shutters fast.

Then it is that he opens a map, and, like Newton, goes "voyaging through strange seas of thought . . ." and not only through strange seas, because maps unfold the best of both worlds, the known and the unknown. They that have eyes to roam between the lines of a map may derive as much pleasure from recognising an old route as from plotting a new one. Photographs speak for themselves, but maps are a jig-saw whose pieces must be assembled imaginatively, like the black-and-white marks which compose a printed poem. I have such a jig-saw beside me while I write. On it I see the blue tints which signify rivers, lakes, reservoirs, and the sea itself, Britannia's other element. Next I see patches that are as green as the woods they represent; and through them the one-legged footprints denoting bridleways and footpaths. Glancing inland a few miles, I sight those mauve humps which tell me that I am 1,700 feet above the waves (a piece of information which we owe to the Victorian cartographer, J. G. Bartholomew, who first introduced the coloured contours). Sometimes a yellow frontier appears, defending National Parks against many forms of profit-taking. Everywhere are thin lines to indicate how narrow the lane is, how inextricably interwoven with others, how primrosed, how middled with grass, how fond of sheep, of right-angles, of tractors parked lengthwise around an unexpected bend.

Modern British cartography is a by-product of war, having received its impetus from the Jacobite Rising in 1745 when the English army suffered so grievously from a lack of reliable maps that General Wade initiated a limited survey which was interrupted by the American War of Independence, whereafter, in 1783, General Roy surveyed parts of London for his own amusement. A national survey was not begun until, in 1791, the French government suggested a bilateral exercise that would fix the positions of the observatories at Greenwich and Paris. Responsibility for compiling Ordnance Survey maps passed from the War Office to the Commissioners of Works and thence in 1899 to the Board of Agriculture, with whose successor it remains.

Even an experienced map-reader finds it difficult to cram a crooked mile into a straight inch. The best guide on a day's march is a two-and-a-half inch map. That and a compass will obviate hit-or-miss decisions as to which of five sheep tracks is the one that reaches journey's end before darkness has dimmed all hope of a bath and a meal and a bed. Maps on the grand scale uncover many things which lesser maps ignore. On a six-inch map I find my homeland writ so large that I might almost count the stiles in the meadow. There, for example, is Mount Whistle, flaunting its breezy name as though it were a mansion and not a cottage alone on a hill. Higher Hobbs Wood is dotted with so many leafy trees that I am tempted to look for its bluebells, which in summer shine like a sea beneath my window. Far below, in the combe, I see the very shape of Boundy's Cottage (Boundy himself long ago departed this life), and along his lane the Bible Christian Chapel (still alive and preaching).

The act of walking may distort our sense perception. Only when it appears in print does the lie of the land answer its own questions. Are those sheep really grazing on the site of a derelict copper mine? Is the Old Rectory only a mile from the cross roads? Do I hoist myself all those hundreds of feet whenever I follow the gated lane homeward? Can a crow reach the sea so soon? Indubitably: the map says so, giving chapter and verse in rods and poles. It is all very strange, like seeing an X-ray photograph of your own heart. No such close-up was possible in 1625 when John Norden published his pioneering handbook, *An Intended Guyde for the English Travailers.* Travail was certainly a synonym for travel, at any rate north of Nottingham: "I have observed by travaile," Norden reported, "that in these Northerne parts the miles much exceed the miles in the South and Westerne parts of the Kingdome . . ." One wonders whether Norden had ever explored the Kentish tracts of Watling Street whereon the eighteenth-century postmen demanded "overtime" because (they declared) the mileposts were separated by more than 1,760 yards. A contrary state of affairs was caused, at any rate in theory, by George IV, whose fondness for Brighton clashed with protocol, which required the Sovereign to inform his ministers whenever he ventured more than fifty miles from the capital. Brighton being fifty-two miles away, the King caused a couple of milestones to be removed, thus ensuring that he could play truant without flouting convention.

Stevenson said that to arrive safely is less rewarding than to travel hopefully. But what if hope is compelled to spend the night on a mountain, or in a ditch, or at a boarding-house whose bedside text exhorts the sleeper to contemplate the wages of sin? Moonshine is indeed Cupid's ally, yet it cannot enlighten a lost traveller trying to read a crumpled map in a dark wood. Wisdom, on the other hand, never allows unforeseen circumstances to hide its map under a bushel of blackness. Wisdom carries a torch, or at least a box of matches.

Have you ever reached a strange village after dark, and then, next morning, discovered how inadequate were your overnight impressions of it? Something of the same trial-and-error occurs when, from a fireside chair, you scan the map of an unfamiliar region. No matter how closely you plot a course, nor how vividly you imagine a scene, still the countryside will take you by surprise when at last you do explore it. That straight sector of lane is not, after all, perceptibily direct; neither does the blue blob create a true likeness of the lake beside the church. Contours will forewarn you against a gradient, but they cannot reveal the vista from the summit. Even so, maps do maintain old acquaintance, and invite new friendship. They lighten our January darkness by offering a painted version of Milton's springtime prospect:

Tomorrow to fresh woods, and pastures new.

2

The Depth of Winter

We are all cast in a mould of thought, both temporal and tempera-
mental. Genes and generations encircle us. Some people cannot
conceive eternity except as an infinite series of passing moments,
which the philosophers dismiss as a naive delusion. Bertrand
Russell confessed that he never could wholly span the gulf between
classical and quantum physics. So with the winter; no matter how
profound our knowledge of plants and animals, we instinctively
regard the dark months as a time of death ... and then we double
the self-deception by speaking of the death of winter. It follows
therefore that when the dead season does die, we greet its heir as
a sign of life, forgetful that if winter really had been stillborn it
could not have propagated spring.

To say that in February the land awakes is a poetic, but scarcely
a precise, statement, because the leaves that will unfold in April
have remained wideawake since they were begotten in September.
The snowdrops bloom like tapers for Candlemas, and every
countryman has seen a shepherd's purse flowering on New Year's
Day. As for our fauna, only three or four species practise hibernation; the others either grin and bear it or, like a squirrel, indulge
siestas, from which they awake in order to feed themselves. True
hibernation, by contrast, seldom stirs, for that would defeat its
purpose, which is to reduce the need for nourishment by reducing
the activity that consumes nourishment. In climates colder than
our own, the marmot undergoes remarkable changes during hibernation; the pulse rate drops from eighty to four per minute; the
body temperature drops from ninety-seven to four degrees
Fahrenheit; and instead of breathing twenty-five times a minute,

the sleeper breathes once every five minutes (and may continue so to live for nearly seven months). Winter, in short, is neither a resurrection nor a re-awakening; it is a germination, and its dynamics may be likened to those of a novelist who, having despaired of ever again flowering, discovers that a stray idea, apparently forgotten, was all the while at work within him, waiting upon those events which act as the catalysts of activity. When Dickens was asked to describe the genesis of his most famous character, he replied: "I thought of Mr Pickwick." . . . which suggests that Sam's master had leaped alive from the novelist's unconscious mind. In other artists the idea lies dormant for years; stirring, perhaps, and then again receding, so that a decade may separate conception from publication. Just so, the blackbird's song recedes, and then announces itself tentatively, and then awhile falls dumb, to re-emerge perfected. Yet we continue to equate winter with death, spring with life; and our habit is so stubborn that the first breath of spring will cause us to glance backward, wondering whether we really were alive during winter. It is idle, in such mood, to recall the tingling walk, the dawn-pink snow, the fireside night. A snatch of thrush-song or a glint of grass persuades us that the past six months were somehow less alive than the coming twenty-four weeks. The illusion is understandable because half a year has passed since we stacked the garden chairs, moth-balled the swimsuits, discarded the sun glasses. Light is a synonym for life, but darkness belongs to the tomb, at any rate in human imagination. The first days of February tax our patience, for it is then that the depth of winter seems both unfathomable and everlasting. Even the Highland Scot, born to a sun-starved climate, shares Christina Rosetti's *eithe genoimeen*:

> Gone were but the Winter,
> Come were but the Spring,
> I would go to a covert,
> Where the birds sing.

Persons of riper years find that the winter too closely resembles their own season. Few men possess the good fortune and equable foresight which inspired Ronsard's last words: "So do I go from my own place as satiated with the glory of this world as I am hungry and longing for that of God." Another wise man, Joseph Addison, declared: "Human life turns upon the same Principles and Passions in all Ages." Does it? Glancing at the headlines, or listening to the news, we may feel inclined to dismiss Addison as out-of-date. With timeless attitudes tumbling about us, and strange manners in places high and low, we remember Mirabeau's announcement that the French Revolution was about to breed a new society: *"Novo ordo rerum nascitur."* Mirabeau was right; a new society did arise; and with it the guillotine and a young artilleryman named Bonaparte. Myself, I back the best of the old ways to outline the worst of the new, especially in February, when many small calendars tell a hopeful time of year. Like old friends, those calendars are more welcome than any novelty; and the less they change, the better we like them; catkins, for example, the wayside "kittens' tails" . . . has any countryman ever cried: "Same old blasted catkins again"? Or the thrush, singing from a wind-bent bush . . . has any countryman ever cried: "Can't it find a new tune for a change"? Or the snowdrop and the crocus, shining like good luck among woods, around gardens, beside lanes . . . are they in some way less relevant to the human situation than is the latest crime that has been committed in the name of liberty, equality, fraternity? Or the lambs' beseeching sound; or the blackbirds on bare boughs, unaware of our electronic Bartoks; the lengthening light that allows a pre-supper session with the flower beds; a primrose opening its yellow parasol . . . has anything new been said of those things, these past thousand years? Will anything new be said, these next thousand years, unless by science?

Some countryfolk would like to hunt six days a week, and spend the seventh in their saddle room; yet they are only a small handful, and few of them really do prefer February to May. Spring, after all, is more colourful than winter, more melodious, warmer, drier, gayer. It invites us out of doors, and cheers us while we work within. If we are ill, we tend to feel better; if well, we notice a similar improvement. There is everywhere an expectancy; not the hushed sort—the autumnal lull before a wintry storm—but the bustling kind, for the birds are mating, the sap is stirring, and every countryman shares the foresight of Katherine Tynan:

> In the dark of the year,
> Turning the earth so chill,
> I look to the day of cheer,
> Primrose and daffodil . . .

C

A Person in the Village

At the little Devon town of Bampton, on the edge of Exmoor, they still recall Old Bart Davey *alias* Rev. Bartholomew Davey who was vicar of that parish from the reign of George III to the reign of Queen Victoria, a span of fifty-five years. Himself the son of a Devon parson, Bartholomew Davey received the classical West Country education at Blundells, whence he graduated at Balliol College, Oxford. Having (as we say) looked around, the young vicar chose to marry an heiress, Jane, one of the Govetts of Tiverton. As a result, he was able to live in modest style, at a house larger than the parsonage, where he brewed ale for distribution to the poor (a fact which explains why they frequently called upon him, to enquire after his health). There is a family tradition that Mrs Bartholomew Davey did not care for the colour of her husband's Oxford gown, wherefore she sent him to graduate *ad eundem* at King's College, Cambridge. The college books confirm the degree, but omit its motive.

If you study Bampton parish register you will decide that the vicar served his flock faithfully. If moreover you delve otherwhere—among hearsay and newspapers—you will discover that, besides being a high Tory who rode to hounds, Davey liked to watch cock fighting. In his age he went blind, yet could preach a homespun sermon, and knew much of the Liturgy by heart. I feel an especial interest in Parson Davey; partly because he was my great-great-grandfather, and partly because, like the dodo, his line is now extinct. The last of that line, Sabine Baring-Gould, died in 1924, in his ninetieth year. He was the "squarson"—that is, both squire and parson—of Lew Trenchard in Devon. His biographer said of him: "in his mind, in his manor, and in his parish he had kingdoms which he was content to rule absolutely ..."

Dr Johnson believed that biographies ought to be rewritten every century, so that new knowledge and a fresh assessment might redress the balance. Yet there was a time—a long time, from the sixteenth to the twentieth century—when the biography of an English country parson seemed as perdurable as a standard work. Not until the end of the Edwardian era did the parson cease to live up to his name of *persona* or an important person in the village, second only to the squire. That ascent had been slow, for the average individual priest was certainly poor and probably plebeian: *sicut populus, sicut sacerdos.* Like the majority of his sheep, he lived in a hovel. Not for him the monastic scholarship which became the source and the citadel of European culture until the eve of the Renaissance. Chaucer etched the best type of priest, poor in earthly possessions, yet enriched by pious thoughts and good deeds:

> . . . a povre Person of a town
> Yet riche he was in holy thoght and work.

Such a pastor kept watch over his flock, defending them against a covetous neighbour or an unjust lord. It was Becket, not Henry II, who won the battle of Canterbury. Many an English village witnessed its own Canossa when the priest defied a despot "What-so he were of heigh or lowe estate". Then came the rumpus of right and wrong which we call the Reformation, setting a new status for the parson, who, although he continued poor, ceased somewhat to be of the people. Thus, one of the Caroline rectors of an obscure Wiltshire parish was the poet George Herbert, kinsman to the Earl of Pembroke. Certainly a priest of the new Church of England could do more than gabble a Latin Mass. Several of the Cambridge Platonists were country parsons; so also for a season were Wycliff, Baxter, Jewel, Latimer Ridley, Andrewes, Juxon, Laud. This social upgrading received a stimulus from the English system of patrimony, which compelled younger sons to seek a livelihood away from their elder brother's acres. When Addison praised "the three great Professions of Divinity, Law, and Physick", he was citing an old-established Establishment.

Fox-hunting deists, political evangelists, revivalist High Churchmen, lovers of latitude . . . all came, and some stayed, while the country parson consolidated his position as *persona.* Yet Barchester was never wholly a diocese of placemen. Even the lax Augustan era produced good shepherds: witness Parson Woodforde's Diary, and Goldsmith's *Vicar of Wakefield.* Nevertheless, the crest of that Anglican wave rode parallel with a rising tide of nonconformity which was less a religious than a political gesture whereby the cottage snubbed the manor. John Wesley, the founder of Methodism, lived and died as a priest of the English

Church; yet most of his followers were farmhands and small shopkeepers, to whom theology seemed less relevant than radicalism.

Many Anglican clergymen have now ceased to be any kind of *persona* at all. They are unknown outside their congregation. They earn less than the village grocer. Their opening hours have been taken over by the brewers, unofficially and without compensation. The causes of that decline and fall were not wholly secular, for the Thirty-Nine Articles have proved almost as erosive as the ninety-five theses which Luther unleashed from Wittenburg. But that is by the way.

Historians may yet discover that the Church of England "as by law established" did not soon lose the allegiance of religious Englishmen. It was a priest of the Roman Church, Cardinal Newman, who wrote: "how is it that men, when left to themselves, fall into such various forms of religion, except that there are various types of mind among them, very distinct from each other?" Some temperaments are attuned to high ritual; others, to plainness, mysticism, fundamentalism, middle-of-the-roadery. The English Church contains them all. No other Christian denomination offers so much to so many. Not Rome itself has a cannier understanding of human nature. Insight decreed and continues to obey the opening sentence of *The Book of Common Prayer*: "It hath been the wisdom of the Church of England, ever since the first compiling of her Publick Liturgy, to keep the mean between the two extremes . . ." To keep the mean, however, is not the same as to co-opt every deviation from it. One thing is certain: the English country parson will seem even less personable if his own Church decides to become a Revised Version for the use of those who have hitherto declined to conform with it. All Protestants are at liberty to worship in any Christian church. What more is required . . . unless it be corporate suicide in the waters of ecumenical dilution?

D'Ye Ken John Peel?

They stood in little groups at the foot of the mountain while the Master chided an errant hound. This was John Peel's happy hunting ground, the Blencathra country, though a southron might have supposed that the foxhounds were beagles, because only three horsemen appeared, and they all dismounted when the field moved off. In these rocky mountains two feet are nimbler than four, so the fox is chased on foot, and the clothes fit the terrain. A Shire pack, indeed, would blink at the black-booted, raincoated, trilby-type followers. A spit-and-polished Whaddon Chaser might even need an interpreter when the shepherd remarks to his employer: "Maister, happen owd veexen's in't yon slack. Wullie Thwaite's bairn heered eet afower soon-oop." Meanwhile, a duffle-and-gumboot damsel plunges across the beck, followed by an oil-skinned cleric who, prophetic as Savonarola, points heavenward, knowing that those rifts of blue sky are but the vain gewgaws of the

> spurious spring
> That comes in February to astound
> And, against reason, make our hearts alive.

Eastward the craggy pinnacles of Cumberland and Westmorland flash their answer to the sun; westward they are rinsed with rain; and rainward the field moves off, onamatapeically; slosh, splash, squelch, ooze. Presently hounds speak, and the Lakeland terriers let-go their own shrill salvo, all echoing John Gay's halloo:

> The morning wakes, the huntsman sounds,
> At once rush forth the joyful hounds.
> They seek the wood with eager pace,
> Through bush, through brier, explore the chase.

Like a shepherd, the huntsman can recognise his charges. Unlike a shepherd he can name them: "Magistrate!" he will shout, or "Saxifrage" or "Samuel". So long ago as 1781 Peter Beckford's *Thoughts on Hunting* suggested some names for hounds ... Alfred, Agile, Bowler, Woodman. Nowadays a hound's name usually begins with the first letter of the names of its sire and dam. Thus the litter of Alfred out of Beauty might be called Able, Absalom, Abinger, Abbess, Abraham. Sometimes a hound is called Jones or perhaps Johnson; and if you, too, bear either of those names the effect can be startling, especially when a huntsman abjures Johnson or Jones to "get up with the pack, you bloody old bastard!"

After half-an-hour the gum-booted damsel beings to tire, but the oilskinned cleric soldiers on, for he has indeed waited upon the lord, and now mounts up, unwearied as an eagle, perpetually renewing his strength. Non-hunting foxhunters—of whom I am one—feel no great interest in the chase *per se*, though they know that hunting as at present conducted is less gruesome than the wayward wounds inflicted by distant marksmen defending their flocks against a ruthless predator.

After about an hour, having reached a height from which a

large part of England is visible, I usually take leave of the pack, allowing it to press on, while I eat and drink and am merry. If the weather turns foul I return to base and bath. If—as does sometimes happen—the weather holds fair, I roam so far and wide that my return coincides with the hunters, who have been known to applaud my stamina after an especially arduous run. As a rule, however, the weather is neither fair nor foul, but a blend of both, fanfared by those faraway sounds "that would waken the dead, or the fox from his lair in the morning".

John Peel himself lived at Caldbeck, a village whose inhabitants coined a proud saying: "Caldbeck and Caldbeck fells are worth the rest of England." The name Peel, of course, is a north country one. Some holders of it were famous, like Sir Robert Peel, the second baronet, who became Prime Minister and the first man ever to take a Double First at Oxford. John Peel, by contrast, was content to remain a yeoman and to marry a yeoman's daughter, Mary White, of the neighbouring hamlet of Uldale, where you can still see her old home. Since the four parents disapproved the match, Miss White one night jumped from her bedroom window into the arms of her fiancé who, mounted on his father's best horse, galloped across the Border to Gretna Green, whose farrier joined the runaways at the anvil. Tradition says that Mr and Mrs Peel senior had indulged a similar nocturnal elopement. Wishing to make the best of what they still regarded as a bad job, the two families persuaded the young couple to be married decently by the parson at Caldbeck church. On my last sojourn at Caldbeck I was invited to wear a "coat so gray", of the sort which is called 'hodden', an ancient Scottish word, meaning a mixture of undyed fleeces. Although the garment was a century old, it felt warm and weatherproof.

For more than half a century John Peel kept a pack of hounds, so that his fame needed no other spur in a land of foxhunters. He became a legend while he lived; a typical Cumbrian estatesman who thought little of riding ten miles to a meet, then walking and trotting twenty when he arrived, and another ten, in darkness, to his farm. He died in 1854, and was buried near the church door at Caldbeck, there to be visited by so many pilgrims that the years have worn a path beside his grave. Peel's fame rests as much on a song as on his prowess as a hunter; and during an earlier visit to Caldbeck I sat in the room where the words of that song were composed by John Woodcock Graves, at a cottage facing the inn. Graves himself described how he set to work in Peel's presence while snow beat against the windowpane; "We sat by the fireside hunting over again many a good run, and recalling the feats of each particular hound, or narrow breakneck scapes when a flaxen-haired daughter of mine came in, saying, 'Father, what do they say to what Granny sings?' Granny was singing my eldest son with a very old rant called 'Bonnie Annie'. The pen and ink for hunting appointments being on the table, the idea of writing a song for this old air forced itself upon me, and thus was produced impromptu, 'D'ye Ken John Peel with his coat so gray?' " Those words might never have migrated beyond the Border counties had not their tune lifted them thither; not the tune which Granny sang, but a more polished air, the work of William Metcalfe, who sang in the choir at Carlisle Cathedral. In 1868 Metcalfe chanced to hear Graves' song being sung to that "very old rant called 'Bonnie Annie' ". Admiring the words, but finding much amiss in the music, Metcalfe improved the latter to its present form, which became the march of the Border Regiment, and is known throughout the world. Yet the final word lies with Graves, for when he had finished the verses, he sang them to John Peel, "who smiled through a stream of tears which fell down his manly cheeks; and I well remember saying to him in a joking style, 'By Jove, Peel, you'll be sung when we're both run to earth.' " And he was, and he is, and he will be.

Leap in the dark

The day was so cheerless that not even good news could have brightened it. Glancing at the mist-hidden mountains, I remembered Crashaw's poem, "On a foule Morning, being then to take a journey":

> Where art thou, Sol, while thus the blind fold Day
> Staggers out of the East, loses her way
> Stumbling on night?

The uneventful air declined to answer; not one whiff of it touched my cheek. The mist seemed to have drugged all activity. Sheep had ceased to bleat, birds had ceased to fly, dogs had ceased to bark. Meanwhile I plodded on, uphill and down, through country-side grey as a battleship in twilight. And whenever I reflected that my journey had been undertaken for pleasure, I overheard the voice of Rimbaud, plumbing the depths of his own stupidity: "*De profundis Dominie, suis-je bête!*"

At the cross-roads, being uncertain which way to turn, I found myself reading the signpost, though I knew all its names by heart.

Down the four lanes I gazed, unable to decide which of them looked the dreariest. "Oh well," I muttered, "it doesn't much matter anyway." So I chose any way, the way to Cwman. But not even that uneventful decision fulfilled itself, because I soon wandered from the lane, up into the clouds, following a track to Maesllan, the farm that had first set me to plough, all those years ago. Were there six gates on the track, or seven, or nine? "You've forgotten," I said, as though to deepen the gloom. That there were four gates I proved by opening and shutting them, but at the fifth a ewe dodged through, so I spent several minutes failing to catch her, and ended up at the third gate.

Even before setting out I had been a good way from anywhere, but by this time I was a bad way from anywhere because the light, if you could call it that, began to dwindle, and my boots sprang a leak, and I suddenly remembered that at the third gate there was a misleading path which, unless it were detected and shunned, led straight to Moussorgsky's Night on the Bare Mountain. Had I followed that deceptive path? A ruined farmhouse reminded me that I had not. As though to console its own melancholy, the place produced the first event of an uneventful day . . . one snowdrop in the rubble, braving a February fog. Still reluctant to feel cheered, I uttered the sort of sound that we mean when we write "Brrrh!" However, it becomes difficult to remain morose unless your temperament is congenitally sullen, so I went down-hill at a brisker pace despite the boulders and a stream that set my rubber soles flapping with every footstep. In darkening mist I sat down to make-and-mend, or so I thought, until examination showed that I was wearing the wrong boots, a decrepit gardening pair, instead of a hale walking pair. The leather soles, in fact, were as tattered as the rubber. After three more miles the rubbers came adrift, and lay like jetsam in the mud, revealing my toes, dismal as ten picaninnies who had migrated to the chilling murk of a Welsh month. Proceeding at reduced speed, I reckoned that I would arrive fifty minutes too late for the tea which I had promised myself with friends. Then the leather soles gave way, and after them the heels, so that I came very near to not liking February, nor the dog, nor myself, nor Wales, nor anything to do with Wales. Indeed, such was my ill-temper, I would at that moment have applauded even the most piffling dispraise of Cymru . . . such, for example, as Beatrix Potter's complaint: "the Welsh railways are past description . . . When mushrooms are in season the guard gets out to pick them."

Presently a slight easing of muscular tension told me that I had at last reached level ground. Sure enough, the semi-lane became a minor road; and after half-a-mile I sighted the flicker of firelight through a farmhouse window, and willow patterns on a white tablecloth, and from the brown tea-pot a wisp of aromatic steam, and from the kitchen a woman's voice: "Dewi bach, toast is ready."

"But Mam . . ."

"Ready, I say. So leave that old pig till afterwards. And mind you wipe your boots."

If only I spoke Welsh, I thought, I too would wipe my boots, and leave the pig till afterwards, for this was Cardiganshire, a land wherein poets were powerful, and hospitality not yet supplanted by the tourist trade. A weary traveller had only to poke his head round the door, and say:

> *Ni dorson ein crimpa',*
> *Wrth groesi'r sticeila',*
> *Yn dyfod tuag yma—nos heno.*

Though I had no more Welsh than would bid good-morning, I slip-slopped into the byre where Dewi, evidently the grandson, was preparing to leave the pig till afterwards. Suddenly the invisible voice added a postscript: "And Dewi, bring the honey."

"O Rupert Brooke," I murmured; and then I took a leap in the dark by saying aloud *Ni dorson* etc, but in the prose of my own language which, when he heard it, caused Dewi to enter the kitchen: "Mam," I heard him say, "there is an Englishman."

A long pause followed, not raising my hopes. Even the dog turned away, willing me to accept the inevitable. I was about to do so when Mam's voice once again drifted through the dark.

"What's that you say?"

"An Englishman," Dewi repeated.

"Here? On Sunday?" Mam's voice receded. "Tell him we don't need any. We use the Co-op."

"No, no," cried Dewi. "This one has walked, he says, and is wet, and would thank you for a cuppa."

"Is he respectable?"

"Very poor boots, Mam."

"O drat the man!"

My falling hopes fell flat, but revived when Mam herself appeared, as pretty as she had sounded, sixty-five-roses-and-cream, with a pat of golden butter on a plate, and behind her the rainbow of a beechlog fire. She looked down at my boots and then up at my face.

"I have seen you before," she decided.

"Oh?"

"Many years ago."

"You could be right."

"I *am* right." Then she remembered. "Lampeter it was, with the English family from Maesllan."

"Correct," I nodded.

"Dewi bach," the door was opened wide, "bring another plate."

A Song for All Seasons

The rain came in. The wind came in. The smoke came in. Wondering who next would enter uninvited, I began to feel that the house was not mine at all, but a common lodging place, a hilltop hospice for any fugitive from the weather. Since attack is sometimes the surest defence, I left the fugitives in possession while the dog and I dared the winter whence they had escaped. Now all countryfolk enjoy winter, but none enjoys it overmuch. Winter is the most economical of the four seasons; a little goes a long way.

The dog and his master, meanwhile, squelched down the 1-in-3 lane, pursued to port and starboard by two streams bearing a cargo of straw, twigs, leaves, fleece, bracken, mud, and a farmhand's filter-tipped fag-end. At seven hundred feet a wind nipped invisibly between the rain and the mist. At five hundred feet we sighted what appeared to be a sack that had acquired Dunsinane's mobility, and was now strolling along the top of a drystone wall. Presently the sack turned toward us, and then it resembled a wigwam wherein the farmer's face was framed. Like most other people who live in a remote and sparsely populated parish, the farmer and I enjoy our brief encounters, and have sometimes stretched them to cover half-an-hour's discussion of sheep or of ponies or of persons; but on this occasion the bleakness of the day was reflected by the brusqueness of the duologue.

"Rainin' a bit."

"A bit."

"Good-day."

"Good-day."

Returning home via a less dizzy gradient (it is only 1-in-4), the dog and I faced the same sort of spate that had tried to poop us while we were descending, for each stream carved a fairway through the frostbitten surface, and on either side of the lane the bedraggled bracken drooped like sodden toast. At the summit I paused, largely from habit, because most days of the year offer a glimpse of Dartmoor, thirty miles away; but this day of the year revealed only a steaming wraith that might have been a heifer, thirty feet away. Being by trade a poet, I found some consolation from leaning on a gate, and there composing a song, which began:

> Every year, at about this time,
> When the wind veers east, and the catkins sway,
> And the daylong dew is rinsed with rime,
> And the sky forever old and grey . . .

There I stopped, partly because my songs are so old-fashionable that no one nowadays will publish them, but chiefly because my nose was dripping.

When the lane bent left and right I paused again, because clear weather brings the Exmoor peaks so close that you feel you need only stretch an arm in order to stroke them. Once more I saw merely a misty apparition, which I took to be a sheep because it bleated. All round lay the most spectacular landscape in Devon, but everything was shrouded except the lattice-bare hedgerows and a few yards of muck-spread lane. However, the wind began to abate, lapsing from viciousness into sullenness; a vivid contrast with the previous day, when bright sunshine made the snowdrops seem like guests who had outstayed their welcome. Does an Englishman ever cease to be amazed by his own climate? I doubt it. "The wind blew so keen . . . we felt ourselves obliged to seek the covert . . . The trees almost *roared,* and the ground seemed in motion . . .' So wrote Dorothy Wordsworth in her *Journal* on 1st February 1798. Next morning she reported: "a warm pleasant air. The sun shone . . ." Alas, that same evening turned sour:

"The wind rose very high . . . The room smoked so that we were obliged to quit it."

In one of his stupid moods Dr Johnson declared that a man is a fool if he writes without being published and paid. True poets do indeed appreciate payment on publication, but they seldom write solely in the hope of obtaining it. Their motive is deeper and more demanding. They sing because they must. So, once again I leaned on a gate, this time finishing the second stanza:

> Every year, I begin to think,
> "The winter is long. I can bear no more.
> My bones are brittle. The spirits sink
> Like a seaman lost on a loud lee shore."

Somewhere in the gloom two sheep coughed, so uncannily like an asthmatic human being that I whistled the dog, and away we went, into the mist. I knew that we were descending, of course. Memory said so, and the muscles of my legs said so; but the signpost, which ought to have said so, remained invisible until I came within ten yards of it; and then it dripped, mournfully yet without emotion, like a hired mute. Although there was still an hour to go before teatime, the murk had cast a long winter evening throughout the day; another instance of spoiling a good case by overstating it. Buttered toast and a blazing fire are among winter's best boons, but does anyone enjoy having to switch on the light in order to see his luncheon?

There is this to be said for non-publication; it is a great enemy of prolixity. Had Milton assumed that *Paradise Lost* would never be printed, he might have stopped short after the first five thousand lines. I was already ringing the changes on a theme for the third and final stanza of my own poem when I heard something which brought me to a halt, and kept me there, forgetful of the gloomy twilight. Most people would associate the sound with summer, yet it occurs during part of every season. Having heard it—brief though it was, and tentative—I thanked it for completing my song:

> About this time, and every year,
> As the waters close above my head,
> The first bold blackbird brings me cheer,
> And I rise, and revive, and am comforted.

3

On the Brink

The valley preserved an air of privacy, curving among the hills, like a prehistoric riddle. The path from the summit was so steep that you had either to tread warily or to lope lithely, trusting that the hedge at the bottom was strong and not too prickly. Both sides of the valley were plumed by woods whose buds waited on the sun, as though eager to crown the bare slopes with a halo of Chiltern beeches, the pride of Buckinghamshire, and the envy of England. The poet John Davidson praised those beeches in prose: "The Chilterns," he declared, "are famous for their beeches; none are finer than those that grow on this estate [Chequers]. High up on knolls they stand, letting the light hide among their fluted stems. In a bay that runs deep into the hill they throng together on either side, masses and clouds of foliage— a green sea cleft asunder by some enchanter's rod." Looking up at an especially tall tree, I seemed to overhear Alice Meynell's question and answer:

> Whose is the speech
> That moves the voices of this lonely beech?
> Out of the long west did this wild wind come . . .

The slope on this side of the valley was grazed by six Herefords and one horse. I noticed, too, a piglet, which puzzled me until a man appeared who chased the vagrant into the lane with much cursing and squealing. In the end he caught it and carried it home, and for the most of the way the piglet protested *fortissime*. When silence returned I glanced up, and saw sunlight polishing the furrows on the far slope where part of a ploughed field was as tawny as chocolate. In another field someone had lit a bonfire, from which a flame shot out, redder than holly berries.

Few vehicles ever used the lane, so the setting remained peaceful, though in March never silent, for this was the brink of a season as well as of a summit. Birds flitted above hedgerows, buoyed rather than bowed by the responsibilities of parenthood. Whenever the wind veered, I heard a tractor from the invisible end of the valley; and behind me, in the wood, two aspens rubbing noses like horses. All in all, it was a scene of expectancy merging with achievement because the sun waxed while the winter waned. Winter itself might violate that merger; snow and gales might confirm the violation; but nothing could seize spring's inner fortress; that was inviolate, as Swinburne understood:

> I reach my heart out toward the springtime lands,
> I stretch my spirit forth to the fair hours . . .

In the north country, no doubt, a hill farmer would dismiss that prospect as premature. Snow lies late on Carter Bar; in Anglesey a wind retards the grass; in Sutherland they may not harvest till October. Not so among the South Hams of Devon whose lanes are already speckled with violets, studded with primroses, dancing with daffodils. Nevertheless, the whole of Britain echoes to a new time of year; "We've a guid stock o' firewood. I'm thinking I'll no' cut any more" . . . "We'm just away shopping to Barnstaple. I told my husband last night, the birds are singing, I said, and I haven't a thing to wear for spring" . . . 'Oi stopped 'alfway up'ill and oi said to meself, it must be spring, oi said, 'cause oi'm sweating loike a ruddy pig" . . . "Evan Morgan's ewe dropped her twins this morning, and then she went away and came back with a hat-trick. There's productivity!" . . . "Hast ever seen the sun snowing? Nay, lad, nor have I. One o' these days happen they'll get their weather forecast reet."

Wonderful beyond words is spring; literally miraculous or worthy of marvel. It is more than a renaissance. It is an embellishment of life itself. Art alone can express something of the yearning that rises like sap when the catkins fall. Little children hold the secret, and some old people rediscover it, but in most the magic withers, or is stunted by care and the naive worldliness which we call sophistication. Once gone, such innocence never wholly returns. Paul himself lost something to young Saul, even as our poets lost something to their mediaeval masters. Thomas Campion caught the last breath of that spring, and Herrick copied it; whereafter we gobbled the tree of scientific knowledge, and have ever after suffered indigestion.

Spring is lyrical or it is nothing. Spring is rural or it is nothing. Yet most Britons are townsfolk to whom the season reveals only an intermittent glimpse. No brook babbles in Manchester, no lamb frisks through Birmingham, no nightingale sings in Berkeley Square. Never before have so many people been so eager to regain their birthright, their part in the pageant of spring while it unfolds from the daffodils of March to the bluebells in May. Spring is so old that nothing new can now be said about it. Even the mediaeval lyricists were repeating Vergil. And before Vergil, spake the prophets: "For, lo, the winter is past, the rain is over and gone . . . the time of the singing of birds is come . . ." Quiller-Couch was descanting on the centuries when he invoked the warm west wind:

> West wind, awake! and comb
> Our garden, blade from blade—
> We, in our little home,
> Sit unafraid.

Nothing new, then, can be said. Even those who seek ingenious ways of stating that fact find themselves out-dated by their own desire to sound original. But as I stood on the brink, listening to a wren, I felt no need of novelty. It was enough to hear and see what an English poet saw and heard seven centuries ago:

> Between March and April
> When spray beginneth to spring,
> The little bird hath her while
> In her language to sing.

Tips for the Rat Race

Even his wife calls him Ratty. The Inland Revenue probably computes him as a Rodent Officer. By any name he is part of the rural scene, having spent half-a-century in Warwickshire, travelling

D

its lanes, tramping its fields, waging war against rats, mice, rabbits, and moles.

I first met him while I was a guest at a moated Hall whose barns and byres bristled with rodents. Seeing his estate car on the far side of the bridge, I assumed that the man himself was a young technologist, curtly pressed for time. Instead, I found a grey-haired cottager, built like a jockey; so unpressed for time that he liked to lean on a gate, discussing rats, gipsies, budgerigars, crops, the weather, and eccentric neighbours. As for his technology, it consisted of an old tin (containing rat poison) and the mouthpiece of a metal spoon (soldered to three feet of stair rod). If—unlike most people—you use the word 'technology' as it ought to be used, which is to connote, not a lump of lifeless machinery, but an art or a craft, then you will rightly insist that Ratty is indeed a technocrat, steeped in decades of trial and error, of practice and theory, of new ways and old.

Some farmers regard Ratty solely as a part-time employee. Having briefed him, they expect him to go about his business. But the Hall receives him as much for himself as for his mission. So we sat in the kitchen, taking coffee and cake while we discussed Muscovy ducks and moleskin waistcoats (of which more anon, as the man said to his creditors). Then, refreshed and informed, we gumbooted through the mud, exploring sheds, barns, and the moat itself.

"Ah!" Ratty pointed to a nest behind some logs. At once his devil-supping spoon deposited a mound of white powder near the site. He glanced at my hostess: "When I first came here," he reminded her, "you were alive with 'em. I was using this stuff by the hundredweight." Again the spoon fed. "But you've been very good, you have. Not like some people I know. They fill their shed with old papers, old curtains, old apples . . . and then they phone up and say, 'Ratty . . . they've come back.' " He turned to me: "Wouldn't you come back if someone offered a warm house with all mod. cons. and free lunch vouchers?"

Peering and prodding like Sherlock Holmes, the rat catcher recited the rapid life-cycle of his quarry. Thus, the period of gestation among rats is only three weeks. Within a month of birth the young can fend for themselves; ten weeks later they begin to breed; and within thirteen months one pair of rats may compile a family tree of eight hundred-and-eighty children, grandchildren, great-grandchildren, and so forth.

"Ratty," I said, when he had gone the rounds, "I'd like to join you on your next job. Where is it?"

He pointed to a house over the hill, occupied by an elderly spinster: "There's times I think she feeds 'em by hand."

So away we went, among lanes and cottages that Shakespeare may have seen when he played truant or went poaching. Having arrived, we once more plodded through mud while Ratty scanned crannies, holes, and other likely sites. "Mind you," he remarked "this stuff won't kill dogs. Not unless they eat it by the pound." He halted in the doorway of a shed that was littered with old carpets, decaying newsprint, rotting apples. "See what I mean? There's no end to it. And there's no end to vermin either. A female rat—or doe, as we say—she'll conceive again only an hour after she's dropped her litter."

"How many are there in a litter?"

"Seven maybe. Sometimes eight."

"But surely I've seen more than that?"

"You may have seen more, but they weren't all from the same litter 'cause the females have a habit of nestling up together. But what was I saying just now? Ah, yes, about waistcoats. Years ago I'd have given you enough moleskins as a present. But now," he shook his head, "If you was to say to me, 'Ratty, here's twenty quid', I still don't think I could get 'em. It's the labour, you see. The money. Now that waistcoat you were talking about . . . the one your dad gave you . . . hundreds and hundreds of moles had to be skinned to make that. And you don't skin a mole in a minute."

At last we called it a day, having fought a good fight against pests that once ravaged mankind with plague, and would do so again if they were allowed to foul our food and water. It was sentiment, not sanitation, which impelled Coleridge to revere the life of rodents: "They play the very Devil with us " he complained "but it irks me to set a trap. 'Tis as if you said 'Here is a bit of toasted cheese: come little mice! I invite you!' When (O foul breach of hospitality!) I mean to assasinate my too credulous guests. No! I cannot set a trap."

My brief participation in the rat race ended at the pied piper's cottage where we inspected his aviary of prize-winning budgies and afterwards went indoors to meet Mrs Ratty, who not only ran the flower department (a miniature Kew Gardens) but also supplied the wine cellar ("Parsnip, elderberry, cherry, the lot").

Presently I heard a tinkle of glasses, and Mrs Ratty inquired whether I would take a drop.

"One," I replied. "And no more."

She winked at her husband. "Tell him," she said, enigmatically.

Ratty's mouth twitched, crafty as one of his arch-enemies: "We'd a gent here recently who could swallow whisky like it was water. Before he left he took some wine for the stomach. And after that he took some for the road. Fair old Timothy that gent was. Anyway, about an hour later his wife rings up to say he hasn't arrived home. Well, naturally, the missus and me we feel a bit worried, so I goes out to look for him. Three mile down the lane, there he is, parked in his car, snoring like a 'potamus. So I give him a nudge, and when he comes to, he looks up and says, 'Ratty, you old villain, you've sozzled me.' "

Ratty himself regarded his lifelong crusade with gratitude. "I've had a wonderful life," he said. "Always my own master. Always out and about in the open air. Ah, and I used to take the wife and kids with me. Times we've had, I can tell you. Especially when there was plenty of rabbits about. We'd just make a fire, bring out the knives and forks, and take pot-luck. Wet or fine, we always enjoyed ourselves." And again came the glad thanksgiving: "Wonderful life I've had. Wonderful!"

The Winds of March

Straight from the Steppes it came; ruthless, erosive, unlovely. Nothing could escape the biting blast. Some villagers gave up trying to escape, like the baker whenever a customer entered: "Every time that damned door opens I can hear my 'lectric light bill going up." Even the postman—that rubicund all-weatherer—was glad to regain the warmth of his van. Only the shepherd seemed invulnerable, riding a reinless pony while he clasped a new-born lamb in each arm.

Hearing hooves in the yard, the farmer's wife glanced through the kitchen window as the shepherd arrived. "Poor little mites," she murmured, and forthwith practised her own preaching by setting a pan of milk on the stove. Next minute—shawled and shivering—she was in the yard.

"The danged old ewe wouldn't take 'em," the shepherd explained. "Reckon her's joined the woman's liberation movement. All her wants is less work and the right to get fed not doing it."

The farmer's wife weighed the two foundlings in the scales of her hands: "Both seem healthy enough," she decided, "considering they'm twins."

"The boss was lucky, Missus. I just happened to be on the moor when they was dropped. Another hour o' this wind and they'd have been goners. So mind how you handle 'em."

"Handle 'em?" The hausfau looked up at the horsemen. "Thomas Gurney," she said, "You'm getting long in the tooth *and* short of memory."

"Me?"

"Yes, you. Didn't the boss marry his shepherd's daughter?"

"I only meant . . . "

"I know very well what you meant. You and your woman's liberation."

"But . . ."

"But I've handled lambs afore now. Ah, and I've dropped three o' my own. That's more than you'll ever do, Tom Gurney."

Gurney wheeled his pony in retreat.

"And don't 'ee go sneaking away like that."

"I've . . . "

"I've a hot cup o' tea for this weather. So come inside, and get it."

"Women," muttered the shepherd, and then went inside, and got it.

Away on the moor, meanwhile, the doctor's white coupé was bumping along a track which to him seemed endless until at last a wisp of smoke appeared, and after that a chimney pot, and finally the roof and upper storey of a cottage, apparently the last dwelling this side of eternity. An old woman opened the door, her pink-and-white complexion shadowed by anxiety.

In the kitchen a greybeard dozed in an armchair. The doctor turned to the wife: "Why isn't he in bed?"

" 'Cause he won't go."

"In that case, I shall. Back they way I came." Pause. "Did you hear me, Jim?"

"I heard all right," Jim replied. "The trouble is, I don't like what I did hear. 'Tis only a cough."

"Do you want to live to be ninety?"

"I'm damned near that already."

"At the moment, I'd say you were nearer the churchyard."

"Because of an old cough?"

"Because of an old heart. Now open up your shirt."

Five minutes later they were all taking tea and saffron cake while Jim spoke his mind: "Doctor, 'tis a waste o' public money. Seven mile you've come, and seven mile you'll go, just to tell me what I've been telling her these past ten days . . . there ain't nothing wrong with me. And to prove it, I'll sing 'ee the first six verses of . . ." But the second verse was swallowed in coughing.

"Jim," said the doctor, "I'm twenty-eight, and in this sort of weather I take good care never to sit in a draught." He glanced over his shoulder. "Just look at that curtain. The one by the door. It's moving the whole time. Every year this east wind kills hundreds of people who really would live to be ninety if only they'd go to bed and keep warm."

"Oh, very well. And you may as well ring up th'undertaker while you'm at it."

"There's no need to do that. Shall we see you at the darts match?"

"How can 'ee, if I'm in bed?"

"But the match isn't till Saturday week. You've got another eight days."

"In bed? Now look yere, doctor, that's sheer plain murder that is. In fact it's worse . . . it's compulsory athanasia."

Outside, the doctor said: "Make sure he takes that medicine. I'll look in again the day after tomorrow." He held the old woman's pulse while he spoke. "Keep warm, both of you." Then he dropped the wrist gently. "There's no need to start worrying. He's still in good shape. Much better than he was last week. If he's sensible he really will be at the darts match. Oh, and by the way, my wife says will you kindly let her have the recipe for those saffron cakes."

On his way home, in the heart of the moor, the doctor halted because a blue pool had appeared on the ocean of grey cloud. Minute by minute the pool gew larger, edging the greyness farther and farther to the west. With a glance at his wristwatch, the doctor clambered out, opened the boot, took an ash walking stick, and strode through the heather. Sometimes he paused, swivelling his head in order to catch the bleatings that came up from sheltered pastures far below. During one of the pauses he used his stick to scoop a shallow grave for a lamb whose arrival and departure had taken place unnoticed by any human being on earth. "Poor little chap," he said, because he was that sort of man. And then he went on, rejoicing in the life around him, because he was that sort of man also.

Presently he consulted his watch, hesitated, sighed, and returned to the car. By this time the sky had become a willow pattern of blue and white whereon the clouds scudded so swiftly that their mosaic changed even while the doctor watched it assembling. Suddenly it occurred to him that the winds of March were the heralds of spring, as it were "The voice of one crying in the wilderness, Prepare ye the way of the Lord, make his paths straight."

Old Faithfuls

The house keeps itself to itself. Not even the tallest Tom could peep over the encircling walls. Cottagers call in the Manor, but guidebooks usually describe it as the Hall. By whatever name, it stands outside the village, at the end of an avenue of rhododendrons and some copper beeches. Seeing it for the first time, you would probably say: "That's a fine old farm." Closer inspection might revise your verdict: "Or is it a small manor house?" You would certainly feel puzzled by a line of oaks which, although they grow beside cornfields, were surely planted as ornaments of a park.

Like their house, the occupants are reticent. You will never see their photographs in the glossy magazines; no gossip writer ever mentions them; no television camera peers through the keyhole of their privacy. Yet that family lived in that house, and were lords of that manor, five centuries ago. Indeed, their genealogical tree spreads its branches so wide that they encompass a large part of the history of England. There is, for example, a

tradition that the family's earliest members were shepherds during
the reign of Henry II. Toward the end of the fifteenth century they
acquired a grant of arms, served as knights of the shire, and—
having co-opted an earl's daughter by marriage—used her dowry
in order to build the Hall. The earl, alas, allied himself with some
rebels, and was soon afterwards so heavily fined that he felt
obliged to borrow his daughter's dowry; wherefore the family cut
their losses by halving their ground plan. Had the earl *not* meddled

with treason, the Hall would have acquired another wing and a
third storey. By minding their own business and by tending their
own acres the family retained a modest prosperity which was
shared among the retainers, as is proven by a brass in the church,
commemorating one squire who endowed an almshouse "for
nyne poore widowes". In or about the year 1803, when the family
finances were especially precarious, their almshouse collapsed—
fortunately, it was empty—and the rubble went to a builder who
used some of it for roadmaking (the forecourt to a neighbouring
farm is still known as Widows' Walk).

Unlike most of the local gentry, the family adhered to the Old Faith, thereby forgoing all hope of preferment at Court and of prestige in the county. In 1536 one of Thomas Cromwell's Royal Commissioners dined at the Hall, having spent the day in preparing the death warrant of a nearby monastery. It is possible that the family expressed their disapproval of his desecration. We shall never know. But we do know that, on the following Christmas Eve, the Hall received a royal visitation by proxy; in other words, Henry VIII and his *novi hominess* stole the family cattle, felled many of the parkland trees, and exacted crippling fines. For the next three hundred years the family lived as quasi-aliens in their own land; suspected as traitors, reviled as idolators, and for much of the time disbarred from the professions, the universities, or any leadership in public life. Seeking better things in the Roman Catholic colony of Maryland, one of the younger sons served awhile under Sir Walter Raleigh, and it was he who started the family's long association with the Royal Navy, for his loyalty was such that the Queen not only employed him against the Armada but also allowed his family to hear Mass in their own chapel, at a time when popery was a password to prison and the scaffold.

During the '45 a posse of thugs set fire to the stables, having been bribed (it is said) by a London mercer who, like Ahab, coveted a property which he could not buy. Less than half a century later, during the Gordon Riots, three crackpot Baptists tried to shoot the squire, but were either so blind or so drunk that they merely grazed his left thumb. In Queen Victoria's reign, when the last of the anti-Catholic laws was repealed, the family once again sent their sons up to Cambridge, yet the alienation persisted, and was echoed by an English Jesuit, Gerard Manley Hopkins:

> To seem the stranger lies my lot, my life
> Among strangers.

When I last heard of him, the present squire commanded a warship. His younger boy was a midshipman; the elder, a barrister whose legal knowledge may enable him to minimise the fines that are now imposed on families who have maintained an estate for several centuries.

Despite its straitened means, the Hall is so well-esteemed that it confirms the wisdom of Dr Johnson when he said: "Riches do

not gain hearty respect; they only procure external attention."
However, it would be wrong to assume that the family take no
part in local affairs. On the contrary, they are governors of schools
and hospitals. They actively support the Conservative candidate,
the beagles, the British Legion, the Council for the Protection of
Rural England, and all who prefer the Latin to an English missal.
In theory, as an old county family, they know everyone; in practice, and for the same reason, their choice of friends is eclectic.
They avoid pimps, pop singers, and property developers, but are
au fait with O'Rory, an endearingly dissipated pedlar, who once
confessed that he was not bound by the temperance pledge
"because, do you see, I was tight when I signed it, and it's a
terrible thing to be confounded by your own inebriation. The
truth is, I'm anti-pathetic to water. Didn't our blessed Lord
gain great glory by turning the stuff into something drinkable?"

The chapel, of course, is still used, though it no longer main-
tains its own chaplain. The domestic staff—a Spanish widow
and her son—are likewise of the Old Faith; and I believe that
neighbouring RCs sometimes share the services of a visiting priest.
The villagers accept this state of affairs, and are content to remain
non-protesting Protestants. I remember hearing some of them
discuss what the family would do if the Pope should order the
faithful to depose the Queen of England. The casuistry soared so
high above any conceivable reality that even the Presbyterian
grocer concluded by remarking: "Well, I don't suppose the
Pope ever will."

Hilaire Belloc said: "Our civilisation is splitting more and more
into two camps, and what was common to the whole of it is
becoming restricted to the Christian, and will soon be restricted
to the Catholic half." That was a partisan prophecy, yet it may one
day be fulfilled because the minority who still follow the Roman
way of worship may one day become the minority who still
follow the English way of life.

The Hub and the Spokes

Not even in Bond Street had I seen a finer display of window
dressing. Indeed, it was more than window dressing, for the wares
overspilled on to the pavement: coal-scuttles, cheese, underclothes,

grapes, gumboots, candles, carpets, aspirins, transistors, walking sticks, crême-de-menthe, ploughshares, broken biscuits, cloth caps, saddle soap . . . a stocktaker's nightmare, varied as the poet's portrait of Thame Fair:

> Pins and needles, cotton-thread,
> Eiderdowns and featherbed,
> Paper windmills, gaudy ties,
> Sticky strips to snare the flies,
> Paste for searing pimple-spots,
> Evening bows with ready knots,
> Nails and hammer, awl and brace,
> Flannel, worsted, velvet, lace . . .

Where was this embarrassment of riches? In Manchester? No. Norwich? Never. Crawley New Town? Wrong again. It was in the far north of Scotland, a region so thinly sprinkled with shops that many tradesmen describe themselves as General Merchant, thereby assuring the customer that he has not travelled fourteen miles solely in order to buy a box of matches or a loaf of bread. Such enterprising examples of capitalism prove that 'centralisation' has not yet conquered Caithness nor Holy Island nor the Lizard Peninsula. London itself is rightly regarded as the seat of government and the foundation of finance, but people who live a whole day's journey from a sizable town continue to view their own terrain as the hub or centre of things. The capital—whether it be Paris or Pekin—is merely the far end of a long spoke. Centralisation acknowledges that fact, and counters it by means of 'decentralisation'. Once a year, for example, the postman presents me with a Demand for Rates, which I am able to accept equably because the sum scarcely exceeds sixteen pounds. On the back of the Demand I find a postscript from the North Devon Water Board: "Collector will attend at the following places." Among those places are (I quote verbatim) "Rackenford, Church Room" . . . "Rose Ash, Post Office" . . . "Brayford, Mrs Gammins, 2 The Villas". Some of the rendezvous sound especially interesting, as, for instance, "East Wortlington, Stucley Arms Cottage" and "Umberleigh, Collector's car near Auction Field". As all the world knows, the population of Umberleigh exceeds sixty-seven. As for East Wortlington, you will not need to be reminded that it possesses a thatched rectory.

Since my domestic water comes from my own fields, I do not pay the annual rate of twenty-five un-Englished pence; but I do sometimes watch the collector at his vehicular receipt of custom or in one of those private houses which, by happy chance, stand at no great distance from a public one. Some people, however, seem less than grateful to the North Devon Water Board. Handing over his twenty-five pence, a shepherd exclaims: "I do wonder why we bother to pay. There's a bloody great river just across the meadow. And last year it sank my sofa." The riverside consumer glances over his shoulder as a second customer appears: "Now *that* fella certainly don't need to pay. You can see from yere . . . so far as water is concerned he's a total abstainer. He even shaves hisself in beer."

The Mobile Library is another form of de-centralisation, a very curious form whereby ninety-nine people out of a hundred read a man's book without paying him for that privilege. The baker expressed the injustice vividly: "If one o' my loaves could feed ninety-nine customers I'd be out o' business before I opened the shutters." In this part of the world not every book-borrower seeks the companionship of books. One housewife, marooned on the moor, informed me that she had asked the Library to obtain *Cruden's Concordance* and *Life of Hiawatha*. When I remarked on the catholicity of her reading, she replied: "My dear soul, I don't read 'em. I just like having the van up for a chat."

Once or twice each summer I am visited by gipsies who act as carriers along their route, delivering eggs to the Manse or a harrow from the smithy. If I purchase a number of clothes pegs, an attendant dusky girl rewards me with a song, rather like the lady in *Kubla Khan*:

> It was an Abyssian maid,
> And on her dulcimer she played . . .

Instead of "singing of Mount Arbora", however, the maid breaks into "Honey, I'm just mad about Manhattan".

Many country folk are solicited by heirs of the itinerant pedlar. While I was staying at a Welsh farm my hostess opened the door to an Oriental person who had climbed two thousand feet, and forded several streams in doing so. Unslinging his pack, he exclaimed: "Missee, I have pretty carpets, hairbrush, bonbons, razor blades, smash bits, dry batteries . . ." We bought a comb, if

I remember, and then led the pedlar into the kitchen, where, over a cup of tea, he expounded Zen; performed a kind of Indian rope trick; and at the front door smilingly returned the wallet which he had borrowed from his host's hip pocket.

Dwellers in lonely places are liable to be visited by less amiable exponents of de-centralisation. Thus, two men lately knocked at my door, having (as I afterwards learned) parked their stolen bicycles at the foot of the hill. The spokesman wasted no time in sales talk: "Got any hantiques, guv?" Before I could reply, the junior partner uttered a *caveat emptor*: "No junk, mind. Me and my colleague we're coinossers." Even had I possessed one, I would not have revealed the whereabout of a Louis Quinze clock. My suspicion deepened when the spokesman enquired whether anyone was at home at the big house.

"Which big house?" I asked.

"Any big 'ouse, We're not particular."

I shook my head, and began to close the door, a gesture that did not meet with approval.

"Nar wait a minute, guv. All we want to know is . . ."

"Good-day."

Fortunately, the sound of the dog at my heel, and a glimpse of the spurs against the wall, convinced the antiquarians that I was a Philistine and no friend of Chippendale.

A Rosy Prospect

Nothing is so piquant as a rosy prospect. It resembles the fragrance from an empty box of chocolates, and it promises that the box will soon be full. Though it must sometimes fade, the prospect constantly recurs, like pockets of warm air through a valley. It is the most congenial of all fellow travellers; silent without surliness, never obtrusive, yet always at our beck and call. Noah saw it when the dove descended. We see it when the daffodils arise. And having seen, we suppose that the glimpse was a mirage, for March is a teasing month, the season of Wordsworth's celandine

> That shrinks, like many more, from cold and rain;
> And, the first moment that the sun may shine,
> Bright as the sun itself, 'tis out again!

Although the thrush has outworn the rapture of novelty, his song sounds even more pleasurable because the ear is attuned and therefore better able to interpret. Farmers quizzing their meadow are apt to blink, wondering whether they, too, have sighted a mirage; but a second glance confirms that the grass really is greener. Twilight lingers like a child at bedtime, reluctant to say good-night. Indeed, the entire spectrum has mellowed, for whereas the brilliance of a December day was caused by the sun's decline, the sun in March mounts higher, so that it shines rather on to the head than into the eyes. The hard gloss of winter gives way before the pastel shades of spring.

If we seek a formal salutation to the season, we must consult the poets, and especially the mediaeval poets who, weary of salted meat and smoky hearth, prayed for the first wind that should bring warm rain:

> O western wind, when wilt thou blow
> That the small rain down may rain?

March is the month of Mars, that warlike god. Swinburne in Northumberland spoke of "fierce March weather". Sir Walter Scott in Roxburghshire turned the other cheek on "weather boisterous as March." Sir William Watson improvised on the proverb which says that March comes in like a lion: "roaring," he called it, "maned, with rampant claws." Yet he allowed that the beast sometimes changes its spots, "and bleatingly withdraws".

Though we look for it in January, and may have greeted it seventy times, spring takes us half-aware. Despite her country lore, Mary Webb was surprised by certain small calendars in a Shropshire lane:

> I did not think the violets came so soon,
> Yet here are five . . .

When Christina Rosetti walked to Wordsworth's cottage she heard as well as saw the signs: "Lambs athirst for mother's milk." Edward Thomas heard them, too, noting that March gives "twelve hours singing to the bird". Andrew Young watched the March hares going mad "with that serious game of love". J. M. Synge detected a more restful response: "Buds are opening their lips to the South." Thomas Gray became as eager as a bee "to taste the honeyed spring". William Drummond bathed in

spring showers: "The clouds for joy in pearls weep down."
Even while W. H. Davies sheltered from a "stoatlike wind",
he knew that the prospect was not an illusion: "Spring, for very
sure, is born." For G. M. Hopkins the season was beauty's
summum bonum: "Nothing is so beautiful as spring." And the
greatest of them all accepted the rough with the smooth when he
saw the daffodils

> That come before the swallow dares, and take
> The winds of March with beauty.

Poetry, however, is merely a special version of the paean which
every countryman overhears when he talks to a shepherd, or
enters the smithy, or calls at the pub. Though it is older than
Englishry, the salutation utters the latest slang. Says a Devon
postmistress: "Smashing morning, midear." Says a Suffolk
fisherman: "Just the job for drying my nets." Says a Pennine
ploughman: "That owd blackbird mun think 'tis May Day." In
Lucretian phrase, spring is the delight of men and gods, *hominum
divumque voluptas*. The youth of the year overtakes us so gradually
that its progress may seem imperceptible, like a man who cannot
decide whether to get up or to sink back; he opens his eyes, then
thumps his pillow, then looks up again, and then once more sinks
back. Closing the door on leafless trees and frosty stars, we put
away all thought of spring lest our pride and our patience are
mocked. Opening the door next morning—to be greeted by blue
skies and a mild breeze—we put away all thought of winter lest
our patience and pride are confounded. And even while we welcome what is about to come, we mourn what is about to go:
"There'll be no more fires soon. What a relief!" . . . "Soon
there'll be no more fires. What a pity!"

Whether he relies on poetry, or prefers to speak in his own
tone of voice, a countryman longs for the spring, and feels
thankful when at last he receives it. Horace hailed the sun as a
"good captain", imploring it to revive the cold earth: *Lucem
redde tuae, dux bone* . . . But nowadays one must be careful what one
says about the season. In some quarters it is safer to say nothing.
Approving Chaucer's delight in spring, W. H. Hudson emphasised
the danger of expressing a comparable ecstasy: "Is it conceivable,"
he asked, "that any poet of this time could have such a thought,
or having it, would dare to put it into words? If he did, what

a ridiculous, extravagant person he would seem, to be sure."
Behind that 'extravagance' lies William Allingham's yearning:

> Bring back the singing and the scent
> Of meadowlands at dewy prime;
> Oh, bring again my heart's content,
> Thou Spirit of the Summertime!

Spring is the universal tonic and a well-tried panacea. Under
its benign influence tedium becomes contentment; contentment
becomes happiness; happiness becomes happier. Even the
botanist, with his understanding of earth's winter activity, sees
the spring as a phoenix reborn above the ashes of October. To
them "that travail and are heavy laden" the prospect will sometimes lighten their burden, and often brace the courage which
supports it. Spring combines the zest of desire with that peace which
the world cannot give. It is both anticipation and realisation; the
act and the aftermath; and it knows no time, but is itself eternity,
for it resurrects the past, and kindles the present, and remembers
the future. Spring is life's response to life.

4

Laughing in the Wind

On 15th April in the year 1802, William Wordsworth and his sister Dorothy went walking near Grasmere. Having returned home, Dorothy sat down to describe the walk: "When we were in the woods beyond Gowbarrow Park we saw a few daffodils close to the waterside. We fancied that the lake had floated the seeds ashore, and that the little colony had so sprung up. But as we went along there were more and yet more; and at last, under the boughs of the trees, we saw that there was a long belt of them along the shore, about the breadth of a country turnpike road." Many people have admired a fine show of daffodils, but no one has portrayed them more vividly than did Dorothy Wordsworth in her *Journal*: "I never saw daffodils so beautiful. They grew among the mossy stones about and about them; some rested their heads upon those stones as on a pillow for weariness; and the rest tossed and reeled and danced, and seemed as if they verily laughed with the wind . . . they looked so gay, ever glancing, ever changing."

Unlike his sister, Wordsworth did not write when he returned from their walk. On the contrary, he went straight to his book-shelves, seeking something to read: "He brought out," said Dorothy, "a volume of Enfield's *Speaker*, another miscellany, and an odd volume of Congreve's plays." And that was that, or so it seemed. The sister eclipsed the brother, and prose prevailed where poetry dared not tread. Two years later, however, Wordsworth recollected in tranquillity the daffodils which his sister had pressed promptly between the pages of her *Journal*; and having recol-

lected, he reconstructed that waterside walk and the daffodils near Gowbarrow Park:

> Continuous as the stars that shine
> And twinkle on the milky way,
> They stretched in never-ending line
> About the margin of a bay:
> Ten thousand saw I at a glance,
> Tossing their heads in sprightly dance.

The Daffodils belong to the large family of *Amaryllidacea,* and are known to botanists as *Narcissus pseudo-narcissus,* a misleading name for two reasons; first, because it implies some radical difference between daffodils and narcissi; second, because it has no connection with Narcissus, the classical youth who fell in love with his own beauty. As a botanical term *Narcissus* comes from the Greek *narkissos,* meaning numbness, a reference to the druglike effect of some plants. William Turner, the Tudor botanist, had great difficulty in sorting the flower's various names: "When I was taking a holiday in Norfolk," he wrote, "a little girl hardly seven years old met me as I was walking along the road; she was carrying in her right hand a bunch of white flowers; as soon as I saw them I thought to myself those are Narcissi . . . But when I inquired the name no reply was forthcoming. So I asked the folk who lived in the neighbouring cottages and villages, what was the name of the plant. They all answered that it was called '*laus tibi*': I could get no other name from them."

First recorded in 1548, the word "daffodil" is a variant of the Middle English "affodill", whence Asphodel or King's Spear, the flower that was said to greet Persephone's yearly return from Hell to Earth. When Herrick wept to see the early death of "faire daffadils" his Devonshire parishioners still used the old country name, daffodowndilly. The wild daffodil they called a Lent lily, a name that has survived among countryfolk. It seems poetically just that Herrick himself—with two other poets, Homer and Horace—is, so to say, propagated by a variety of daffodil, *Poeticus,* bearing his name; a form of fame which Parnassus shares with certain other immortals, of whom I had never heard until, in an idle moment, I opened a gardening book, and there they stood . . . Mrs Walter T. Mare and Mr C. J.

Backhouse. And behind them loomed a very mixed bag . . . King Alfred the Great, Madame Plemp, Lady M. Boscawen, the Duke of Bedford, the Queen of Spain, and Miss Willmott.

On my part of Exmoor both the wild and the cultivated varieties are as rife as weeds. They nod from the top of high-banked Devonshire lanes. They shine like giant primroses through the wood, and like pools of sunlight under hedges. In churchyards they seem to remember the dead, especially those whose graves are anonymous mounds. Farms and cottages are festooned with daffodils bristling *en masse* from drystone walls, or singly wherever a slither of soil exudes between chinks in the cobbled yard. You could pick the flowers all day, and still the spoliation would be no more than a single thread torn from a yellow carpet. Happily, I have no need to pilfer, because my own acre of England was planted with daffodils that have multiplied for two centuries. I first saw them when I arrived to inspect the property, during one of those springs whose late arrival, followed by precocious warmth, had retarded the snowdrop while speeding the daffodil, so that each wove a white and yellow mosaic in a corner of the orchard, as though to verify Kilvert's rubric: "There is usually one day in the spring when the beauty of everything culminates and strikes one peculiarly, even forcing itself upon one's notice and a presentiment comes that one will never see such loveliness again at least for another year." The loveliness, I felt, ought not to blossom on a deserted air, out of sight of the house, and marooned among nettles. I therefore began to transplant the bulbs; not one by one, but in barrow-loads, pressed down and overflowing. Although the bulbs were mine, and mine the land, I felt as though I were a thief, the more so because—having many other tasks to perform—I worked late, digging by the light of a hurricane lamp, furtive as a body-snatcher in the night. Today those flowers mark the alpha and the omega of my acre; lining the drive, lighting the paths, spanning the orchard, sprinkling the hedgerows, and generally indulging what Masefield called "the never-quiet joy of dancing daffodils".

No British county lacks daffodils. Walking once from Land's End to John o'Groat's, I greeted them as fellow-travellers and guides to our climate. By mid-March they were at their best in Cornwall; by mid-April they were at their best in Cumberland; and on May Day they lit the banks of Loch Ness, confirming

Crashaw's vernal observation: "All things are full of supple moisture."

Adam and Eve

On remote farms in the mountains, and along many suburban streets, an Eastertide motif is provided by the lawn mowers' metallic music. The fruits of their labour—scent, colour, neatness, repose—ought to shame those graceless idlers whose gardens are a wilderness of flowerless soil, of hay-high grass, of weeds, leaves, dustbins, cartons, bottles, cinders, bus tickets, and rusting motor vehicles.

The Book of Genesis, you remember, contains an allegory which states that "God planted a garden eastward in Eden"; that the serpent opened Eve's eyes to the fact that she had no clothes on; that Eve imparted the revelation to Adam; and that "the eyes of them both were opened, and they knew that they were naked; and they sewed fig leaves together, and made themselves aprons". Sometime later, Milton depicted the banished couple as they made their exit from the Garden of Innocence:

> They hand in hand, with wandering steps and slow,
> Through Eden took their solitary way.

Milton, however, saw the bright side of that abysmal Fall. Although Adam and Eve had lost Paradise, they were not utterly downcast when they went in search of an earthly Eden:

> Some natural tears they dropped, but wiped them soon;
> The World was all before them . . .

There is a tradition that Dean Swift chose to be married in a garden; not by a vicar in sunshine, but by a bishop in moonlight. Assuredly it was a garden path which led him up the ladder of preferment, for he became secretary to Sir William Temple, friend of King William II , who often called at Temple's home near Farnham. During one of those visits the King showed young Swift how to sow asparagus in the Dutch fashion, and was so pleased by the pupil's skill that he offered him a commission in the cavalry, which was rather like offering a botanical brevet to Bonaparte.

Swift's contemporary, the poet Shenstone, seems to have been the type of gardener whose zeal becomes obsessive, consuming his income, his leisure, his conversation, his dreams. Having acquired an estate at Halesowen in Worcestershire, Shenstone wasted his patrimony on creating a Lover's Walk, a Vergil's Grove and Grotto, and a maze of temples, arbours, fountains, and naiads. So many sightseers arrived to admire the poet's garden that his neighbours, resenting such intrusion, acted as unofficial guides who, according to Dr Johnson, "took care to defeat the curiosity which they could not suppress, by conducting their visitants perversely to inconvenient points of view, and introducing them at the wrong end of a walk . . . injuries of which Shenstone would heavily complain." Shenstone himself—an aesthetic rather than a practical man—was content, as he put it, to live "embowered in trees, and hardly known to fame". He valued his garden, said Johnson, "merely for its looks; nothing raised his indignation more than to be asked if there were any fishes in his water." Johnson then depicted the obsessive gardener: "Shenstone's house was mean, and he did not improve it; his care was of his grounds. When he came back from his walks, he might find his floors flooded by a shower through the broken roof; but he could spare no money for its reparation."

The doyen among Caroline gardeners was John Evelyn of Sayes Court near Deptford in Kent, which he transformed from a hundred acres of grassland into what he called *Elysium Britannicum* or a British Eden. South of the Court he set two bowling greens, each planted with cypresses, divided by gravel paths, and flanked by fruit-bearing walls. The eastern wall overlooked a Milking Close where cows grazed, shaded by eight walnut trees. Beyond the bowling greens Evelyn set an avenue of limes, three hundred yards long, leading to the main gate. His private garden, westward of the house, was filled with flowers and herbs, and crossed by gravel paths and grass walks. There he kept an aviary and the transparent beehives which caused his fellow-diarist, Samuel Pepys, to remark: "You may see the bees making their honey and combs mighty pleasantly." Nursery and kitchen gardens supplied the Court with flowers and food.

Evelyn's Eden contained a litany of ingenious and ornamental features: the Oval Garden, for instance, planted with evergreens "for birds, private walks, shades, and cabinetts" . . . the Grove, planted with a thousand evergreens and several hundred oak, elms, beeches, ashes, and French walnuts . . . the Promenade, a grassy walk, twenty-one feet wide and a hundred and seventy-six yards long, bordered by codlins and pearmaines . . . a miniature banqueting hall for the children . . . an island summer house surrounded by raspberries, mulberries, and asparagus. Unlike Shenstone, the owner of Sayes Court was both practical and artistic, for he adorned the unfinished manuscript of his garden manual with more than sixty sketches of implements, from rollers and rakes to greenhouses and watering cans. Such blending of theory with practice would have pleased the author of *The Garden*:

> Delicate are the tools of gardener's craft,
> Like a fine woman next a ploughboy set,
> But none more delicate than gloveless hand . . .

Two own a fine garden is not necessarily to be a good gardener. The Augustan magnates—those grandees of horticulture—employed a professional landscaper who, like Capability Brown, re-arranged Eden, in a manner better-suiting his client's aversion from unruly Nature. Hills were brought low; valleys were raised up; elegant bridges were built, to distract attention from the fact that no river ran thereunder.

True gardeners, on the other hand, employ little assistance, or none at all, like Parson Woodforde of Babcary in Somerset: "I have," said his *Diary*, "been very busy all this day in planting my Peas and Beans and Radishes . . ." A year later, in 1765, Woodforde wrote: "I have been busy today in pruning the apple trees in my garden here . . ."

Some gardens are zoological rather than botanical, as Theodore Hook discovered when he visited Captain Marryat in Norfolk: "There were," he remembered, "animals everywhere; calves feeding on the lawn; ponies and a donkey under a clump of larches . . . a jackdaw sat on the shoulder of one of the little girls . . . there were also an aviary, rabbits, pheasants, partridges, cats, dogs . . ." One of the Misses Marryat fondled a pet rat which had just killed a ferret; and the Captain himself was followed by a tame seagull. No suburban garden can vie with Marryat's zoo nor with

Shenstone's sightseers; yet there are many small lawns and many backyards whose colourful neatness illuminates a text which Evelyn borrowed from Genesis when he declared: "As no man can be very miserable that is master of a garden here; so will no man ever be happy who is not sure of a garden hereafter . . . where the first Adam fell, the second rose."

Public Right of Way

"How many miles to Babylon?" That question was both asked and answered by an old English folk song: "Three score and ten." When the weary traveller inquired whether he could get there by candlelight, the song replied: "Yes, if your legs are long." Not even Midsummer Day is long enough for a walker who would cover seventy miles, but in April the lengthening light invites a countryman to bestir himself and limber up. T. S. Eliot, a non-walking Londoner, believed that "April is the cruellest month . . ." Well, any month will seem unkind if you sit indoors, and think it so. Baudelaire himself would have felt better, and therefore have written better, had he gone for a walk more often, and laced his absinthe with castor oil,

From certain kinds of suffering, if nothing can be done to ease them, we must turn away in dumb compassion; but when an easygoing man takes no hard exercise for six months, and insists on going to bed late after meals which his muscles neither request nor require . . . then, I suggest, a spoonful of compulsion ought to be added to his overdose of self-pity. Make him hasten forthwith into the nearest fresh air, there to walk until his legs have stirred his liver without straining his heart. He may not discover that he has travelled to Damascus with dazzling insight; he may fail even to solve whatever personal problem seems to him to be the only one in existence; but he *will* have earned his supper and a good night's rest.

Is there still a nip in the air these April mornings? All the better for walking; nice people do not care to sweat overmuch. Are the young leaves still playing at hide-and seek? All the more reason to find them, as you certainly will, spun like a green haze on sheltered hedgerows. Does the forecast speak of snow? Let it.

April can make fools of us all, and does not gladly suffer weather-
men. Is it fooling them already, parching a soil that begs a drink of
water? Then slacken your speed. Rest beside a stream. And if a
passing busybody chides your idleness, carry the fight into his
own camp, like the militantly pacific shepherd:

> I sit with my feet in a brook;
> If anyone asks me for why,
> I hits him a whack with my crook—
> "It's Sentiment kills me," says I.

Above all, please yourself; *laissez-faire*; make your own rules, and
never fear to prove them by inventing exceptions. Some men
choose to travel in silence. "I cannot see the wit," said Hazlitt, "of
walking and talking at the same time . . ." Not so Coleridge,
who talked himself into ditches, against walls, and across foot-
bridges that were not there. Thoreau, by contrast, composed
while he paced: "the length of his walk" said Stevenson, "made
the length of his writing." Country lanes, green roads, public

footpaths: each invites, and all prosper according as we use them well, or ill, or not at all. Edward Thomas emphasised that lanes, like limbs, need to be exercised:

> The hill road wet with rain
> In the sun would not gleam
> Like a winding stream
> If we trod it not again.

Nor would our footpaths, the envy of the world; with what kindliness and courage were they granted, or wrested, for the benefit of cottagers who had no other beaten track to the church, the inn, the farm, the highroad. There always have been landowners who dispute old rights as meanly as they withold new ones; witness the famous action of Boteler *v* Cecil, when the latter, who had lately been created Earls of Salisbury, were the most powerful family in Hertfordshire, ruling like regents from Hatfield House. One of their neighbours, Sir Francis Boteler, claimed that, in building their house, the Cecils had violated public right of way across the land. Once a year, therefore, he asserted his right by riding up the steps of the north doorway, thence through the inner rooms of the House, and so out via the south door.

Few men, one feels, have ridden their horse through a mansion or indeed through any building that was not a stable. Among the elect was Simon de Montfort, who, on Good Friday, 1264, rode his horse through the nave of Rochester Cathedral, a distance of one hundred yards. According to *Flores Historiarum* the Earl and his rebels so looted and profaned the cathedral that "the holy places were made the stables of horses and filled with the uncleanness of animals and the filth of corpses." Another and more reverent of the elect—I name him with proper diffidence—was the author of these words, who, having been sent by the BBC to ride the Roman Fosse Way from Lincoln to Devon, found himself invited to ride through the White Hart Hotel at Moreton-in-Marsh, along a cobbled pavement that had formerly been an entrance for coaches, but was now part of the dining-room. Guests, rider, and carpets remained unscathed, but the horse was visibly disturbed by its unaccustomed *entr'acte*. I recently revisited the Foss, this time on foot, being curious to learn whether and to what extent it had deteriorated since my previous journey.

Between Cirencester and Bath a sector or two was impeded by fallen trees and the passage of tractors and cattle. Farther west—at Babcary in Somerset—the Way had become an impenetrable coppice. On the whole, however, I was agreeably re-assured. You can still walk for hours, following the footsteps of the Legions along this green and ancient road.

A right of way offers a right of way and of nothing more. It does not convey the land to the public who walk upon it. Trespass is a matter for lawyers, of whom I am not one, but a few facts may help to guide the wayfarer through that legal labyrinth. First, do not be deterred by *Trespassers Will be Prosecuted*. Trespassers will not be prosecuted. Only the Crown can prosecute. Trespass is not a crime; it is a civil offence, for which the offender may be sued by a fellow subject. Second, a landowner can ask trespassers to leave his property; and, if they refuse, he may lawfully eject them by using "reasonable force". Third, the Courts will not usually punish a trespasser who has damaged nothing, stolen nothing, and generally behaved in an orderly manner. In a lifetime of wandering I have seldom met a landowner who objected to my walking through his fields, so long as I neither trampled the crop nor stampeded the stock.

He was a wise walker who first said: "Always follow a foot-path." And Stevenson, too, was wise when, looking back on his own fieldfaring, he declared: "Tomorrow's travel will carry you, body and mind, into some different parish of the infinite."

All over Britain

All over Britain the blackbirds are singing. Imagine, if you can, the total volume of song which at any given moment hovers above this kingdom. Even in translation the mediaeval Welsh of Dafyd ap Gwilym echoes the music:

> This morning, lying couched amid grass,
> In the deep dingle south of LLangywyth's Pass,
> While it was yet neither quite bright nor dark,
> I heard a new and wonderful High Mass.

To the birds, no doubt, their "High Mass" is simply a part

of the busines of living. How fortunate we are, that the necessity of one species becomes the luxury of another. It is as though our tap-room talk were to the birds the very music of the spheres. But, of course, you cannot imagine the total volume of spring song in Britain. You can only sample an infinitesimal fraction of it. To me lately the music came from the banks of the River Nene at Fotheringhay in Northamptonshire, where an ancient church overlooks the site of a castle at which Mary Queen of Scots was executed, "apparalled," said an eyewitness, "in a kinde of joye." While I walked beside the river it seemed that the song kept pace, flying from tree to tree, saying the same unforgettable thing, over and over again. I heard it next day, along a Roman road, Dere Street, near the Scottish border at Chew Green; and soon afterwards on a road in Eire, the home of Patrick Kavanagh who, being himself a poet, claimed kinship with the birds:

> And we are kindred when
> The hill wind shakes
> Sweet song like blossoms on
> The calm green lakes.

And in Herefordshire I heard the song, echoing down the lanes of Stoke Lacy and among Masefield's *vin de pays*:

> A wine of life, from apple and from pear,
> Gushed each September in the orchard there . . .

As though to prove that it was a truly national anthem, the song reached me while I climbed the mountainous tract from Cwmann to Maesllan in Cardiganshire; it led the way to Swyncombe in Oxfordshire; it awaited me at Blakeney in Norfolk; it awoke me at dawn in John o'Groat's; and when I followed the sunset above Dromara in County Down, lo, the song went before, beckoning like a lullaby to bed.

Summoned by that song, villagers end a hibernation which has overslept into March. Sometimes they awake dramatically, as at a certain Hall in the West Country, which from Martinmas until Palm Sunday appears to be unoccupied. No one is seen to enter it, none to depart, except the once-weekly woman who looks-in to make sure that the place is still there. If a stranger ever does pass by he probably remarks: "What a pity that such a lovely old house remains empty." Had he been a native he would have known that, one April morning, the backdoor would creak on its hinges, grazing the flagstones; and out would come an old lady, bent like a hunchback, with a lilac-coloured shawl over her head, and in her left hand a bamboo cane, tipped with a lightweight hoe. Then, without needing to stoop—for her arched spine could bend no further—then the old lady would tip-tap at the weeds, moving more slowly than the snails which she disturbed. Sighting her from a hill, Farmer Crowcombe says to his collie: " 'Tis spring, my lass. Th'old girl's gardening." When he comes along-side the moss-covered wall, Crowcombe switches-off his tractor at a spot where a breach allows him to talk without trespassing.

"Morning, milady."

Milady nods, without turning.

"I see you'm merry and bright again."

Milady utters a sepulchral cough which could be either a denial or an affirmation.

"I do truly love to watch 'ee swishing through they old weeds."

Milady replies with a sharp hiss, directed against a cat that is about to pounce on a nest.

"That frightened 'en!"

This time her ladyship does turn: "I hear," she says, "that it was a good season."

"Foxhounds? Ah, middling good. But I always did say, 'taint never been the same since you gave up the mastership. Reckon you'm the only master as was ever blessed by a bishop."

"Bishop?"

"He drove down here to induct the new rector, and just outside the church gate his car ran over the fox."

"I don't remember."

"But the bishop did. He came up to me afterwards, and he said, 'Who's that woman uses such terrible strong language?'" Crowcombe looks about for his collie: "Ah, well, I must get cracking. Yere, Melody. Hup, girl." He peers over the breach again. "Any time you want anything, milady, just you let me know, and I'll send a man down."

"Thank you, Crowcombe. By the way, how is your little grand-son?"

"My little . . . ? He's walking out."

"Arthur?"

"With the gamekeeper's daughter. They'll be married come Michaelmas."

"Crowcombe, it is time we died."

"Ah, don't 'ee believe it, midear. If only I could 'oist 'ee on an 'orse, you'd be up with the field and . . ."

But the hinge has creaked, the door has closed, and the cat sidles around the wall, waiting to pounce.

Crowcombe turns to his dog: "Poor old girl," he mutters, glancing back at the closed door, as though to emphasise his sympathy. "She's had a lot o' sorrow in her time, Melody. More'n a fair share, if you ask me." He aims a stone at the cat, switches on the engine, and with one hand knocks out his pipe as he bumps home to dinner, whistling like the blackbirds all over Britain.

Evensong

There is an evening as well as a dawn chorus among the birds; and each inspired Edmund Blunden to coin a wise word from two Greek ones, *Ornithopolis* or the city of birds, within whose gates all may hear the music, as in the Golden Age:

> Through trees and chimney-pots the news is told,
> With loud-tongued gossip of an age of gold.

The full evening chorus spans less than twelve weeks. On June 13th, 1802, Dorothy Wordsworth's *Journal* noted an effect of rough weather: "Since Tuesday 8th . . . we have had no Birds singing after the Evening has fairly set in." Down in Hampshire, however, Gilbert White found comfort from "such birds (singing birds strictly so called) as continue in full song till after midsummer". Among those later singers he cited the woodlark ("continues to sing through all the summer and autumn"); the wren ("all the year, hard frost excepted"); and the linnet ("breeds and whistles till August").

There is no single moment at which you can say that the evensong has started; none at which you know the end has come. It is all crescendo and diminuendo, conducted by the sun itself, whose rising and setting affect the birds' metabolism. When the

light falters, the evensong opens; when the light fades, the evensong closes. Many have tried, and each have failed, to trace the
whole genealogy of oral communication. Richard Jefferies
believed that the swallow sings verbatim: "He literally speaks to
his fellows. I am persuaded you may almost follow the dialogue
and guess the tenor of its discourse." Verbatim or not, Thoreau
detested the owl's belated adagio. He described it much as
Shakespeare would have described our avant-garde literature:
"Expressive of a mind which has reached the gelatinous mildewy
stage in the mortification of all healthy and courageous thought.
It reminds me of ghouls and idiots and insane howlings." Rose
Macaulay compiled a brief *solvitur cantando*: "the nightingale jugs,
the robin warbles, the wren tweets, the goldcrest (or is it a
long-tailed tit?) zee-zee-zees, the Dartford Warbler pittews, the
hedge-sparrow chirrups, the linnet trills." Some moorfolk
maintain that the lapwing pew-its rather pee-wits. And if that
sounds too poetical, let the man of science tune himself to
A. F. C. Hillstead's analysis of a blackbird's song: "Duration is
from three to five seconds, and repetition occurs approximately
eight times a minute." Whether we regard it as speech or as music,
birdsong seems to confirm Darwin's belief "that musical notes
and rhythm were first acquired by the male or female progenitors
of mankind for the sake of charming the opposite sex" . . . and,
he might have added, for the sake of challenging the same sex.
W. H. Hudson steered a middle course between anthropomor-
phism and Behaviourism: "When," he said, "a modern philosopher
suggested that the aesthetic sense, the sense of beauty in all things,
is but an overflow of the sexual feeling, he was not spinning it all
out of his own brain, but had taken the sexual selection theory at
Darwin's own valuation, and made the sex feeling *the* root instead
of making it one of the many distinct elements contained in the
root."

The birds' evensong differs from their matins, for whereas
dawn utters a challenge, dusk sounds a truce, so that ecstasy
gives way to serenity, or at any rate to repose. Both dawn and
dusk evoke a domestic dialectic; and one suspects that the birds
find it easier to awake than to retire, especially when spring has
delivered the first clutch of nestlings. This would explain why
the evening chorus is interspersed with a dissonance suggesting
back-chat and back-bite. Like human parents, a bird may need

to repeat the word "Bedtime" and then to emphasise it with a tap of the beak or a minatory flutter of the wings. One must not press the analogy, but is it not possible—even among birds—that a paterfamilias sometimes lingers overlong in the luxury of liberty, and is curtly summoned to resume the cares of office?

Only an eclipse of the sun has power to halt the chorus or to quicken its arrival. Come rain, come shine, the music never falters. Though a gale may break the daffodils, Ruth Pitter's prophecy is fulfilled whenever we hear

> The old unfailing choirester
> Burst out in pride of poetry.

We do not fully understand the factors which, after sundown, compel birds to sing more blithely than at any time since daybreak. Perhaps the cool air invigorates them. Perhaps they anticipate the pleasures of rest after toil. Perhaps they fear "the perils and dangers of this night", and are concerned to warn their kind against cats, foxes, and egg-lifters. Certainly the blackbird utters shrill alarm calls, swooping low over the meadow.

Some birds, of course, sing by night; and two of them were named after that fact. When Keats heard the nightingale he turned away from life:

> Darkling I listen; and, for many a time
> I have been half in love with easeful Death . . .

A skylark, too, will sometimes shatter the midnight silence. When Ralph Hodgson heard him he envied *la vie Bohème*:

> To pay the world nor tax nor toll
> Save with his melic labours,
> To claim in turn nor due nor dole
> Save peace and gentle neighbours . . .

But nightjars, nightingales, owls, and nocturnal skylarks are exceptions, proving the *Ornitholpolitan* rule that lights-out means pipe-down.

The most eloquent evensong is a monopoly of high moorland. Thus, on a hill above Honeymead, in the solitude of Exmoor, the chorus will continue long after it has ceased in more populous regions. Surveying the sparse hedgerows and solitary trees, you marvel that such bleakness should evoke such music. Perhaps, after all, the silence makes the volume seem greater than it is, even as a pin seems loud when it echoes down the aisle of a midnight abbey. Always there is one bird that outsings the rest; and usually the bird is a skylark. One by one the others retire— thrush, curlew, pippit, robin—but the lark lingers, lost now amid the darkness which it dares. Only when it veers westward can you glimpse the dim dot, simultaneously a sound and the notation thereof, rising and falling among the stars; so that a rapt observer, turning at last to his own nest, murmurs Izaak Walton's grateful Amen: "Lord, what music hast thou provided for the Saints in Heaven, when thou affordest bad men such music on Earth!"

F

5

The Youth of the Year

A great change has come over the land. Even the people of Poplar notice it; even the Old Lady of Threadneedle Street, fume-foul and deafened at the receipt of custom. They have seen it in Manchester whenever they gazed skyward between smoke-scarred warehouses. In Glasgow, too, the change is felt, visibly inaudible above the Gorbals. Cardiff greets it bilingually. Belfast responds despite the backstreet bullies. All Britain responds, though only in the countryside is the greeting total, because there alone the change appears in all its glory—the glow of young green leaves.

Many townsfolk cannot understand what all the fuss is about. Bred among bricks and mortar, they share Dr Johnson's illusion that life begins somewhere between Pinner and Putney, and that beyond those far-flung outposts it dies of sheer fresh air. At the other extremity, a few people regard the change as a profoundly important fact of life, universal yet so private that it passes into their veins, and thereafter eludes a formal expression, like Luther's negative definition of the holy spirit: "If thou feelest it truly in thy heart, it will be such a great thing to thee that thou wilt rather be silent than speak aught of it." Midway between those extremes stand the majority of countrymen, who are silent only insofar as they choose a poet for their spokesman:

> What is so sweet and dear
> · As a prosperous morn in May,
> The valiant prime of the day,
> And the dauntless youth of the year . . .

Sir William Watson's question is answered by every bird that now whistles while it works throughout the day, feeding and fending a brood. Not until April returns shall the land resound with such a *sursum corda*. Only for two more weeks can the green haze shine with such translucence.

In March the year was young; in January, younger still; but those were seasons of infancy and childhood, whereas May is earth's adolescence, comparable therefore with those aspects of youth which, among human beings, reach the zenith of gaiety, idealism, and physical allure. One would suppose that mankind had by this time become accustomed to the changing seasons, yet spring continues to take the world by surprise; and none is so amazed as those who, having feared that the miracle must fade with youth, find in the end that time was on their side, for the shedding of an egocentric skin has revealed pores which remain unclogged by passion and a passing mood. Like Wordsworth, maturity seeks "the depths, but not the tumult, of the soul". So, by an apparent paradox, the youth of the year is autumn's twin and winter's also.

Three rubrics stand at the head of my own country calendar. They are the first snow, Christmas Eve, and May Day. Each transcends its parish roots. For example, hearing a cuckoo or watching the lambs, I think of people and places whom I have met and hope to meet again, southward from Caithness to Cornwall. Is the water-miller's wife at John o'Groat's still 'spotting' the seabirds that fly from the firth? Are the daffodils still flowering by the banks of Loch Ness? Do the violets still shine at Toller Whelme in Dorset? Are the rooks cawing above Charles Reade's old manor house at Ipsden in the Oxfordshire Chilterns? My friend the warden of the Northumberland National Park: is he certain that the last snow has thawed on the coldest gully astride the Cheviot? How warm are the wavelets which lap the foot of Exmoor at Heddon's Mouth? That old man who was mowing the verge beside Tennyson's church in Somersby on the Lincolnshire wolds: will he whet his scythe again this year? On Sarn Helen East, a green Roman road through Wales: is there any sign yet of those blue-bells where the Sarn fords a stream near Aber Bowlan? At Joseph Conrad's old home in Bishopsbourne beside a Roman road through Kent: is the lane still an avenue of beeches under a green sky flecked with blue? At Kirkby Lonsdale in Westmorland, the apple of Ruskin's eye: does Jonty Wilson still send the sparks upward from his anvil? On Holy Island, palmered by pilgrims across the sand: does the vicar still keep watch over the ships by night, pacing a coastguard's tower? Down the green lanes of Warwickshire, into the hamlet of Honington: do the Wilkes family remember the years when we made hay while the sun shone above Marshal's Farm? That track to The Bield at Prestwood in Buckinghamshire, as deeply imprinted on my memory as it is itself imprinted with my footsteps: does beauty still catch her breath, seeing the view therefrom, Chiltern-high and crowned by beechwoods? *Eheu fugaces*; how fast they fly, the slowcoach years.

Yet all is young today; young the primroses flanking the Severn at Quay in Gloucestershire, once a port-of-call for many barges, now an inn alone beside the water; young, too, that Roman road above Fring in Norfolk, where I see the miles of rising wheat, and then glance northward at the ruined windmill and beyond it to the sea. All, all is young; yet older than the Romans when they saw it. Old therefore and young was Laurie Lee's spring song:

> If ever I saw blessing in the air,
> I see it now in this still early day
> Where lemon-green the vaporous morning drips
> Wet sunlight on the powder of my eyes.

May has been called the merry month. It is also a munificent month because each receives from it according as he gives, and every donor finds himself rewarded by a season

> When nothing that asks for bliss,
> Asking right, is denied,
> And half of the world a bridegroom is,
> And half of the world a bride.

Straws on the Wind

We were sitting on a chimneypot; a predicament less uncomfortable than it sounds because a cushion of straw lay between the pot and the posteriors. We were, in fact, thatching a roof.

More precisely, Thatcher was thatching while I looked on, occasionally passing a whimbel or hoisting a yelm.

"In these parts," Thatcher remarked, "we use wheat straw. Up in Lincolnshire they use reed. And according to my son the Scots use heather. This yere," he slapped his cushion, "is unthreshed straw. If it looks a bit untidy 'tis 'cause the stuff's been broken."

"How long," I asked, "will a straw roof last?"

"A sight longer than you will."

"And reed?"

"I once helped my old Dad thatch a reed barn in Norfolk. That were forty years ago. And the roof's near as good as when we made 'en. You can't beat thatch. Warm in winter, cool in summer."

"But it has its risks."

"So's petrol if you set light to 'en." He leaned forward, addressing the lane below: "Boy, more yelms needed." Then he glanced at me: "Anyway, you can get fireproof thatch nowadays."

The straw that was hoisted up the ladder had been prepared or yelmed during the previous week, when Thatcher and his son spread handfuls on the ground, and then sprinkled them with water. More handfulls followed, the whole was turned over, and the sprinkling began again. When the straw was about to be used, they gathered it into bundles or yelms which were wedged between the prongs of a fork or jack; six yelms making one load or burden. Having been hoisted to the roof, the first burden was placed on the left of the thatcher, who worked from right to left, starting at the eave, ending at the ridge. Each segment or lane of straw was two-foot-six-inches wide, a comfortable arm's length; and each lane was secured by means of hazel rods, held down by hazel pegs. When a yelm had been pegged into position, it was beaten with a spud or flat piece of wood (Norfolk reed thatchers use a leggatt with corrugated surface). Although he may have under-estimated the risk of fire, Thatcher had certainly not exaggerated the longevity of his handiwork. During the 1870s, for example, Richard Jefferies met a Wiltshirewoman who was more than a century old: "She reckoned her own age," he wrote, "by the thatch on the roof. It had been completely new thatched five times since she could recollect." The average life of each thatching— twenty years—would have been longer had the cottager felled the trees which dripped on to the roof in wet weather.

Meanwhile, after tea, Thatcher arranged the yelms so that they overlapped on both sides of the steep roof, forming a ridge tile, ready to be combed by a nail-studded stick. His son was trimming the eave with a pair of shears and a long knife whose handle swept forward, parallel with the blade. A casual observer would have noticed only the interplay of badinage and silence while father and son got on with the job; but a keener eye perceived that their movements were rhythmic, leisurely, confident, effective. Edmund Blunden was justified when he praised the craftsmanship of twentieth-century England:

> The scythesman and the thatcher are not dead,
> Or else their ghosts are walking with a will;
> Old England's farms are shrewdly husbanded,
> And up from all the hamlets jumps old skill . . .

And not only from the English hamlets, for in parts of rural Ireland thatch is the rule that implies exceptions. Wales, too, has its thatch despite a surfeit of slate. Even in Scotland I have counted many thatched cottages, some of them wearing a rope net secured by heavy stones, as a defence against gales.

Instead of complaining about his hours of work, Thatcher suddenly glanced up at the evening sun: "I'll say this for spring," he muttered. "It may keep everyone waiting, but when it does arrive it don't give a chap no excuse for hanging around." After another interval of busy silence he remarked: "The party as lives yere wants a dolly on top." He then produced a straw blackbird which he had plaited with affectionate skill. "Purtiest sound you ever heard." Having descended the ladder—at no great speed, for he was past sixty—he added: "The blackbird's song, I mean. Do you know what th'old vicar said? If a man can't rejoice when he hears a blackbird, he said, then damme there ain't nothing on earth as *will* help 'en." Being a truthful man, Thatcher qualified his quotation: "Maybe the vicar left out the 'damme'."

It was pleasant to see Thatcher set an arm on his son's shoulder while the pair surveyed their day's work. "Not bad," he exclaimed, "not bad at all." And then, since they lived in different villages: "Seven o'clock tomorrow, boy. There's nothing like a dab o' dew for wiping the dust off your boots."

Craftsmanship is a gift or genetic attribute. Practise makes perfect, but inheritance bestows the perfectibility. The best-made objects are handmade: clothes, shoes, tapestry, pictures, pottery, furniture, paper, saddlery, books, toys. Mechanical processes are by definition merely parts of the whole, but a craftsman completes every process of his trade. Give him a piece of wood, and he makes a door. Give him a lump of iron, and he makes a weathervane. His product works well, wears well, and looks so well that we delight to see it regardless of its function. You may catch a glimmer of craftsmanship in a besom broom; more still, in a well-layered hedge. At its highest—a Chippendale chair or an illuminated manuscript—craft becomes art. Unlike the average wage-earner, a true craftsman lives for his work. Because of it he awakes each morning with zest; and at the end of the day he is impatient for another zestful tomorrow. His higest wages are love, so that he will sometimes work without material profit; perhaps at a loss.

There is a legend concerning a mediaeval mason who aspired to carve the high altar of a new abbey, where all might see his skill. Instead, he was set to work in a crypt so dark and deep that none ever went there unless upon an errand. Being human, the mason rebelled and grew embittered. One day, while he was carving listlessly by the gloom of a narrow grid, the mason heard a voice: "My son, I have no need of eyes. I can see in the dark." Ashamed of his bitterness, the mason cast away his worldly pride, and from that day onward worked only for the spirit that was within himself, which men then called the grace of God. Centuries later, they say, the great abbey decayed and at length fell to pieces. All its proud carvings mouldered in the dust, or were carted away to make roads. But the dark crypt stood intact; and when men learned once again to prize such things, they flocked to see that crypt and to marvel at the mason who in lonely twilight had carved with as much zeal as though he were decorating the high altar.

An Old English Custom

Such days do dawn, even in May, even in England. If we kept a diary we might discover that they dawn less seldom than we supposed. This day, May Day, had dawned so well that the pessimists shook their heads, saying: "Mark my words, there'll be rain before noon." But no cloud appeared; not even the wisp that is smaller than a man's hand. So, as we stood in the little town, awaiting the great moment, we admired a milk-white May-pole and its rainbow of ribbons.

"They're coming!"

The two words grew to a murmurous salutation; and sure enough, from a narrow side street, they did come . . . a brass-bright cart-horse hauling a new-painted hay wain, and in the wain as pretty a country lass as ever excited Mopsa's envy, and around her a train of little girls; all wearing white, all bearing bouquets. A cheer went up from the crowd while some of the mothers wept, and others smiled, to see their own beauty born again, even as the spring was reborn. In short, there are places where May Day is still a simple-hearted junketing to greet the spring as John Clare greeted it:

> Come, Queen of months, in company
> With all thy merry minstrelsy . . .

No one knows how many ancient customs are observed in England, nor how many recent customs have swelled that number. The simplest division is between the well-known and the not-well-known. The former include the Magdalen College May Day Matins at Oxford, the Pancake Race at Olney in Buckinghamshire, the Well-dressing at Tissington in Derbyshire, the Hobby Horse at Padstow in Cornwall, the Dunmow Flitch in Essex, the Exmoor Pony Fair at Bampton in Devonshire, the Pie Poudre Court at Bristol. The latter include the tug-of-war (across the River Thame) between Ickford in Buckinghamshire and Tiddington in Oxford-shire, the Hornblower at Bainbridge in Yorkshire, and the Easter dole of bread-and-cheese at St Briavel's in Gloucestershire. But a litany of names and addresses is a lifeless guide to the treasury of old English customs. Consider, for example, the Easter revels at Hallaton in Leicestershire, which began three centuries ago, when the rector was granted some land on condition that, in lieu of rent, he provided a communal feast of ale, bread, and hare pie. Hares being always elusive and sometimes unseasonable, the pie now contains beef or some other meat. Midway between Hallaton and Medbourne, at a place called Hare Pie Bank, the rector blesses the pie and then cuts the first slice, whereafter the crowd scrambles to grab a portion of the remainder.

When that mêlée has subsided, another arises . . . the so-called Bottle Kicking Match between Medbourne and Hallaton (I say "so-called" because the bottle of beer is a cask, accompanied by two "empties").

Not all of our customs are annual events. Some occur only once in a lifetime. Others may lapse for decades, perhaps for centuries. Thus, near Checkenden in Oxfordshire stands Wyfold Court whose lease requires that the occupants shall present a red rose to the Sovereign if he or she should happen to pass that way on May Day; which the Sovereign seldom does. Several celebrations are neither annual nor yet unpredictable. One such began two centuries ago when John Knill, sometime Customs officer at Saint Ives in Cornwall, built his own mausoleum, but never occupied it. Even so, he did reward the ten little girls who, every five years, on Saint James' Day, July 25th, were to dance around his tomb, to the tune of a violin, for a quarter of an hour, singing the Old Hundredth. The reward for that rollicking Requiem was shared with the fiddler and two chaperones. The obsequies have been shortened, and the reward reduced, but the custom still takes place every fifth year.

Some customs are observed many times a day throughout the year, as at Sandwich in Kent, where the Borough Council exacts a toll for the use of its bridge across the River Stour. Tradition says that a toll has been exacted ever since King Canute granted ferry rights to Christ Church Priory in 1023. When the corporation built a bridge in 1754 all vehicles paid to cross. In 1968, however, a motorist not only refused to pay the toll but also invoked the Law to quash it. But it is an old saying that Time never runs against the King; wherefore the judge upheld the council's ancient right. A few customs are inherited like a title. Perhaps the oldest of them belongs to the Dymokes, lords of the manor of Scrivelsby in Lincolnshire, who for six centuries have been hereditary King's Champion, bearing the Royal Standard at a Coronation, and, until the reign of George IV, appearing there in armour, to challenge any who denied the new Sovereign: "If any person of what degree soever, high or low, shall deny or gainsay our Sovereign Lord George the Fourth . . . to be the next heir . . . here is his Champion, who saieth he lieth, and is a false traitor . . ."

In the end, however, brevity must be content to litanise a few of England's uncountable customs: Mytholmroyd Pace Egg, Hot

Pence of Broughton-in-Furness, Verderers' Court in the Forest of Dean and in the New Forest, Ripon Hornblower, Ambleside Rushbearers, Fenny Stratford Poppers, Bampton Morris Dancers, Helston Furry Dancers, Tichborne Dolers, Allendale Torchbearers, Widecombe Fairers, Sedgefield Footballers, Cooper's Hill Cheese Rollers, Painswick Church Clippers, Chipping Campden Scuttlebrook Wakers, Wishford Grovely Proceeders, Hastings Sea Blessers, Andover Christmas Mummers, Abingdon Ocksters, Hungerford Hocktiders, Haxley Hood Gamesters, and (since the 1960s) Bideford Round-the-Houses-Racers. Most of those customs are echoes from an England that was 'merrie', not in a tipsy but in a sober meaning of the word, which suggests a willingness to take both the rough and the smooth without being bowled-over by either. Some of the customs have died; others ought to be allowed to die because they perpetuate dead attitudes. Yet there remains a residue of colourful pageantry which recalls things that are worth remembering . . . the deliverance from disaster; the munificence of a King or of an obscure village benefactor; our reliance on seed-time and harvest; things temporal and things spiritual; matters of high estate and those other matters that are unknown except among the countryfolk whom they concern. Each has its place in the index to the story of England.

Breakfast in the Garden

Breakfast is like an opening batsman. Much depends thereon. Many people nowadays are content to gulp a cup of coffee, bolt a slice of toast, puff a whiff of smoke, skim a page of newspaper, and then scurry to swell the hordes of other ill-fed folk who likewise spoil the best part of the day by anticipating the worst.

Leigh Hunt wrote an essay on the subject, which offered some good advice: "Persons," he said, "must not come to breakfast with a face sour enough to turn the milk." Such sweetness is more easily prescribed than achieved. On first waking, we must bridge the chasm between night's *alter ego* and our everyday identity. Morning, in short, solicits both a tonic and a sedative that shall make dreams bearable, and daylight acceptable. Breakfast in the garden offers just such a soothing apéritif. When May is merry, the world greets you as it welcomed Edward Thomas:

> The glory of the beauty of the morning,
> The cuckoo calling over the untouched dew;
> White clouds ranged even and fair as new-mown hay . . .

One glimpse of that glory is more stirring than liver salts, more supple than yoga. As though refreshed by sleep, the hills stand tiptoe on their own verve. The air warms without wearying. And

how many human families are at that very moment emulating the birds which flit to and fro, feeding small yet vocative mouths *con amore* and occasionally with admonition. There is something amiss with the man who cannot adjust his perspective to the sun's. If now and again he does adjust it, he will understand why Thomas Bewick pitied the sluggards who know the dawn only from hearsay: "I have often thought," said Bewick "that not one-half of mankind knew anything of the beauty, the serenity, and the stillness of the summer mornings in the country, nor have ever

witnessed the rising sun's shining forth upon the new day."
When Robert Louis Stevenson was exploring the Cevennes
he made a memorable early meal, but of a sort so frugal that it
dented rather than broke his fast: "away towards the east," he
wrote, "I saw a faint haze of light upon the horizon . . . Day was
about to break . . . I drank my water-chocolate . . ."

My own summer breakfast is served on a lawn in a wood up a
hill, from which—through a well-placed gap in the seclusion—I
see a skyline of moorland. Since the nearest really large town is
fifty miles away, and the village an hour's walk, it follows that the
meal proceeds serenely, the more so because I never disturb it
by reading a newspaper. Any doctor will tell you that news of the
world seldom favours the gastric juices. Certainly the world's
fear and folly must be swallowed, but it is best to imbibe them *after*
breakfast, when the flavour of food gives way to the business of
earning it.

And what of the menu? I hope I shall not be charged with
straining after originality when I remark that food is a matter of
taste. It is also a matter of muscle. The designer of women's
hats, who regularly retires at 1.30 a.m., will not share the *bon
apétit* of a man who toils ten hours in a hayfield. Myself, I am
mere English, which is to say an egg-and-baconian. North Pole or
the Sahara are all one to me. Wherever I wake, it is to bacon and
eggs. I have eaten them in a Force Nine gale while the ship tried
to steal the food from my mouth. I have eaten them on trains, in
Transport Cafes, at five-star hotels, cottages, castles, rectories,
manors, farms, monasteries, lighthouses, and on the tops of mountains. In heat-waves I have eaten them, and in blizzards. I have
eaten early (at 3 a.m. on Salisbury Plain) and I have eaten late (at
noon in *Noah's Ark* off Dodman Point). And always I have ended
with toast and marmalade. Izaak Walton would therefore have
agreed that mine was "a good, honest, wholesome, hungry
breakfast", enjoyed at leisure, with no thoughts save gladness,
and no intrusions beyond those which Edward Thomas relished:

> The heat, the stir, the sublime vacancy
> Of sky and meadow and forest and my own heart . . .

Lest I should ever feel tempted to transform an earthly garden
into an ivory tower, my breakfast is sometimes enlivened by news
of a pleasant world, as when a distant tractor breaks its own fast

with a belch, or a bee bumbles above the antirrhinums, proving that first-come is best-fed. Wise in his generation, a robin waits beside the breakfast tray, head cocked like a terrier trying to learn English. While spreading the marmalade, however, I overhear two voices. The first voice is raised by those self-styled 'realists' who dismiss all quietness and every cornfield as archaic relics of sentimental escapism. Replete and at ease, I suffer their folly gladly; and soon its echo fades away, unanswered because unanswerable because inane. But what of the genuine realists— the undoubted grapplers with truth—who, as they run to catch their train, protest that I mock them by depicting as universal a routine which is a privilege of the few? To them I answer thus: first, consider it possible that some privileges have been purchased at the cost of luxuries which are nowadays rated as necessities; second, gardens never were confined to the countryside. For example, I know an elderly spinster who lives in a London suburb, miles from a green field and from her place of work. Yet every fine morning sees her breakfasting on a patch of grass by the backdoor, among birds as clamorously companionable as those that share my own bacon rind, True, she has no sheep beyond the hedge, no skyline of wooded hills and purple moor, no sea within a morning's walk, no postman reporting *viva voce* on a friendly world. Nevertheless, that wise and working woman breakfasts in the sun, thereafter feeding her birds, watering the flowers, and plucking a weed while for one precious hour she forgets, as Edward Thomas forgot,

> how pent I am,
> How dreary-swift, with nought to travel to . . .

No one travels nowhere. Even the realist counts his footsteps to the grave. So, having removed the breakfast dishes, I burden the tray with a pile of blank pages, knowing that a daily quota of them must be filled with words. Sometimes I live even more dangerously than that, for I leave the words unwritten, and whistle the dog, and go track the Barle to its source on the roof of the moor, or head north-west to the sea, or follow the first signpost that spells Arcady. This morning, which promises to be a scorcher, I shall play a lazier truant by sitting where I am, listening to the birds, while the unwritten pages wait trustfully upon a Pentecost that has never failed them.

County Folk

The word 'county' can be traced via the French *comte* to the Latin *comitatus,* meaning a regional overlord. The word 'shire' descends from the Anglo-Saxon *scir,* meaning official responsibility. In 1647 'county' was being used of territorial nobility and gentry; nine years later it was used to connote any native of a county. In 1860 'the Shires' became a foxy name for Leicestershire, Rutland, Northamptonshire, and those parts of Lincolnshire that are hunted by the Belvoir.

Which of the counties is the oldest? Some Kentish people claim that theirs was created in 445 by Hengist and Horsa, a brace of buccaneers from Jutland. Historians, however, eschew such hindsight because the genesis and early evolution of counties are lost in the mists of antiquity. The counties themselves grew more important, their boundaries more precise, though never immutable. Until 1884, for example, Norhamshire in Northumberland was part of County Durham. Less than half-a-century later the village of Ibstone passed from Oxfordshire to Buckinghamshire (writing of Buckinghamshire in 1862, J. J. Sheahan observed that Ibstone "is situated partly in this county and partly in Oxfordshire, the boundary line passing through a room in the manor-house. The Church is in Oxfordshire"). Sometimes a county border appeared to have been drawn by a blind man, as at Halesowen (now annexed by Worcestershire) which formerly belonged to Shropshire, though it lay thirty miles from that county, and was surrounded by Worcestershire and Warwickshire. It is fitting that such absurdities should be corrected, but the tradition-loving countryman will regret that, during the 1970s, many county borders were changed, and not a few deleted, in order to gratify Burke's sophists, economists, and other miscalculators. The upheaval boxed the British compass, for much of the ancient topography of Scotland and Wales disappeared overnight, and large chunks of England were uprooted and dumped down where they did not belong, did not wish to be, and were not welcome. Rutland, the smallest English county, fought valiantly for survival, but was overwhelmed by the administrative ocean of Leicestershire. Westmorland, too, went down,

that little land of lakes and mountains. All of the fallen will be
mourned by those who believe that 'economic growth' and
'regional efficiency' are less valuable than the awareness of
belonging to a county which is steeped in centuries of pride,
privilege, and obligation. County patriotism, in short, now
seems old fashioned, and may soon become archaic. The men of
Cardiganshire—like the men of La Vendée—will be less than
names to the hagglers in a European market place. So, once
again, we go to school. Having forgotten our shillings and pence,
our rods and our poles and our perches, we must remember not
to say: "Oakham is the capital of Rutland."

Unlike Scotland and Wales, whose basic divisions lie between
north and south, England is so much a kingdom of counties that
her country folk still observe a dual allegiance, to the whole and to
that part wherein they were born, or have set their roots. The
result is a lyrical and at times libellous litany of personal preference.
Thus, William Brown, a Tavistock man, saluted Devon:

> Hail thou my native soil! Thou blessed plot
> Whose equal all the world affordeth not.

In 1594 John Norden became, as it were, the public relations
officer for Essex; "This shire," he declared, "is most fatt, frute-
full, and full of profitable thinges, exceeding (as farr as I can finde)
anie other shire ..." Michael Drayton, on the other hand, preferred
his native Warwick:

> The shire which we the heart
> Of England well may call.

No county is so small—none so remote nor seemingly unim-
pressive—that it has not bred affection. John Constable, a native of
East Bergholt in Suffolk, avowed that he loved "every stile and
stump, and every lane in the village". John Clare set Northamptonshire to poetry. Thomas Bewick set Northumberland to prose,
which he enhanced with his own engravings. Wordsworth *was*
Westmorland, his "dear native regions". Tennyson retained a lifelong rememberance of "deep peace on this high wold" at Somersby
in Lincolnshire. Sir Walter Scott crowned Perthshire as "Queen
of the Highlands". Ieuan Gwynedd saw in Merionethshire a
glimpse of Paradise. Quiller-Couch spoke for Cornwall in three
words: "The delectable Duchy." John Masefield confessed: "The

Herefordshire scene had its part in making me, and profound influence on my work." Gilbert White found what he sought in Hampshire. Thomas Hardy made Dorset the hero of his novels. Arnold Bennett put Staffordshire on the map of literature.

Loyalty by adoption may prove as steadfast as loyalty from birth. Did not French-born Belloc serve Sussex with a fervour fierce as Kipling's? Even a non-residential allegiance can become famous, as with W. H. Hudson, who was born in Buenos Aires, and spent much of his life in a London boarding house, yet claimed to be a Wiltshireman by virtue of "a certain adaptiveness in me, a sense of being at home wherever grass grows ..." Most moving of all, perhaps, are the tributes from the exiles, which do not pretend to be what we call objective assessments, but are love songs whose chief merit is their ability to kindle the warmth which other men feel toward other places, as in Rupert Brooke's nostalgia:

> For England's the one land, I know,
> Where men with Splendid Hearts may go;
> And Cambridgeshire, of all England,
> The shire for Men who Understand ...

Songs such as that are international because they were written in the heart's Esperanto, and can be understood throughout the world.

All this, of course, is older than the counties themselves. Two thousand years ago a Latin poet rejoiced in the hills of home: *Sulmo mihi patria est.* And still the cry goes up. Lancastrians utter it when Yorkshire loses the Wars of the Roses. Buckinghamshire utters it when the men of Ickford yearly tug a war against men on the Oxfordshire side of a stream. Cornwall utters it whenever a non-Cornishman appears. So, after all, the English counties are not dead. Even if they should one day lose their identity, and become part of a planners' fief, still their history will abide, their landscape remain awhile unchanged. Still, therefore, some of their sons and daughters will approve the example of William Hine, a twentieth-century antiquary, who ended his letters with a homely phrase: "Yours in the love of Hertfordshire."

G

The Woods in May

The woods reach the summit of splendour in mid-May, that brief and brilliant time which carries the freshness of April to the brink of June. Each tree becomes part of a green cathedral, suffused by sunlight streaming through the latticed clerestory, as though to conform with Andrew Marvell's design:

> The arching boughs unite between
> The columns of the temple green . . .

When you gaze up at them, the leaves seem to filter the sun so that their greenness becomes a silvery haze, against which the twigs stand out like ebony veins. The bark of an oak is made to look even more venerable by the youthfulness of its foliage. Old trees are more of a piece with winter. Their boughs—bent as if with rheumatism—seem appropriate to that season. Half-uprooted by March gales, an aspen nudges an elm, each creaking like ships alongside a quay. The saltwater sound grows uncannily reminiscent whenever a breeze touches the branches, for then a sigh is heard, as of waves receding over shingle. Meadows beyond the wood are yellowed with buttercups; whitewashed with daisies; dappled with dandelion, clover, and sorrel. Footpaths are speckled with violet and primrose, and the cuckoo calls like a metronome, automatically saying over and over again that spring has reached its prime. Gilbert White noted a neighbour's observation of the cuckoo: "About Selborne wood, he found two singing together, the one in D, the other in D Sharp . . . and about Wolmer forest some sing in C." The wood's perennial undergrowth is scattered by squirrels supple as frigates riding a seaway. The squirrel's tail (or rudder-cum-anchor) moves so swiftly that it seems never to curve, but always to be caught at the conclusion of a jerk. From time to time the dog gives chase, but the squirrels scramble for safety, and he is left to growl up at them, wishing no doubt that heaven had rewarded his angelic disposition with the customary aerial attributes.

Some woods are watered by streams whose spray reaches the primroses, causing them to quiver. I have watched a wren fly through the spray and then repeat the process several times, apparently because the showerbath was agreeable. Wherever it enters a shaded zone, the woodland stream grows grey, but on re-entering the sunshine it turns as blue as the sky. If, like Gideon, you drink from such a stream, you will detect a difference of opinion between Nature and the Water Boards. Water, however, is not the only refreshment which the woods provide. At Looseley Row in Buckinghamshire they will tell you that manna or celestial food was once found among the beech woods. I first heard the tale some forty years ago, when I called at the Pink and Lily, a hilltop tavern where Rupert Brooke used to stay. The landlord assured me that a gamekeeper had picked up a piece of paper among the trees, signed by Brooke himself, and bearing these words:

> Two men left this bread and cake
> For whomsoever finds to take.
> He and they will soon be dead;
> Pray for them that left this bread.

Brooke's brief grace appeared in the Memoir which Sir Edward Marsh contributed to the first edition of the collected poems, but was afterwards found wanting, and is now a curio, quite eclipsed by the poet's praise of

> The Roman road to Wendover
> By Tring and Lilley Hoo . . .

Few wayfarers can expect to find free food in the woods, yet May offers gratis a different sort of manna. For example, one sector of my garden is hedgeless and unwalled, and from it I step into a wood whose bluebells achieve the same maritime illusion that John Masefield noticed near his Oxfordshire home:

> There lay a blue in which no ship could swim,
> Within whose peace no water ever flowed.

Although Masefield was past eighty years old when he wrote those lines, the bluebells still retained their ability

> To consecrate the spirit and the hour,
> To light to sudden rapture and console . . .

The bluebells of Scotland are the harebells of England, a tall plant, unrelated to the true bluebell, which thrives on open moorland,

and remains in bloom for several weeks because the lower buds open one after another from the base upwards. The plant's botanical name is *Campanula rotundifolia* or the bell-flower with rounded leaves. Since the leaves often disappear before the plant has bloomed, very young botanists may be puzzled to account for the *rotundifolia*.

Sunrise and sunset show the bluebells to their best advantage. At first light the trees—like man himself—are dim and not yet wideawake. Presently, however, the birds begin to stir, and within a few minutes their clamour fills the land. Some say that the dawn chorus is merely a symptom of territorial aggression; others, that it contains an element of Wordsworth's joy:

> Then sing, ye Birds, sing, sing a joyous song!
> And let the young Lambs bound
> As to the tabor's sound!

Entranced by such music, and forgetful that he has come rather to see than to hear, an early-riser may miss the precise moment at which the sun peers above the hill, like a wand conjuring colour from pallor; leisurely gilding the lily; silently performing a feat beyond the range of manmade noise to follow. Now indeed the bell-like sea turns blue, and the roof above it green, and green also the shores of grass. From topmost twig to rooted bole, the beeches, so lately gnarled and grey, shine smooth as olives. Primroses preen their saffron silk, and the fallen leaves fade away like old soldiers, one beneath the other, into immortal humus. Deep through the wood flows that static sea, surging among creeks and backwaters, lapping a surfless coast, so easy on the eye that its pastel panorama exerts a fascination which mere brilliance could not sustain.

At sundown the pageant of dawn is repeated in a lower key and from the other hemisphere. The cuckoos clamour, the beeches shine, the bluebells surge. And when the rest of the wood has turned grey, one patch of sunlight abides—perhaps only a few inches on a single bough—marking the place where day nails its last ensign to an ultimate mast.

6

Water Music

"Come," they had said, "whenever you like. The boat will be there." So I came, and found a mahogany skiff, seventy years old, shimmering in the morning sun. Removing a green tarpaulin, I admired the rope, coiled shipshapely in the bows; the sculls, set parallel with the keel; the rudder lines, lashed to the wicker-backed seat; baler, boat-hook, and anchor all stowed trimly. The dog, alas, was not a sea-dog nor even a fresh-water sailor. He is a Lakeland terrier whose experience of such things was as limited as Jan Ridd's when he confessed: "I had seen a boat nearly twice before, but the second time my mother found it out, and drew me back." After some unsteady exploration, the land-lubber decided that his own quarters lay for'ard among the spare cushions.

Our port of embarkation was a raft alongside a meadow half-hidden by willows that seemed rather to smile than to weep, so warm was the air; so cheerful the church clock just then striking seven; so stately the Chilterns sloping to the Thames, and in places overhanging it as though, like cattle, they had come to drink. Attended by birdsong and an inquisitive horse, I cast-off and headed upstream, occasionally leaning on the sculls, and, when I passed under a bridge, touching the sunless arch with fingertips that turned green with age. To port and starboard, young summer wore a Sunday best, for the corn was still green, the hay already cut, and the scent of honeysuckle drifted across the river. This was the water music of Debussy's *En Bateau*.

Presently I entered a creek, where I lay down in the sun, hearing and feeling time pass; not regretfully nor impatiently,

but with introspective detachment, as though a great play were unfolding. I had with me a fishing line and a copy of Walton's *Lives,* rather like the man whom Robert Bridges encountered when he, too, explored an Oxfordshire backwater:

> Sometimes an angler comes, and drops his hook
> Within its hidden depths, and 'gainst a tree
> Leaning his rod, reads in some pleasant book,
> Forgetting soon his pride of fishery.

After a while the book slipped from my hands, and I said: "What is the loveliest sound on earth, not made by men?" What, indeed? Is it a summer wavelet on a sandy shore? Is it the lark, bestirring a tardy sun? A cuckoo, calling winter's knell? A nightingale, crying for the moon? Can it be a robin, pledging his loyalty when September steals another summer from our store? Or the sound of water, gobbling a heather-hidden course across the moor? Can it be Tennyson's timbre, "the murmur of innumerable bees", informing our closed eyelids that the sun looks as golden as it feels? Or is it a blackbird, weaving his song through sun-filtered leaves, bidding us be brave when we must, and gay while we can, because life holds no proven reply to the questions which we would wish most to answer?

Meanwhile the day wore on while I continued upstream, nosing among creeks, wandering across meadows, and twice slipping over the side to swim. At noon on the towing path a farmhand answered his grizzling junior: "Give over, boy. Oi 'ad more fun on three quid a week nor wart you git with twenty. Ah, *and* oi didn't need to pay tenbob for a tannersworth o' baccy. Oi dare say toimes was 'ard for some of us. For most of us, if you loike. But by golly, boy, if we ever did git a bob to spare, then the damned thing was worth twelve old pence, not foive point summat o' these bloody new 'uns." Far astern, glinting in the sun, I saw what Quiller-Couch had seen:

> Lissom oars and backs that swung them,
> Eight good men in the good old times . . .

Good indeed, though now so old that I marvelled that I, too, had once toiled like a slave in a Dark Blue galley.

In mid-afternoon I tied-up to a tree, stepped ashore, and followed a lane into Ewelme (pronounced U-elm), where they laid Jerome K. Jerome, creator of the immortal boating trio. How vividly he voyaged the Thames, how variously; at one moment a guide ("Nuneham Park is well worth a visit. It can be viewed on Tuesdays and Thursdays"); at the next, a poet ("The river . . . flinging diamonds from the mill-wheels, throwing kisses to the lilies . . ."). In Ewelme, under a painted tomb, they laid also Chaucer's thrice-married grand-daughter, Alice, Duches of Suffolk, who with her third husband received from Henry VI his licence to "found a hospital at their Manor of Ewelme, in the County of Oxford, and settle a sufficient endowment, not exceeding the yearly value of 200 marks, for the maintenance of two Chaplains and thirteen poor men . . ." There the mediaeval almsfolk gave thanks at Compline: "God have mercy on the sowle of the noble Prince Harry the Sext and on the sowles of my Lord William, sum tyme Duke of Suffolk and my Lady Alice Duchess of Suffolk hys wyfe our first founders and on their fadyr and modyr sowles and all Christen sowles Amen." That rose-red almshouse is still a haven for superannuated souls.

The light was failing when I returned to the boat for coffee and sandwiches. I must have supped leisurely, because a church chimed eleven as I turned downstream. An afterglow of daylight lingered in the west, faint as the reflection from a distant furnace. The air remained warm, spiced now with many sorts of scent from hay, leaf-mould, byre, barn. The moon lay like a scimitar on the water, studded by sapphires that were stars. Sometimes a fish arose, quivering the galaxy. All birds having gone to roost, the stillness sounded double-deep when an owl hooted seven times. After that, I could hear droplets splashing from the sculls into the river, which shone like steel. The green trees were sable; the hills above them, darker than black. Voles and mice rustled from the banks.

In Queen Victoria's time this empty fairway surged with the bow-wave of barges plying between Cricklade and the Nore. Now there was only one craft, a white pleasure boat, tethered like a swan to a tree. Hearing my rowlocks, the owner thrust his head through a pool of light from the cabin.

"Lovely evening," he remarked.

"It is indeed."

"Don't often see an oarsman at this hour."

"I suppose not."

"Ah, well. Goodnight." I could hear him smiling. "And *bon voyage*."

The boat reached her moorings in a silence so profound that every movement evoked a clatter. Still inquisitive, the horse came to see what all the noise was about. When I offered him two lumps of sugar, he accepted them amiably, with tremulous upper lip, while the dog looked on, dew-drenched and drowsy. Having left all things as I had found them, I glanced gratefully at the boat; and the church across the meadow capped my glancing Grace with one Amen.

On Time's Cycle

Poets are not renowned for normality. Their public utterances can seem as childish as their private lives. Nevertheless, they do sometimes act rationally, and speak wisely, as did W. B. Yeats when he urged J. M. Synge to explore the Aran Isles: "Live there," he wrote, "as if you were one of the people themselves." Synge followed that good advice, and out of it came the plays which reveal him as a master of country talk, for he found among the Aran islanders a race of men and women who in their everyday converse spoke poetry as naturally as now the English utter their "O.K." and other telephonese. Yet the English are not wholly without the gift of tongues. Even in the Saxon counties you will catch an echo of the wit and lyricism which Synge culled from the lips of Irish peasants.

I had the good fortune to spend the best years of my boyhood in north Buckinghamshire, at a time when that region really was remote. The other day I returned there, and was gladdened by a familiar tone of talk: "Oi wouldn't warnt to speak no different nor wart oi do. It's 'ow they learned me. And wart were good enough for my old dard, oi reckon t'aint too bard for me." During that revisitation, I remembered especially old Sewell, the bicycle man, whose workshop was an upper storey in a side street of the village. I can still hear his paternal advice when he considered my request to hire a bicycle, at a time when I was saving-up to buy one. In those distant years Sewell always addressed me as "Master Peel", though the sounds he uttered were more like "Marser Poil".

"Now look 'ere, Marser Poil," he would say, "oi aren't agoing t'oire you no boike, not unless you swear solemn as you won't never 'ang on the barksoide o' them lorries. T'ain't safe, for one thing. Not nowadays t'ain't. Oi've seen them lorries doing near twenty moile an hour. And for another thing, oi've a great respect for your grandard. Oi reckon th'old gent wouldn't loike to see a member of his farmly 'anging on the barksoide of a lorry. Wart's thart you say? No, Marser Poil, 'ee still wouldn't loike it, not even if the lorry was only going ten moile an hour."

At that point the bicycle man would twist his benign features into a frown: "You real surprise me, you do. Oi don't never let my Cyril 'ang on. And 'ee's a soight older nor wart you are. And another thing, Marser Poil . . . oi've 'eard say you're to go to Hoxford one day. Well, oi'll tell you now, no young gentleman won't never git t'Oxford by 'anging on the barksoide of a . . . wart's thart? Git there by train? Maybe you will, but thart don't make no difference to wart oi'm saying. And even if you did git there, oi reckon they wouldn't be very pleased, not when you arroived they wouldn't. Oi reckon they'd think, Wart would 'is old grandard say?"

In the end, of course, I did swear solemn, and duly received the bicycle: "Thart'll be two bob a week for the 'oire, plus a tanner deposit just in case. And mind you bring bark both them mudguards. Thart t'other young gent... the one as you kindly introduced ... 'im as is a vicar's son . . . well, the less said about thart one the better. Why? Oi'll tell you why, Marser Poil . . . it's 'cause oi aren't never seen a boicycle come bark in such a state. Oi told 'im straight, 'When oi give you thart boike, Marser Lawson, it 'ad a chain and a pump and a bell and a . . . and now where are they?' oi said, ' 'cause oi don't see 'em.' " It was useless to plead benefit of clergy on behalf of Master Lawson: "Oi dare say 'ee was in a 'urry to git to church, but if 'ee'd gorn a bit slower 'ee'd ha' stood a better chance of seeming pleasing in the eyes of 'is Maker... ah, and my old boike wouldn't ha' been messed up." Even so, Sewell never did take the deposit: "No, oi don't really warnt your tanner. You go and buy yourself some sweets. So be a good boy, loike wart oi said, and then you'll henjoy yourself and maybe not git any punctures."

Sewell never thought it strange that a potential Oxonian should save-up in order to buy a bicycle, but he would have thought it very strange indeed had anyone bought a bicycle without paying for it: "Young charp come down from London last Sartday. Warnted my friend Ted to buy two 'undred poundsworth o' farm tackle. 'Two 'undred?' says Ted. 'Oi think you've come to the wrong place,' he says. 'It's the Bank of England you warnt.' 'O no,' says the charp 'You can 'ave that tackle for fifty quid down, and pay the rest as you please.' So old Ted goes and 'as a look at the stuff, and then he says, 'Oi got two 'undred quid. Oi got two thousand. Ah, *and* a bit more. If oi warnted,' he says, 'oi could buy thart lot cash down in foivers.' 'Then why don't you?' says the charp. 'For two reasons,' says Ted. 'First, oi don't loike your loine o' talk, trying to git folks to buy wart they don't need and can't afford. Second, oi don't loike your loine o' tackle. In fact, oi more than don't loike it. Oi think it's a load of old junk.' 'Thart,' says the charp, 'is a bloody lie.' 'Strictly speaking,' says Ted, 'you're 'alf-roight. So let me put it this way . . . your tackle is a load o' *new* junk.' "

Few folk nowadays would go cycling for pleasure on Watling Street, but in those years a small boy could safely wobble while he watched the Royal Scot racing north to Glasgow, or the Irish Mail south to Euston. And the by-lanes—doomed to be submerged beneath the concrete of Milton Keynes New Town—they were fairways for farmcarts, for ploughmen riding homeward side-saddle, and for the village constable on a Sunbeam roadster (the mere sight of his helmet could nip the bud of any breach of any peace at any time in any place).

If Sewell's machine were due to be returned at noon, my grandfather required me to deliver it one hour beforehand; not because he declined to pay an extra tuppence, but because that kind of punctuality was then the rule among that sort of person. And Sewell always returned the compliment by making fair allowance for a week's wear-and-tear over flinty lanes: "No, Marser Poil, oi don't reckon thart's a real dent. Looks more loike a bit o' stone flew up. Could 'ave 'appened t'anyone."

To me in those days Sewell seemed infinitely old, a wizened creature, with a few grey wisps and a nicotine thumb. I know now that he was not much above fifty, that he had married late in life, and that the twinkle in his eye was a true register of the kindness of his heart. Good cycling, Master Sewell: if I ever do get there, perhaps I shall find you free-wheeling in Paradise.

Midsummer Night

What a thing it is when you stack the garden chairs at the end of a perfect day, assured by the weather forecast that you will be doing the same again tomorrow. Drained of all definable colour, the western sky sinks into a furnace whose sparks are cloud wisps, mother-of-pearling the universe. Marooned among twilight, one thrush sings a challenge to the darkness.

"You can't surely be gardening at this hour?"

You pause, wondering what to say. In the end you mutter: "Just coming." Then, as though to justify your absence from indoor domesticity, you clink the hoe against some stones half-visible under a rose tree. Suddenly you glance up, perplexed. After several moments, you understand; the thrush has stopped singing; the land is asleep.

Presently a scythesman ambles down the lane, his blakeys as rhythmic as a metronome. Knowing that he has been overtiming in a meadow nearby, you wander up the lane for the pleasure of quaffing his new-mown hay. Few folk use the lane, but tonight the traffic is heavy—three people in three hours—the latest of them being an uphill farmer who has met his downdale son-in-law. Their talk drifts across the meadow.

"Hello, Dad. Out for a stroll?"

"Just airing the dog. How's that ram o'yours rubbing along?"

"Not so good, I'm afraid."

"Had the vet to 'en?"

"Three times."

"What did he say?"

"Exactly what you said."

"Not exactly, boy, 'cause I never mentioned nothing about three times three guineas."

"I know one thing. If I ever do catch that bloody dog I'll shoot 'en. What's more, I told her so. 'Oh,' she said, 'I'll prosecute you.' 'Begging your pardon,' I said, 'but you won't, because there's only one person as can prosecute, and her's the Queen. And I don't reckon Buckingham Palace is likely to come down yere on account of a dog's been chasing my sheep.' "

"Her didn't like that."

"And she said so. By the way, how's Ma?"

"She's like her daughter and all other women . . . inclined to be feminine."

"Oh?"

"Wants to have the kitchen papered."

"Papered? The kitchen? But dammit . . ."

"That's just what I told her. 'For near three hundred years,' I said, 'that kitchen's been rubbing along all right wi' a dash o' whitewash.'"

You hear a match being struck, and presently the whiff of shag arrives, followed by Dad's inquiry: "How's my daughter?"

"Bit like her Ma by the sound on't. Wants a holiday abroad.'

"Broad? What's wrong with Weston-super-Mare all of a sudden?"

"Her's been reading they travel brochures."

"Well, boy, you know my advice. Either you'm master in your own house or the woman is equal. You can't have it both ways 'cause as soon as she *is* equal she starts acting superior." A second match is struck, and once more the smoke smothers the hay. "Was Dick down the Wheatsheaf tonight?"

"Oh, ah. Getting a bit wobbly nowadays."

"Give'en a chance, boy. Dick Davey was near too old for the Kaiser's war. Ah, well, I must be getting back. But bear in mind what I've told 'ee . . . if you start gadding abroad, and I start papering the kitchen, we'm both of us likely to outstrip the cost o' living. Come on Lassie, girl, You don't want no rabbits this time o' night."

And away they go, uphill and down, fainter and fainter into moonlight, hay-scent, stillness.

All the sparks have left the sky now. The pale blue deepens. Stars appear, as though to warm their fingers at the faint glow of the faded furnace. A scythe gleams like a silver gap in the hedgerow. You feel suddenly very wise, as though you had discovered the non-meanings of life: the shopping, cheque-cashing, investing, insuring, and all other of those palpitations which Charles Lamb diagnosed as "the quick pulse of gain". Even the busiest body renews his strength when he turns to the abiding hills. Elections will be forgotten; dynasties will fail; the topheavy towerscape of technology will one day seem as archaic as a hand-loom; men themselves may commit *hara kiri* on the altar of their own spleen. In the midst of change, not all of which augurs well, it is good to grasp the best aspects of stability. So, in the end, your discovery was no more than a neglected platitude, one of many that were first propounded thousands of years ago.

"What *are* you doing out there?"

You return just in time to reply by dragging the lawn-mower into the shed. En route a bat flits past, making you flinch. Still reluctant to retire, you linger in the light of the moon and in the peace of your own corner of the kingdom, understanding that each region is part of a mosaic, and that all are restful, moonlit, quiet: Fenland dyke, Thames-side garden, Cornish quay, Scottish loch, Welsh mountain, Leicestershire covert, Dorset forest, Kentish orchard, Hampshire chalk stream, Surrey heathland.

"I suppose you know it's past midnight?"

You do not know, neither do you care, because, tomorrow being Sunday, tonight is a *nox non,* on which, like Robert Nichols, you are content

> To brood apart in calm and joy awhile
> Until the spirit sinks and scarcely knows
> Whether self is, or if self only is
> For ever . . .

Sometime later—perhaps a long time later—you go timelessly upstairs; and having opened the bedroom window, you share Hilaire Belloc's hail and farewell:

> The moon on my left,
> And the dawn on my right,
> My brother, good morning,
> My sister, goodnight.

Cutting a Long Story

Round a bend in the towing path I came on a small Georgian bridge, handsomely designed, as such things usually were. Beyond the bridge stood a lock and the keeper's cottage which suggested human activity and the busyness of barges. On approaching nearer, however, I saw that the lock was in ruins, and the cottage no longer a keeper's. Much could be learned by examining the lock, the quality of its timbers, and the skill with which they had been fashioned to fulfill a function. Who in our own time would leaven the needs of industry with a sprinkle of artistry? The cottage, too, combined usefulness with comeliness, and seemed likely to outlast many houses of the mid-twentieth century. Lock and cottage illustrated the rise and fall of horse and of coal; the latter supplanting the former until, after little more than a century, it was itself supplanted, this time by petrol. Next time, by what? John Rennie, who built the canal, would have been astounded by a dereliction that had become common when Edward Thomas described it:

> Only the idle foam
> Of water falling
> Ceaselessly calling,
> Where once men had a work-place and a home.

The canal itself resembled an endless lily-pond, from which many fishes plopped up, making me feel as though I had intruded on their privacy; or was it only one fish—a kind of freshwater submarine—shadowing the stranger who continually paused to swish nettles, to spear algae, to pluck flowers; sometimes leaning on a gate, sometimes snoozing in the sun; never seeming to have either a purpose or a destination. Now and again a bird chiff-chaffed, but summer had set its somnolence on the scene, and the sun itself invited a siesta. Even when activity did occur, it held a dreamlike quality, symbolised in the cob that glided past, followed by his mate and two cygnets, as in Andrew Young's waterscape:

> How lovely are these swans
> That float like high proud galleons
> Cool in the summer heat,
> And waving leaf-like feet . . .

The towing path remained in fair condition; the fields beside it teemed with sustenance. Acres of barley waved like blond beards on a breeze. Poppies stabbed the green wheat, pleasant enough to young eyes, but to old memories a wound won in Flanders long ago; perhaps a mortal wound. Sometimes a new-mown meadow sent sweet swathes across the water. On a hillock among elms I sighted a church tower and the amber eaves of cottages; but of mankind I saw nothing at all. It was as though the fields had sown and scythed themselves unaided. This was Wiltshire, the land of *Welsaetan* or Saxons who lived on the Wylye, a tricky river, liable to flood (the Old English *wil* meant 'a trick'). Glancing at the wooded hills and thatched roofs, I understood why Vita Sackville-West confessed: "If I did not happen to belong by birth and tradition to Kent, I should like to live in Wiltshire."

During the course of the next mile I stumbled on an old man who was lying asleep, full-length across the towing path, at the very moment when I happened to round the bend while scanning the sky. So far from being annoyed or alarmed, the veteran sat up, scratched his sunburned stubble, blinked at the sun, and remarked: "If you 'adn't woke me I'd ha' missed my dinner." He yawned and stretched. "Just walking?"

"Just walking."

"Interested in canals?"

"In everything."

Still yawning, he rummaged in a poacher's pocket, from which he extracted a leather wallet, fastened with two rubber bands; and from that he produced a faded photograph whose colours resembled *café-au-lait*: "My uncle took that picture. Gentleman by the name o' Timothy Grass. See them barges? You won't never see 'em again. Not on this cut." He returned the picture to its place among other historic documents: "Daft, isn't it? The roads choked with traffic, the canals choked with weeds."

Sitting down beside him, I offered my tobacco pouch, which he sniffed: "Classy stuff, this." His little finger just contrived to enter the bowl of an undecarbonised pipe: "I first started with a brand called Old Mother Mitchell's. Penny a twist it cost. They used to say that if a chap could smoke it for six months he wouldn't die of anything except old age." Suddenly he pointed to the water: "They're rising like bubbles this morning. 'Tis always the same when I haven't brought my rod." He gave me a sidelong glance: "You a fisherman?"

"I used to be. But never like Izaak Walton."

"Walton?" Again he scratched his stubble. "I don't recollect no one o'that name. The king-pin on this cut is Fred Simmons. Real marvel, old Fred. One look at his float, and the fish come up fried in their own batter." He suddenly glanced over his shoulder and then up and down the canal, as though he were looking for someone. Perhaps he *was* looking, because, in a lower tone of voice, he said: "Strictly speaking, you're supposed to have a fishing licence. But if you ask me . . ." He paused: "However, as you haven't, I won't."

"Poachers?" I suggested.

"People," he countered, "without a fishing licence."

After that, we eschewed generalities, and turned to himself in particular. He was, he said, a retired shepherd: "But the master packed it in, and a syndicate went over to wheat. Anyhow, the gentleman I was telling you about . . . old Tim Grass . . . now his father sailed from London to New York by way o' this very cut. He took a barge up the Thames and then another one along the cuts till he reached Bristol. And there he stowed away on a cattle boat. He was only a lad, mind you. And when he came home again he was near ninety. But the poor old buffer hadn't been here above a week afore he died o' heart failure conducted by unnatural causes. You see, they'd forgotten to tell him about the railway round Savernake, so when he heard a train coming through the trees he was that shook he fell down dead."

"How sad."

"That's what his daughter said. In fact, she wanted to sue the railway, but the lawyers advised against. They said something about the House o' Lords, and as the daughter was a Liberal she told 'em she'd rather let the dead rest in peace."

At that moment a distant church chimed noon, and the old man asked how far I was likely to walk.

"For ever," I replied, gazing at the interminable path, the limitless sky, the infinite fields.

An English Summer Day

All a long day, at an average speed of three miles an hour, I travelled through Norfolk, a land of water, wildfowl, wheat, woods; lapped and sometimes lashed by a hundred miles of sea; for centuries the richest corner of the kingdom, thriving on agriculture and the village crafts that served it. By some miracle of fortune and foresight, East Anglia played no part in the

Industrial Revolution which marred so much of England.
Industry regarded the region as a backwater, but was eager enough
to be fed by its farmers. Not even Norfolk, however, wholly
escaped the tentacles of Mammon. Thetford has changed from a
country town to a factory site; King's Lynn sold itself for a mess of
lorries; and Britain's Common Profiteers hope to extract much

money by 'developing' the east coast ports and their hinterland.
Nevertheless, nine-tenths of Norfolk is deep country, rich country,
quiet country, sane country. During my own exploration the
weather and the season conspired to enhance those boons. The
corn was as green as grass; the leaves thicker than in May and
scarcely less lustrous; the sun, strong yet tempered by a breeze.
In short, it was a perfect English summer day, with one white
cloud sailing a blue sea so leisurely that its course might have
been plotted by W. H. Davies:

> What is this life if, full of care,
> We have no time to stand and stare . . .

The map had forewarned me that my route would be secluded, but only the route itself was able to depict the solitude, for the lane rambled like a trickle of water seeking its own level while mile climbed on mile without ever sighting anything more populous than a farm among fields. Two cuckoos called a time of year, and when one of them stopped, the other answered its own echo. Small hills carried little woods which harboured blackbird and chiff-chaff and robin and wren, all whistling while they worked. Noticing a distant scarecrow, I blinked because the heat haze gave the effigy the power to sway. Closer inspection showed that the metronome was a man, hoeing a leguminous ocean.

Toward noon, when the sun outshone the breeze, I sighted a stream, and lay full-length in it. The dog, by contrast, preferred to emulate those Romans who claimed that their palate could detect from what sector of the Tiber a fish had been taken; having savoured a mouthful at one place, he did the same at another and then at a third, as though each offered a unique vintage. Thus refreshed, we continued our journey, marvelling at the plentitude of corn and vegetables, and admiring the farmsteads which reminded us that the scene was not an idyll *ab initio,* but rather the latest fashion in a landscape which had been a forest, was then tamed somewhat by the feudal system, more than somewhat by the Georgians, and finally perfected by the Victorians. These were the pastures praised by Defoe because, he said, their cattle "thrive in an unusual manner, and grow monstrously fat; and the beef is so delicious for taste . . ."

Slowly the day wore on, moving full-circle over an England as it used to be until traffic and aircraft had compelled even their devotees to seek refuge from the storm of increased productivity. Yet this uneventful seclusion was an illustrated history book, for I had begun the day at Blickling Hall, Norfolk's stateliest home, whose Jacobean *noblesse* seemed rather to be a part of than an addition to the scene. There, in an earlier mansion, Anne Boleyn spent her childhood; and thither she may have glanced when they led her to the block, briefly and bitterly recalling the years when, as Edith Sitwell imagined,

> My step light and high
> Spurned my sun down from the sky
> In my heedless headless dance . . .

From Blickling I proceeded by way of Gresham, the *Gaers-ham* or grazing farm, nowadays a hamlet, though once the site of the palace of Harold, last Saxon King of England; whereafter it became the seat of the Greshams, one of whom, Sir Thomas, built the first Royal Exchange at about the same time as another, Sir John, endowed Holt manor house as a school that was to educate W. H. Auden, Sir John Betjeman, and the first Lord Reith. In this same hamlet stands Chaucer's Farm, so-named because the land had belonged to the poet's son, who sold it to Sir William Paston. Not long afterwards the house was attacked by the private army of Lord Moleyns, a covetous neighbour. Defended only by Dame Margaret Paston and twelve servants, the place resisted so stubbornly that the besiegers were obliged to mine it. You can still see the grasscovered foundations.

All those events were now mere photographs on the wall of faded memory. But Hodge had not faded, for at six of a sun-stroked clock, when I entered an inn, to drink cider, there the man was: "I been hoeing all day," he announced, "and damme I'm that thirsty I could swallow a brewery." The land and the sea breed a type of man not elsewhere to be found on earth. At Gresham, I felt, the outlook was deeper and less discontented than at Thetford's car-crammed traffic lights.

Soon after seven o'clock I reached the North Sea, which had inspired Defoe to compose a prayer for those in peril on the deep: "If," he declared, "the ships coming from the north are taken with a hard gale of wind from the S.E. or from any point between the N.E. and S.E. so that they cannot, as the seamen call it, weather Winterton Ness, they are thereby kept in danger of running upon the rocks about Cromer . . . or stranding upon the flat shoar between Cromer and Wells . . ." If the ships could not anchor and ride the gale, their only hope was "to run into the bottom of the great bay I mention'd, to Lynn or Boston, which is a very difficult and desperate push: So that sometimes in this distress whole fleets have been lost together." Wherefore Defoe anathematised these waters as "one of the most dangerous and most fatal to the sailors in all England . . ." nay, worse, for he added "I may say in all Britain." My own arrival proved more auspicious. The calm sea was bobbled by fishing boats. Even at nine o'clock the air felt warm. An hour later, all passion spent, the sunset suffused a wood wherein one thrush was so enamoured of the day that he continued to sing its praises, or so it seemed to a spectator. When at last the thrush retired, an owl uttered the praises of night, whereupon the dog and I rustled a homeward path through starlight.

An English summer day is a *raison d'être*, unfolding to the poet's leisured wonder:

> A poor life this, if, full of care,
> We have no time to stand and stare.

7

Beside the Stream

It was a scene that would have delighted Constable or Crome.
One cow stood knee-deep in the stream, her tail like a pendulum
swatting flies with predictable rhythm. The stream was the
Warwickshire Stour, tree-lined and so leisurely that a pigeon's
feather passed slower than dawdling pace under the bridge near
Honington Hall. Heavy with sorrel, a patch of uncut grass stood
as high as corn. When the ghost of a breeze passed over it, the
sorrel rustled awhile before resuming a summer siesta. Below the
bridge, the stream looped indelible loops, like a man who has
wearied of his own doodling. Twice it bent back on itself, as
though to confirm Maurice Lindsay's syllogism:

> Beyond the dappled fields cows sit on their shadows:
> The river runs over its ancient argument . . .

In the second field below the bridge an angler gazed into the
water; not Narcissus-fashion at his own reflection, but at the
float, which was painted red and white, plump as Mr Micawber
waiting for something to turn up.

"Any luck?" I asked.

"The light," he replied, "is too strong. But yesterday I caught
my supper. Anyway," he smiled, "it's peaceful here, and warm.
What more do you want?"

"Nothing," I agreed, and went my way.

Shakespeare may have walked beside the Stour. Without doubt
he knew the nearby hamlet of Barcheston, whose name—like a
true Warwickshireman—he pronounced "Barson" (Master

Silence, you remember, dismissed Falstaff as a hamleteer, "Puff of Barson"). Meanwhile the stream played hide-and-seek among light or shade; sometimes venturing into the glare, sometimes seeking the shelter of overhanging boughs, sometimes hiding behind tall grass. Silver snouts plopped up, wrinkling the surface, though never within reach of a float. A rat swam across and then sat in the sun, doing nothing; which is often the best thing to do, especially beside a stream in July. Somewhere far-off a dog barked, a car whined, an aircraft droned; but they soon passed, and were mere sound and fury, signifying nothing in the life of a summer day.

Not every water is as idle as the Stour. Walking once between Forsinard and John o'Groats, I reached a stream so active that within twenty yards it transformed itself from a trickle to a cascade. Or there is Wordsworth's Duddon—praised in twenty-four sonnets—tumbling seaward from the Langdale Pikes, leaping so many cataracts that the spray hovers like mist,

> Thridding with sinuous lapse the rushes, through
> Dwarf willows gliding, and by ferry brake . . .

A more domesticated motif is intoned by the stream that was set to music by Tennyson:

> With many a curve my banks I fret
> By many a field and fallow,
> And many a fairy foreland set
> With willow-weed and mallow.

No man can make a stream, though some have helped a stream to make the most of itself. In the Warwickshire parish of Whichford a friend of mine has on his land the smallest volume of water that can properly be called a brook. This he adorned by mowing the grass alongside and by planting it with flowers. To create an illusion of breadth, he bridged the brook with a plank (three feet long) and then contrived a waterfall (eighteen inches high). So, whenever the brook is in spate, he sleeps to a splashing lullaby. A louder music comes from Devon, where the River Heddon lopes among woods to the Severn Sea, arriving between two ramparts of Exmoor, nearly a thousand feet high. "What a sea-wall they are," wrote Charles Kingsley, "those Exmoor hills! Sheer upward from the sea a thousand feet." The path beside that last lap is an amphibious idyll of skyline moorland, sheep-grazed pasture, carpeted daffodils, and white-lipped waves.

Some streams stir the imagination in much the same way as does the photograph of a famous man taken during his childhood. The Thames, for example, rises in a Gloucestershire meadow near Kemble, beside a plumply recumbent statue of Neptune *anglicé* Old Father Thames. On most days of the year the source is as dry as a mirage because the Isis or infant Thames flows underground until it reaches the Cirencester road. Once or twice in a lifetime, however, a prolonged deluge will cause the spring to gush, so that the fields are flooded, and Rob Roys paddle a passage from the very feet of Father Thames. The Severn, our longest river, rises from the summit of Plynlimmon near Llanidloes in Montgomery-shire, where the river board has erected a signpost above the spring which Tacitus called Sabrina—Milton's "Sabrina fair"—thereafter to wander among the Welsh Marches.

One or two streams have witnessed the making of history. The classic example is the Rubicon, which Caesar crossed en route to capture Rome. Many people assume that the crossing represented a feat of military skill. But the Rubicon was only a brook. Its fame lay in its role, for it marked the limit which Caesar, as a serving general, could not lawfully overstep without permission from the Senate. Lacking that permission, he took the law into his own hands, and broke it, and thereby made a brook immortal. Shades of imperial Rome flow through the Welsh mountains above Llandovery, carried by a stream which heard the tramp of horses, the oaths of men, the clang of shovels. And when at last the procession had passed out of sight, the stream found itself cros-sing a Roman road, Sarn Helen East, at a place called Aber Bowlan, deep among woods. Many feet forded that stream in the years when the road served the Roman gold mine at Dolaucothi. Nowadays I doubt that anyone follows the road, unless perhaps a shepherd or some wayfarer with a taste for green tracks through solitude.

In the parish of Burnham Thorpe, near the Norfolk coast, a signpost beside a stream bears these words: *Site of Nelson's birth-place.* Young Horatio saw the stream whenever he passed through the gate of his father's rectory. Is it merely fanciful to think that on that stream his fleet of paper boats foresaw Trafalgar? There can be nothing fanciful in remarking that Britain's two most cultured cities arose where oxen forded the Thames, and where a bridge spanned the Cam.

History, however, is not always a congenial fellow-traveller. There are times when the clash of arms and the fall of dynasties seem strident as well as ephemeral. It is then that the uneventful stream comes into its own, meandering harmoniously through a month when the blackbird still sings, the corn still stands, the sun still shines.

Jack of All Trades

He is a tall man, nearly seventy years old, yet still so widely sought after by farmers that he works as hard as the rest and with a deeper relish than most. Nobody uses his surname. He is not only Jack but also the only Jack, or at any rate the only one who is never called anything else. If you said to villagers: "Where does Mr So-and-So live?" they would pause awhile before replying: "Oh, you mean Jack."

Jack's fame is a measure of the multiplicity of his skills, for he answers Yes to a catechism which William Langland posed seven centuries ago: "Can you pile haycocks and pitch them into a cart? Or can you handle a scythe and make a heap of sheaves? Or keep my corn in my croft safe from thieves? Can you make a shoe, cut clothes or tend cattle? Can you hedge or harrow or herd hogs and geese? Or do any kind of craft the community needs?" And still the breed flourishes. Hilaire Belloc met Jack in Sussex, seventy years ago, at a time when prophets were already predicting his decease: "a man," Belloc commented, "who worked with his hands, and was always kind, and knew his trade well; he smiled when he talked of scythes and he could thatch. He could fish also, and he knew about grafting, and about the seasons of plants, and birds, and the way of seed. He had a face full of weather, he fatigued his body, he watched his land. He would not talk much of mysteries, he would rather hum songs. He loved new friends and old."

But Jack's expertise ranges wider than farming or cobbling or tailoring. He will thatch a roof, build a wall, repair a pump, bandage a fetlock, exorcise a wart. He knows who occupied

Pennywise Farm in 1880, who kept the Tinners Arms in 1914, and who will inherit Peg's Wood when old Joe retires next year. His vegetables are the envy of every gardener at the flower show. When drought has parched the springs, he knows how many days must elapse before they will respond to wind and rain. He is so upright that householders regard him as a kind of lock and key; when he is about, anything can be left around. Antiquarians, geologists, Ordnance surveyors, archaeologists, journalists, detectives . . . all may find themselves referred to him, and few are sent empty away. He can out-poach the poacher, but prefers to enlighten the constable. At a time of life when many of his contemporaries are either dead or infirm, he is employed to dig graves: "I don't pretend I enjoy it, mind. 'Tis what you might call a thoughtful occupation. But I knew 'en, dear soul, and his wife, too. Anyway, someone must do the job. Someone will be doing it for me afore long."

At all seasons his complexion is brown, but in August he attains the tan which we call mahogany. While the rest of the village is casting clouts he wears a workaday uniform of cap, moleskin waistcoat, flannel shirt (*sans* collar or tie), and boots so studded with blakeys that they sound like an army on the march. Despite his muscular height, he is commonly assessed as though he were small. "I know a little man who'll plaster that ceiling . . . who'll mow that meadow . . . who'll mend that wheel . . . clear that copse . . . patch that barn . . . cure that calf . . . fix that gate." Some writers portray him as a figure of archaic fey, but the better sort show him as he is ("warts and all" as Cromwell expressed it), more outspoken than his father, less egalitarian than his son. Being a realist he still speaks of 'the gentry', and for the same reason is sometimes puzzled to know whither they have gone, and by whom they are superseded. So far as I can discover he envies no man: "Win the Pools? Not work, you mean? Give up my hens and that bit o'thatching I'm doing for young Joe? Lord, Lord, I'd be dead in a fortnight. Now a fiver now and again, that'd be very acceptable, but you don't catch me committing suicide for the sake o' fifty thousand."

To watch Jack at work is to understand the nature of skill, of industriousness, and of the strength which, by not straining itself, achieves more in half-an-hour than some younger men manage in three-quarters. He is among the elite who have retained pride in their craft, loyalty to their employer, and contempt for men who have not. Above all, he stands fast and gets on with the job at a time when steadfastness seems more difficult than in war, being unsustained by any upsurge of national example. Whatever the task, he fulfils it to the best of his ability, which is sometimes considerable, always conscientious, never shoddy. His own limitations and the background to his childhood narrowed the way ahead; yet he chose the path which he has trodden, and would choose it again: "For I never could bear to bide indoors. I won't say, though, that there haven't been mornings when I looked at the sky and wished I could lie abed till dinnertime." In matters of religion he is an Anglican, less from conviction (his father was a Methodist) than from a love of bell-ringing, which chapels cannot satisfy. His politics are best described as the hopeful despair of a Liberal whom events and commonsense have driven into a Conservative camp ("In my young days the present Tory party would have been regarded as a pack of Bolsheviks").

Although he has spent his life in the same village, Jack belongs to no county, because his *alter ego* flourishes throughout Britain and far beyond. I have met some of them myself; Hitler, for example, which is the affectionate nickname of a German who, having arrived here as a prisoner of war in 1944, married a local girl, and set up as carpenter. When the English perceived that he worked better, and charged less, than any other carpenter in the district, their purse overcame their prejudice, thereby transforming an impecunious alien into a prosperous compatriot. Jack traces his lineage to the first men who built houses, devised implements, launched boats, and tilled fields. He was therefore old when Horace, the Latin poet, hailed him as *Rusticus, abnormis sapiens,* one of nature's philosophers. The poet might have added that Jack was also one of nature's gentlemen, being courteous as much by inclination as by education; independent without surliness; respectful without servility; often able to teach because always eager to learn. The health of his mind and the health of his body nourish each other. Activity is his medicine, and he takes it every day. If he remains as fortunate as he deserves, he will live for another decade or more, reducing his work, but never the satisfaction which it affords.

Does Jack symbolise an irrevocable parting of the ways? Will he find no place in a world where loyalty and labour have been supplanted by laziness and lucre? Or is he a member of that happy breed whom W. H. Davies hoped would one day inherit the earth:

> When will it come, that golden time,
> When every heart must sing?
> The power to choose the work we love
> Makes every man a king.

Blackboards and Blackbirds

A young woman suddenly appeared in the middle of the road, raising her right hand to halt the traffic. I therefore glanced behind, assuming that a phantom limousine must be bearing down. The road, however, was empty. Yet there the girl stood, imperious as a Statue of Liberty in the Scottish Highlands. Looking about for some explanation, I sighted a school among trees, from which a little child appeared, then another and a third and so on until I had counted ten. Good as proverbial gold, they crossed to the far side of the road, and stood there, waiting. Having shepherded the lambs, the teacher lowered her hand, and I moved forward again, still wondering why she had halted me. Perhaps she feared lest my Lakeland terrier was a wolf in English clothing.

Presently we got talking—all twelve of us—and the teacher confessed that the sun and the birds had tempted her: "To heck wi' the curriculum," she exclaimed. "It's a bonnie morn, and I'll no' grudge the wee mites a romp i' the heather." Deciding that valour was the better part of indiscretion, I announced that a civil servant, with whom I had breakfasted at an hotel, was less than eight miles to the nor'ard, outward bound on an unheralded visitation. The teacher thereupon glanced at her wrist watch: "Children," she announced, "We'll hae' just five minutes. And after that we'll return to the marthamarticks." So, we went our own ways.

After about a quarter of a mile I looked back. The sound of merry voices still reached me, and I could still see the school, white as one mushroom on a mountain, symbolising the many others, from Land's End to John o'Groat's, whose teachers create oases of stability in a discontented desert. How different, I thought, from the schools which discharge their products by the thousand, some of them already half-baked in the fashionable mould of undisciplined oafs, aided and abetted by 'progressive' pedagogues and witless parents.

Our village schools are descended from the sixteenth-century Dame Schools, so-called because the teacher was usually an elderly woman. As in a pantomime, however, some of the dames were men; a fact which the Education Commissioners noted in 1837: "One of the best of the Dame and Common Day Schools," they reported, "is kept by a blind man who hears his scholars their lessons and explains them with great simplicity . . ." He was, the Commissioners warned, "liable to interruption in his academic labours as his wife keeps a mangle and he is obliged to turn it for her." William Shenstone attended just such a school, and expressed his gratitude by dedicating a long poem to his guru: "He learned to read," said Johnson, "of an old dame, whom his poem of *The Schoolmistress* has delivered to posterity . . ."

Describing the Cotswolds at the end of the nineteenth century, Mrs Sturge Henderson remarked: "There are secluded hamlets where the sole qualification of the teacher is the fact that her mother filled the post before her, and teacher and taught pursue melodious days in ignorance of the existence of codes and examiners." Although our village schools now acknowledge both examiners and codes, some of them have preserved their intimacy. When I last visited Holy Island, a few years ago, the school contained eight (or was it ten?) pupils, half of whom were the children either of the teacher or of the vicar. Such camaraderie will horrify those Aschams who suppose that education is primarily a matter of accommodation; a supposition not shared by the many country-folk who dislike a system which compels their children daily to travel twenty or thirty miles to and from a school in an alien habitat. Such compulsory waste of time and money is called equality of opportunity. But what of the carpenter's son who, at the age of fifteen, says: "Oi don't warnt any more o' thart blasted 'istory. Oi warnt to work 'longside my Dard." Is it right to deny what may be intuitive wisdom? Is it right to condemn the youth to another year of reluctant fact-finding which, if he wishes, he can practise for himself, as countless others have done, and all the better by practising willingly at a riper season? Even the new universities admit that the day has not yet dawned when dustmen will be required to qualify as doctors of philosophy. Any labour exchange will assure you that some doctors of philosophy may soon be seeking employment as dustmen. Equality of opportunity is neither opportune nor equal when it forcibly retards those who do not wish to use it.

Among the staunchest advocates of a truly rural education was Thomas Bewick, son of a Northumbrian peasant, who taught himself to become a great artist. Bewick held that young children ought not to be haunted by homework and examinations. Potential scholars, he affirmed, would blossom more fruitfully were they held back for a year or two; the rest ought to study the homely aspects of country life . . . flowers, stars, woods, fields, and the wild creatures thereof. If children, said Bewick, "were sent to the edge of some moor, to scamper among the whins and heather, under the care of some good old man who would teach them a little every day . . . they would there, in this kind of preparatory school, lay the foundations of health as well as education". He then uttered a challenge by stating a fact: "Let anyone look at the contrast between men thus brought up, and the generality of early-matured Lilliputian plants, and he will soon see, with very few exceptions, the difference, both in body and mind, between them." In short, Bewick anticipated Dr Arnold's motto at Rugby: "First religious and moral principles; secondly, gentlemanly conduct; thirdly, intellectual ability." Yet Bewick himself was partly forestalled by All Souls' College, Oxford, which required its Fellows to be well-spoken, well-groomed, and not obtrusively erudite: *Bene nati, bene vestiti, et mediocriter docti.*

"Education," said Herbert Spencer, "has for its object the formation of character." Much of what now passes as education has for its object the acquisition of money. And with that object in view a great many parents compel their offspring to enter what they themselves have called 'the rat race'. Yet there remains a minority of children who will not enter that race, preferring instead to become shepherds, gamekeepers, postmen, dustmen, grooms, farriers, farmhands, fishermen. If they continue to study textbooks after leaving school, well and good; if they do not, they may still remain good and well. Nine-tenths of those villagers neither request nor require to be fact-filled after the age of sixteen; and were they pumped till they perished, they would continue to prefer *The Maid of the Mountains* to the *Missa Solemnis*. In any event, education does not start at five years of age, nor end at fifty. Education is co-aeval with life itself.

Cricket on the Green

They say that the blacksmith once swiped a 'six' into the sea. He may have done, but it must have been long ago, when tides were higher than they are now, and blacksmiths brawnier, and the atmosphere less resisitant to moving bodies. The pitch itself is sited majestically, midway between woods and waves, in a setting so enchanting that a coastguard has been known to step on his stumps while sighting a yacht whose tipsy signal announced that she was on fire, out of control, in quarantine and carrying dynamite. Likewise the gamekeeper once missed a 'dolly' because, when it popped past his gloves, he was looking to see whether the pigeon were a partridge.

Mourning Zion, the Israelites wept beside the waters of Babylon: "We hanged our harps upon the willows in the midst thereof." But an English willow smiles when it skims a ball to the boundary. Few sights are more English than a village cricket match, played by men who are *amateurs* or lovers of sport for its own sake. Though they will strive to win, such players can well endure to lose, because their cricket is a game and nothing more. Cricket has a long pedigree, dating back at least to the year 1676, when an English naval officer in the Levant joined with others from the Ward Room at a game of 'krikett'. In 1731 the Honourable Artillery Company were playing what they already called "the old game" of cricket. Hampshire's famous Hambledon Club was only one of several prototypes of all such amiable assembles. Rural, too, was the king of cricketers, Dr William Gilbert Grace, a Gloucestershire man, born at Downend near the Severn Estuary, in a house called The Chestnuts. His father, also a physician, had felled part of the orchard in order to make a pitch whereon W. G. learned to play a straight bat with four brothers and four sisters (not forgetting a dog fielding on the boundary). No other cricketer can vie with his prowess. When he was only fifteen years old he scored 170 against the Gentlemen of

Sussex. When he was eighteen he scored 224 for England at the Oval; and on the second day of the match he was allowed to leave the field so that he might compete at a meeting of the National Olympian Association, where he won the quarter-mile hurdles. In his prime he scored 839 in three successive innings. But his finest achievement was to transmute a trivial accomplishment into a symbol of chivalry. Despite the rancourous tedium which now infects our professional cricket matches, people still describe a dirty trick as "It isn't cricket."

On some village greens the players create the sort of ensemble that was there during the reign of Queen Victoria. Longstop, for example, is a choirboy, wearing a Salvation Army cap so many sizes too big for him that he has twice been winded by a ball whose flight he failed to follow from beneath the eye-shading peak. The butcher still flaunts braces and grey flannels when he strides out to hit-or-miss. The scorer still adds an occasional digit to the board, so that ninety wickets appear to have fallen for thirty runs. The cricket Blue still contrives to get himself 'yorked' first ball. Tall umpires still wear the white coat that belongs to their dimunitive colleague at the other end of the pitch. Gerald Bullett caught the very texture of those amateurs:

> Long-limbed Waggoner, stern, unbudging,
> Stands like a rock behind the bails.
> Dairyman umpire, gravely judging,
> Spare no thought for his milking-pails.

No other game has inspired so much good verse. Andrew Lang celebrated summer in Oxford,

> When wickets are bowled and defended,
> When Isis is glad with "the Eights" . . .

Francis Thompson, himself a Lancastrian, mourned the passing of Hornby and Barlow:

> For the field is full of shades as I near the shadowy coast,
> And a ghostly batsman plays to the bowling of a ghost . . .

John Masefield recalled the Test Match of 1888, when England, needing 85 to win, with all wickets standing, failed to make it:

> . . . our star had set.
> All England out, with seven runs to get.

I

Walter de la Mare loved the village game, its tall stories and bizarre statistics. He once told me of a fielder who stumped both batsmen off the same ball. But I liked best his tale of Edmund Gosse, who, although he had never before held a bat in his life, consented to open for a Literary XI, and then smote the first ball so fiercely that the bat disintegrated. Supposing such incidents to be common, Gosse turned to the pavilion, and in a loud voice cried: "Bring some more bats!" No less exhilarating was Mr Jingle's love of the game, or at any rate of its conviviality: "Stopping at the Crown—Crown at Muggleton—met a party—flannel jackets—white trousers—anchovy sandwiches—devilled kidneys—splendid fellow—glorious."

Like the stream beside the green, village cricket goes at its own pace, which is livelier than that of the professionals. The game, not the result, comes first. If a side makes 80, it has not done badly; if a bowler takes two wickets, he has done well. On the field itself all men are equal. A shepherd will say to his employer: "Maister, try pitching wi' both eyes shut. Happen thou'll git closer on't stumps." If the squire can neither bat nor bowl, he goes in at number ten, and is thankful that his fielding got him there. While other 'sportsmen' watch their televised Test Match, young Ted runs a mile up-lane to spread the good news: "The rector's made twelve! Us only needs four to win."

When at last the stumps are drawn, and girls filch the boys from a rival sport, you may smoke a pipe with the old men, savouring the sing-song of their sentiments. And when the veterans retire to supper, you have the starry green to yourself; and the prospect, God willing, of many matches still to come; and the slow walk home through the woods.

Romany Wry

The best way to explore the Chiltern Hills is to walk, and the best way to walk is the Icknield Way, a pre-Roman road from Cambridgeshire to Wiltshire, which crosses the Hills between Dunstable in Bedfordshire and Ewelme in Oxfordshire. Long tracts of the Way are wide and grassy, venturing where no road dares. On them you may pass a gipsy encampment; not a caravan site with television aerials, but a tent, supported by hazel sticks. Forty years ago, when I lived near the Way, I seldom failed to meet some gipsies there. Today they are few and very far between. Often your luck is out, and you find that the gipsies have moved on, leaving only a circle of charred sticks, and perhaps some litter also.

What is a gipsy? How many of them are there in Britain? Where did they come from? How do they differ from Tinkers and fun fair attendants? Few people could answer those questions correctly, yet gipsies continue to cast a spell on popular imagination, which in turn continues to shroud them with myth. The word 'gipsy' first appeared in 1537, echoing a tradition that the nomads originated in Egypt. Some gipsies justify that tradition by citing the prophet Ezekiel: "I shall scatter the Egyptians among the nations." Modern scholarship, however, sets the gipsies' origins far to the east of Egypt. The wanderers, it seems, came from India; some travelling via Persia and the Caucasus; others, keeping to the south, reaching Palestine and Egypt. Like Jews, the gipsies became a race apart, conditioned by the land they had adopted, yet conserving a measure of their native culture. Again like Jews, they were hounded, sometimes with good reason, sometimes without. Queen Elizabeth I ordered them to quit the kingdom, but they stayed and multiplied. Gipsies today may be Christians, or Muslims, or atheists, or eclectic believers. Their laws and customs vary, like their dialect, which is akin to Sanskrit. The less urban the terrain, the more virile the culture. On the Continent, for example, the tribes or *vitchas* (which may contain anything from a dozen to several hundred families) are led by an elected chief with power to punish. Justice is administered by the *kriss* or assembly of adult males who sometimes impose and execute the death penalty.

No one knows how many gipsies remain in Britain. Certainly we have no official census of their numbers, which may exceed 40,000. Some people classify gipsies into four groups, of which the largest, the Travellers, abound at fun fairs, but are not recognised as Romanies. The second group contains *Didakais*, a mixed breed with a sprinkling of Romany. The third group, *Posh-rats*, are said to be half-bloods. The fourth group are true gipsies or Romanies (*Rom*, meaning either a man or a gipsy; his wife being called *romani*). For my part, I do not see how those groups can be

either numbered or defined. It must suffice to say that the true
Romany is a dying breed. Not long ago, for instance, I passed a
large gathering of gipsies at Appleby in Westmorland. Many of
their caravans had cost more than £1,000; several carried a television aerial; all were equipped with kitchen sinks. One of the
Travellers assured me that he owned property in Manchester,
worth £15,000. A few miles further on, at the village of Knock,
I met another sort of caravan, pulled by a horse, and accompanied
by two small children, barefoot, ragged, radiant. Their black-

haired mother—a girl of nineteen—was startlingly beautiful. The
husband—as handsome as his wife—told me that they lived on
less than ten pounds a week, partly by mending and making
baskets, partly by selling fell ponies. Neither he nor his wife had
been to school. They read little and wrote less. Perhaps that was
one reason why they were happy, strong, and healthy.

I never encountered any gipsies among the Scottish Highlands,
but in the Lowlands I have supped with Tinkers or Tinklers, a
kind of Traveller, whose name recalls their ancestral craft. An
Edinburgh professor has estimated that ten per cent of seven

hundred words used by Tinklers are of Romany origin. The New Forest gipsies used to be famous, but in 1927, having been granted four compounds, they became tame exhibits, like the Red Indians. Wales is the last stronghold of the true British gipsies; and there I enjoyed my most memorable encounter with them, notably along the drover's track through the mountains above Tregaron in Cardiganshire. The old people slept in a horse-hauled caravan, but most of the youngsters occupied makeshift tents. In summer the men eschewed even that cold comfort, and slept on the ground. By the light of two camp fires the elders tapped time while dark-haired youths and girls swirled to the tune of a fiddle (the Romany word *bosh* means a fiddler). How did those carefree citizens earn a living? Many of the women told fortunes, and made mops from gleaned fleece; the men were tinkers, basket makers, horse dealers, and seasonal farm workers. Being congenitally cheerful, they smiled a good deal; but when I asked them to foretell the fortunes of their nomadic routine, the smile became wry: "Who knows?" they said, "The old die. The young are corrupted. Who knows?" Then the smile widened. "Tomorrow we reach Tregaron. There is a farmer there who buys ponies. Good beer, too. A generous man. Pays cash."

In 1775 Gilbert White wrote a letter to his friend, Daines Barrington, which proves that some of our Romanies retain their ancient hardihood: "We have," White said, "two gangs or hordes of gypsies which infest the south and west of England . . . One of these tribes calls itself by the noble name of Stanley . . ." Of the other tribe he remarked: "As far as their harsh gibberish can be understood, they seem to say that the name of their clan is Curleople . . ." Despite their genesis in a warm climate, the gipsies did not flinch from Hampshire winters: "while other beggars lodge in barns, stables, and cow-houses," White went on, "these sturdy savages seem to pride themselves in braving the severities of winter, and in living *sub dio* the whole year round." During a frost White found a gipsy girl lying in his garden "with nothing over her but a piece of blanket extended on a few hazel rods bent hoop fashion, and stuck in the earth at each end . . . yet within this garden there was a large hop-kiln, into the chambers of which she might have retired, had she thought shelter an object worthy of her attention."

Like every other way of life the Romany's has its limitations.

In the mountain a new ballet and the latest news bulletin seem less than urgent. The Romany himself may stoop to mend a basket or to gather fleece, but at least he is not bowed beneath the burden of Atlas. For a little while—perhaps for a long while—he and his barefoot family will go their own way, relishing the wind on the heath, and exercising certain physical and psychic powers which industrialized men have exchanged for a prosperously disgruntled existence.

From Dawn till Dusk

We can measure time with amazing accuracy, but of its nature we know nothing. Even its existence is debatable. T. S. Eliot, for example, believed that "All is always now." If, however, time does exist, we may reasonably suppose that it has done so for a very long while . . . so long, indeed, that the clocks wherewith we reckon it are mere infants, and the wristwatch a newborn babe. King Henry VIII was well satisfied if the palace clocks neither gained nor lost more than one hour in twenty-four. Charles II owned a less erratic timepiece, yet watches were still such novelties that Pepys—when at last he did acquire one—confessed: "I cannot forbear carrying my watch in my hand . . . and seeing what hour it is a hundred times, and am apt to think to myself, how could I be so long without one." Give or take five minutes either way, Pepys felt sufficiently punctual when he walked to an audience with the King.

Time itself was slower to reach the countryside, and seemed to pass there more leisurely than in London. Jacobean cottagers relied on the sun, the moon, and all those other sights and sounds which still guide a villager whose watch has stopped. Even a nineteenth-century farmer might eat his dinner or shear his sheep according to a timescale which we would now regard as scarcely more helpful than a tear-off calendar. Farmer Oak, the hero of Hardy's *Far from the Madding Crowd,* cherished a timekeeper that was "a watch as to shape and intention, and a small clock as to size". At least it never lost time: "This instrument being several years older then Mr Oak's grandfather, had a peculiarity of going either too fast or not at all." In more senses than one the instrument was a stop-watch: "The smaller of its hands occasionally slipped round the pivots, and thus, though the minutes were told with precision, nobody could be quite certain of the hour . . ."

Countrymen and sailors are not left utterly timeless when the clock stops. While living in a boat in Cornish waters I used to gauge the hour by the sky, for on bright days the sun served as a dial whose numerals were the brow of a cliff, the spire of a church, the tip of a mast. The knack is not so simple as it seems, because allowance must be made for the daily alteration of earth's course around the sun. After several weeks I got to within twenty minutes of Greenwich, but was never able to vie with the fisherman who, if anyone asked him for the time, glanced at the sun, and replied: "About ten-past three," or "Coming up to six o'clock." On certain occasions his timekeeping was spiritual rather than temporal, as when he answered a local tippler by saying: "Time you signed the pledge."

The pace of modern life compels most people to glance at the clock hurriedly, with an eye on the minute hand and the next appointment; but one of the pleasures of living in a small boat is the knowledge that for most of each day you need not tell the time at all; and when you do need, you discover that time tells itself to every mariner lying at his accustomed berth. Thus, when he awakes, the sun and the birds may say: "Half-past-seven." Had the birds been more clamorous or less, and the sun's altitude a few degrees higher or lower, the mariner might have murmured: "Four-o'clock" or "Well past nine." Meanwhile his morning wears on, measured by a motley carillon. At 8.20 a.m. the Royal Mail is heard, and occasionally seen, burrowing its way among steep lanes above the harbour; at 9.5 a.m. (Tuesdays and Fridays excepted) the fisherman drags his praam to the water; at 10.30 a.m. (Mondays and Thursdays only) the baker's van reaches a farm beside the creek; at 11 a.m. the ferry arrives; at noon the static jetsam marks high water; when the clock points to 2.15 p.m. the sun is immediately above the second oak on the third hill; and when the boat's brightwork becomes too hot to touch, the time is tea. Soon after seven the shadows slant steeply, reaching the limit of their span while the sun sinks behind the highest point of the peninsula, so that the mariner either dons a sweater or steers for the open sea and another sixty minutes of warmth. Punctual as Big Ben, the evening lighthouse rolls its first beam along the water while boats in harbour curtsey as the last ferry casts off, hooting a farewell time-check. Presently the seaweed reflects a star, flowing at a rate which suggests three hours to high water (tide charts are in the starboard locker, alongside a *Pilotage Manual*). And if further chimes are needed, a thrush supplies them, singing solo from the shrub beyond Quay House.

An out-of-doors man tells the time by looking and listening. If you ask him to define the process he will probably say: "It's just an instinct." But that is to over-simplify the matter, for during those intent moments he takes a number of observations, from which he makes a number of calculations. In the last resort he will rely on his own metabolism, a blend of hunger, thirst, and a waxing or waning of interest in ploughing a field or polishing a stanchion. Busy about his task, such a man is spared the kind of clock-watching which afflicted Shakespeare's Richard II:

> Now time doth waste me;
> For now hath time made me his numbering clock.

Edward Thomas wrote a story about some village busybodies who set great store on "tools, processes and machines for saving time". In one parish alone "enough time had been saved to stretch back to William the Conqueror." At the end of their lives, however, when the timesavers came to examine their dividends, the verdict was not profitable. One of the investors, who formerly enjoyed reading Vergil while sitting on a gate, acquired a car, and at once discovered that his time-saving vehicle prevented him from sitting on a gate while reading Vergil.

Walking two miles to post my letters at a wayside pillarbox, I was lately offered a lift by a motorist who could not understand why I preferred to walk: "It wastes so much time," he protested. When the motorist had disappeared, and the lane resumed its everyday idleness, I took a number of observations, made a number of calculations, and then, as I wastefully walked home, said to myself a number of the words which you have been reading.

8

Away from it All

In late August the countryside looks dishevelled and a shade
weary, like an athlete who, as he enters the final straight, knows
that he will win the race, yet cannot conceal the effort which it
has cost him. Trees long ago lost their springtime lustre, and have
still to gain autumnal glory. Uncut meadows need a barber;
so also do highbank lines, especially when a shower bends bracken,
briar, and the last topheavy foxglove. Embrowned by the drought,
lawns are pitted with a kind of alopecia which reveals the fissured
soil beneath bald patches. Cart-ruts become concrete cliffs; and
they, too, are fissured, split lengthwise like faulted rocks.
Marooned in midfield, a plough resembles the hulk of a warship,
rustily alsinaceous. Tar trickles from main roads. Lanes are dusty
to the tops of their hedges. A robin's song heightens the stillness.
Four weeks ago a villager could have made his way home by
daylight at bedtime; four weeks from now he will accept darkness
at suppertime. But August is neither chiefly dark nor predomi-
nantly light. It is a threshold, a waiting place. Above all, it is a
time when Britons go down to the sea in cars.

Some people have dared to suggest that the annual trek to the
coast is not wholly beneficial. Bravest of those brave is Professor
J. A. Williamson, the naval historian, who complained that
Cornwall has been conquered "by the swelling flood of detri-
balised people from no particular region, hotel-keepers, *rentiers*,
holidaymakers, who constitute the amorphous society of modern
England". As though that were not brave enough, Williamson
scaled the very summit of heroism by denouncing "what is called
the tourist industry, the sale of the country's charms for money, a

species of harlotry". Well, I have lived to see a Sussex cottager rubble his garden into a car park for trippers. I have lived to see a Somerset householder selling glasses of water at two for one half-halfpenny. I have lived to see . . . but so have you, and so much the more will your children. People of mature mind and ample leisure no longer visit Polperro during the holiday season. They avoid Looe, they shun Broadway, and it never occurs to them to enter Lakeland. Even the places which do not set out to attract the crowd—Sidmouth, Sheringham, St David's, Iona, Skye—even they now wilt beneath the motorist who extends his frontier beyond Clacton, Blackpool, Box Hill, and Madame Tussaud's. Yet there is a ray of hope amid the gloom because many of those new frontiers are unexplored by the vehicles that have reached them. The principal victims are those unmercenary residents for whom the sunniest season of the year is darkened by innumerable footsteps passing and repassing their door, cramming their shops, littering their beach, and generally proving that whenever too many people visit a resort worth visiting, the resort ceases to be worth a visit. Within a dozen miles or so of my home is a cove which can be reached only by walking thither. I have lost count of the number of motorists who, when I warned them that they could drive no further, remarked to the family: "No go, kids. We'd have to walk." Bless them all. Long may they continue *in partibus vehiculorum*.

How different are the true explorers who bump their way through a mile of ruts, and then walk half as far again to a beach whereon they need not step among supine bodies. Most of those explorers belong to what we now call the lower-income group. They include clergymen, young married officers, newly-qualified barristers, artists, dons, pittance-pensioners, and many others who cannot and will not imperil the national welfare by striking for the sake of a bigger car or a more colourful television. Such people enrich their holiday by discovering what to look for. They carry a guidebook, and maps which they can read. Even before their holiday begins, they have learned more about local history than some of the natives ever knew or ever will. They have an eye for architecture, both secular and sacred. They are fond of walking, and will enlarge their horizon by motoring to unfamiliar footpaths. Avoiding persons who would seem tedious, they tend to meet those who are congenial; and this they do by instinct and experience, for they have the knack of widening the circle of their acquaintance without lowering the standard which they require of intimacy.

I remember especially the elderly widower, by trade a plumber, who each year cycles along lanes from Warwickshire to a farmhouse near the Cornish coast. He knows a little about flowers, about churches, about inns, geology, castles, worthies, manors. Sometimes he is joined by his grandchildren, to whom he imparts his own spirit of informed adventure. Like the swallow, he is welcomed when he arrives, missed when he departs, and at all times taken as a symbol of gladness. I remember also the Methodist minister and his family who pitch their caravan at a lonely spot near Bamburgh in Northumberland. Yet there is nothing unsociable about them. They greet and are greeted. They enjoy their pint and their gossip. But—because they live and work among crowds—they use their holiday as a retreat therefrom, the better to advance when duty calls. It is a pleasure and a privilege to meet such people. From some of them I learn about my own part of the world; by all I am enlightened about theirs. Differences of age, accent, income, politics, religion . . . those things neither obtrude nor impede when one explorer shares his discoveries with another: "This morning we found a path through the woods. It's not marked on the map, so we asked the farmer if he minded, and he said, No, provided we shut the gates. But that's not all. Just before you reach the sea, there's a thatched cottage with the most wonderful hollyhocks we've ever seen. Such a dear old woman lives in it. She'd been a nurse in New Zealand and Singapore and heaven knows where else. Travelled all round the world. And the point is, it's the very cottage she was born in."

That is a true holiday; not a mere squandering of money nor tanning of torsos, but a change of scene and routine; a blend of idleness and activity; each day revealing something new about the ways in which other people spend their own working lives.

Under the Weather

Of all the many phrases with which Englishmen bewail their predicament, none is neater than 'under the weather'. To an Eskimo in his igloo it will seem perfectly natural that the sun should disappear for months; to an African in his kraal it will seem perfectly natural that the sun should never disappear at all, except at nightime. Such men have no need of barometers. Englishmen, by contrast, regard the barometer as part of their person. Deprived of it, they become like women without a handbag.

Strictly speaking, every adult Briton ought long ago to have acclimatised himself to snow in May, frost in June, and warmth in October. Yet his cynicism is matched by his surprise. Having cursed the climate, he feels amazed whenever it fulfils his own gloomy forecast. Even so, the matter is not a jest. Although the climate can no longer starve us, it may still imperil the farmer, debilitate the holidaymaker, and spread dismay from Land's End to John o'Groat's. Summer, after all, is the season when unseasonableness becomes most glaring and least sufferable. A drenching June draws undue attention to itself, like a tall man whose trousers are hitched at half-mast. It flouts our sense of decency, like laughter at a funeral. It puts everyone in a bad temper by withholding what they regard as their reasonable right. Jerome K. Jerome expressed our summer discontents very aptly when his three men in a boat encountered foul weather on the Thames: "Sunlight," they agreed, "is the lifeblood of Nature. Mother Earth looks at us with such dull soulless eyes, when the sunlight has died away from out of her. It makes us sad to be with her then; she does not seem to know us or care for us. She is as a widow who has lost the husband she loved, and her children touch her hand, and look up into her eyes, but gain no smile from her."

Our climate is regional as well as unreliable. While Jerome was writing those Oxfordshire words, the Eden at Appleby, or the Stour at Shipston, may (in his own phrase) have watched the sunlight "flinging diamonds from the mill-wheels, throwing kisses to the lilies, wantoning with the weirs' white waters". For the past few weeks the weirs' waters have certainly been very white indeed, chiefly because the sky above them was grey. No matter where I awoke—whether in Devon, or in Buckinghamshire, or in Northumberland—my eyes opened always on low clouds edged with mourning for summer's premature decease; on trees plump as prima donnas who, instead of standing still, performed a topheavy ballet; on flowers whose colours appeared unnatural, as though they had been forced to bloom for Christmas.

There comes a time when we no longer say Amen to Miss Sackville-West's water music:

> Now be you thankful, who in England dwell,
> That to the starving trees and thirsting grass
> Even at summer's height come cloudy fleets.

We wait impatiently until we may say with Edward Shanks:

> The fields are full of summer still,
> And breathe again upon the air
> From brown dry side of hedge and hill
> More sweetness than the sense can bear.

Being generally a cheerful creature, buoyed by Santayana's "animal faith in life", the average countryman begins by making the best of bad weather. Trusting tomorrow—or at any rate reserving judgment until the weekend—he sloshes around in gum boots and mackintosh, or removes the mothballs from his scarf, and goes gloved and great-coated into the gale. After a while, however, even the most sanguine temperament declines any longer to pretend that such activities are pleasurable. The land itself looks anaemic, drained (or ought one to say deluged?) of its proper complexion. Instead of flaunting their own various hues, all trees and shrubs wear one of two shades . . . either dark green or darker green. Every river and pond is as grey as the North Sea in November. Cornfields are battered. A second crop of hay waits for the sun to raise it. And while clouds scud across the sky, or skulk there motionless, we reflect ruefully that a veneer of vapour is able to hide the hottest star in the solar system.

Some people are so much under the weather that the barometer may be said to influence a large part of their life. Milton's Latin poem to the springtime, written when he was twenty, reveals its own weather lore: "Do I deceive myself, or has the bounteous Spring summoned inspiration to my side?" In his age the poet cut his cloth to suit a later season, for Mrs Milton said that he "used to compose his poetry chiefly during the winter"; a statement which was verified by Milton's amanuensis, Edward Phillips: "His Vein never happily flow'd but from the Autumnal Equinoctial to the Vernal . . ." Housman's Shropshire Lad sighed because he had outlived twenty springs and summers: "It only leaves me fifty more." Fifty! What of the man who has already outlived that number, and in July—with the days growing shorter—still awaits the warmth which June withheld.

Although it will seem a small thing in the sum total of human endeavour, my heart aches for those summer fêtes that are literally washed out. What loving labour went to the planning of them; what willing hands made light work of erecting marquees, cutting sandwiches, brewing tea, arranging flowers, dressing children; what needy and deserving souls set their hopes on a fine day. *Sed Deus flavit.* The sight of a dozen children huddling in a rain-soaked tent, or of a coach-load of pensioners marooned in their vehicle . . . those things raise the question which perplexed Job himself: "Shall a mortal man be more just than God?" Nor does it help if that question is phrased as a proposition: "All things occur by Mischance."

If summer becomes really vicious, I turn the tables by tilting the calendar. At about seven in the evening, when I might have expected to relax in the sun, I draw the curtains, chuck some twigs on the hearth, add a few logs, strike a match, and welcome back the winter. Sometimes I am glad of the fire. Sometimes I really do need the lamp. It is all a charade, of course; and none of it achieves its purpose, which is to spite the summer and perhaps to shame it into a more seasonable frame of mind. Nevertheless, the pantomime does allow me to express a righteous indignation, and thereby to avoid the mere cynicism of Horace Walpole who, surveying his sodden hay, growled: "Every summer one lives in a state of mutiny and murmur . . . The best sun we have is made of Newcastle coal, and I am determined never to reckon upon any other."

Sometimes, however, a scowling summer steals the last laugh. Finding that the heat from my fire has become intolerable, I draw aside the curtains in order to open the window . . . and am blinded by a blazing sun.

Faith - Hope - Charity

Every year the vicar and the bank manager compile a list of villagers who are eligible to receive gratis a bucket of coal and a pair of blankets, the perennial harvest of a legacy bequeathed by an eighteenth-century yeoman. Forty years ago the competition was strong. Even fifteen years ago there were a dozen candidates. This year not a single villager really needs the gift; in other words, none would suffer through lack of it; a fact that would have amazed the yeoman, to whom paupers were parts of the natural order:" For the poor always ye have with you."

Faith, hope, and charity; of which, says the Bible, the last is first: "The greatest of these is charity." Charity, however, does not mean almsgiving. It means loving-kindness (Greek *charitas*), and may therefore be practised by any widow, even although she cannot bestow one mite. To chide an era for not practising what it never preached is as foolish as to scold an infant for wetting the bed. Wisdom disapproves, but does not blame. Much has been written about the hardships of the poor; little about the efforts to relieve them. Yet I would wager that every English town, and many villages, possess tangible tokens of generosity. Consider, for example, the small town of Buckingham, whose inhabitants received a free hospital in 1312, followed in 1431 by an almshouse which John Barton built and endowed for six poor townsfolk, to whom he gave a weekly pension. In 1583 Dorothy Dayrell increased that pension. In 1856 Elizabeth Gray added another increase. Buckingham's Free Grammar School was founded by Lady Isabel Denton in 1540, thereafter receiving a grant from Edward VI. In 1597 Queen Elizabeth endowed Christ's Hospital for seven poor women; in 1598 the hospital acquired a grant of land from Robert Harris; and in 1629 a grant from Robert Higgins whom the parish register describes as "clerk". The long litany of Buckingham charities includes a grant of land for the poor (from Katherine Aggard in 1574); a yearly gift of money and clothes to five poor widows (from Lady Mary Baghot in 1685); a yearly distribution of food (from Thomas Grove in 1687); gifts of money and clothes to six poor people (from Lady Penelope Osborn in 1695); a large sum of money to Christ's Hospital (from Ann Ellis in 1840); and a Christmas Box for the poor (from Henry Pittam, the town draper, in 1842). Both the very rich and the rather poor made their donations. Thus, in 1667 a Buckinghamshire shepherd, Matthew Nash, bequeathed "a house close and two butts" to provide a Good Friday gift of food to the poor of Quainton, Waddesdon, and Wescott; in 1787, an Oxfordshire peeress, the Viscountess Saye and Sele, bequeathed (in modern currency) £100,000 to build almshouses at Quainton and Grendon, to apprentice village boys to a trade, and to relieve the needy.

Throughout the Middle Ages the Church took upon itself to care for the sick, the destitute, the old. Despite their flaws, the monks were the mainstay of the poor. None knocked in vain; all paid what they could afford, which meant that some paid nothing. By dispossessing the monks, Henry VIII and his newly-rich cronies robbed those whose need was greatest. A vivid instance of that robbery can be seen at Stydd in Lancashire, where the

mediaeval Knights of St John founded an hospice and a church. The hospice has disappeared, but the church remains, more or less intact, a barnlike little place *sans* tower, or chancel, or aisle. In 1728, after a lapse of several centuries, the villagers received a substitute hospice, a Gothic cottage for five old people who had to climb sixteen steps in order to reach a gabled balcony. During the 1960s the almshouse was converted into miniature flats.

Britain is studded with almshouses that were built as the secular successors of monastic charity. In my childhood I used to visit two elderly spinsters whom we called Aunt Lucy and Aunt Fanny, though they might more properly have been called distressed gentlefolk, daughters of a Harley Street surgeon whose legacy either could not or would not foresee inflation and a dearth of husbands. I well remember the row of two-room cottages, spick as proverbial span; their garden tended by the more supple inmates; every doorstep glistening white; all interiors (at least to a small boy) cheerful and equipped with plum cake. There the old ladies spent the evening of their lives, as if they were the very couple whom Edmund Blunden depicted in *Almswomen*:

> Long long ago they passed three-score-and-ten
> And in this doll's-house lived together then.

The small boy could not be expected to understand that the two Misses dwelt under the shadow of an inescapable summons:

> Many a time they kiss and cry and pray
> That both be summoned in the selfsame day . . .

The almshouses at Henley-on-Thames in Oxfordshire stand beside the church, within a stone's throw of the regatta course. These diminuitive Gothic cottages bear an inscription: "Endowed by John Longland, Bishop of Lincoln, 1547. Rebuilt 1830." And they really are diminuitive. Not long ago, for example, one of the almswomen, seeing that I was about to take a photograph of her home, invited me to have a cup of tea. Being above average height, I stooped before entering; but I did not stoop low enough, so that tea was preceded by iodine and lint. Most almsfolk can remember the years when poverty was common. That is one of the reasons why they are grateful to their benefactor. "We remember her in our prayers," said one of the almswomen at Appleby in Westmorland. She referred, of course, to the dauntless Lady Anne Clifford, who not only told Oliver Cromwell to go the Hell but also built the beautiful almshouses at Appleby, choosing local red sandstone, and setting the cottages around a tiny quadrangle.

Let us allow that the public conscience of times past was insensitive to many things which we now regard as evil. Let us allow also that the private conscience of times present too often forgets that old age and loneliness need the kind of intimacy which is best shared among a few, as at Ewelme and the many

other almshouses whose "tiny college" is a haven for superannuated souls.

Journey into the Interior

Not even the dismal weather had deterred them. In hordes they
appeared, quarrelling and gesticulating, like a plague of summer
gnats. "What came ye forth to see?" asked John the Baptist. It
was idle to ask what the gnats had come to see, because at sixty
miles an hour, through mist and rain, they could see little except
the car that was four feet in front of them. On the rare occasions
when I drive for pleasure (I call it "taking the car for a walk") I
never exceed forty miles an hour, and prefer not to exceed thirty,
a pace which allows me to see where I am going. The gnats, on the
other hand, did not wish to see where they were going; they wished
only to get there quickly. Some of them even took the trouble to
shout at me as they shot past. Refusing to be either jeered or
jostled into danger, I kept as close inshore as possible, at about
thirty-five skiddy miles an hour. One by one the gnats nosed into
the middle of the road and then—seeing an oncoming gnat—
swerved back again. It grew monotonous, watching them
squeeze in front, and, having got there, stamp on their brakes,
forcing me to stamp on mine. If it is handled safely, a motor
vehicle can become a public benefactor, so long as its numbers are
controlled, and its use confined to essential journeys. Lacking that
control and safety, it has already become what Llewelyn Powys
called "an invention of Satan, disastrous to every form of civilised
life". It has probably killed or wounded someone since you began
to read these words.

Meanwhile, after three perilous hours, I refused any longer to
be tormented by gnats racing to their pub, their beach, their
fun fair. With immense satisfaction, therefore, I halted the race
by thrusting an arm out of the window, signifying that I was
preparing to turn right, on to what seemed to be the narrowest
lane in Warwickshire. Having turned, I observed through the
mirror that one fool had bumped into another idiot; and there they
both stood, red-faced and rude, while the other maniacs hooted. I
really did feel as though I had escaped from a group of madmen.
Indeed, the feeling became so strong that I pulled up, in a gap

beside a gate, listening to the asylum's distant cacophony. Having made certain that the car was not in anyone's way, I got out and strolled down the lane, thankful to move freely in clean air after sitting for so long among fumes. "That's lucky," I murmured. "It's actually stopped raining." More than ever thankful, I proceeded past a farm or two—very peaceable, very trim—until I sighted a crossroads. "If," I decided, "any of the lanes is narrower than this, I shall follow it." Well, one of them was, so I did, encouraged by a sign that said *Unsuitable for Motor Vehicles*. On I went, through acres of pasture and crops, away from the lunatics, deep into sanity. Suddenly I found myself blinking, and thought at first that I was dazzled by the red brick and white paint of a cottage which just then appeared beside the lane. But it was not the cottage that had dazzled me; it was the clouds, which were thinning so rapidly that the sun broke through, flooding the fields with light and warmth. Still blinking, I reached a brook and beyond it a ford and a timber footbridge; and there I rested, entranced by the beauty of the scene. The birds sang, the brook tinkled, the cottage shone. Presently a dog came up, older even than my own. Having sniffed awhile, the two veterans sat down in the sun, six feet apart, with their backs to each other; a gesture of supreme and mutual trust. When at last a voice called from the cottage, the old dog ambled home, and the stillness grew deeper, heightened by faraway sheep. Had I really spent the past three hours in Bedlam? As though to answer my question, the clouds reappeared, distant yet distinct. I therefore stood up, ready to return by the way I had come. After a few yards I noticed a neat signboard which must have escaped my attention when I arrived: "Tapster Valley Preservation Society," it said. "Help us to preserve this lovely valley now under threat of a proposed motorway." Perhaps I am too old ever to grow wholly accustomed to that sort of shock. Perhaps a part of me momentarily refused to accept the truth, pretending that the signboard was a hoax. After all, one would still doubt one's eyesight if, on the doors of Westminster Abbey, a signboard said: "These premises have been acquired for redevelopment by Superacketeers Ltd." Alas, the Tapster signboard was not a hoax; it was a tract for the times, a writing on the wall, an introit to *Ichabod*.

Don Quixote tilted against windmills, but the defenders of "this lovely valley" find that the whole world of Mammon is in arms against them; a world dedicated to the proposition that the chief end or purpose of mankind is to create a superfluity of sellable objects, and to create them in such a way that they must be replaced soon and often. Instead of buying a good car every ten years, we buy a shoddy one every two years. And the slaughter is either ignored or accepted as the price of prosperity. A howl went up when Max Beerbohm demanded a speed limit of twenty miles an hour, to which he replied with his own brand of urbanity: "Whether," he remarked, "this slowing-down of traffic will cause a great or a small loss of national income, is, I am told, a point on which expert economists are not agreed. What is certain is that it will annually save a vast number of lives." (And, he might have added, a vast amount not only of road-building but also of imported oil, metal, and other hardware.)

Of course, Tapster Valley near Henley-in-Arden is only one example of the way in which life, limb, liberty, and landscape are being sacrificed to the insatiable monster. To some people it will seem an especially vivid example because the valley lies within a forest which Shakespeare made famous: "They say he is already in the forest of Arden, and many a merry man with him; and there they live like the old Robin Hood of England . . . and fleet the time carelessly, as they did in the golden world." If the defenders of Tapster do succeed in causing a diversion, their victory will encourage the defenders of other places to follow the motto of Lady Anne Clifford: "Retain your loyalty; defend your rights." Meanwhile, a group of men—doubtless good husbands and kind fathers—are conspiring to destroy the peace of that valley by subjecting it to the roar of innumerable vehicles travelling at a pace far beyond the immediate control of the speedsters. And one day there will be fog . . .

John Ruskin lived just long enough to witness the beginning of the mechanised attack against our countryside: "Wherever I travel in England," he reported, "I find that men have no other desire or hope, but to have large houses and to move fast. Every perfect and lovely spot which they can touch they defile."

Up the Creek

The sea was so calm that it made no sound against the hull. Yet *Noah's Ark* lay a mile off-shore, drifting toward France at a rate of half-a-knot. Through the heat haze astern, Cornwall climbed meadow-green and barley-brown from sandy caves where the tide meandered like a tongue exploring a tooth. Sunlight scorched the deck, the wheel, the dome of the venerable Kelvin engine. Tar trickled through the bilges. A thermometer in the cabin registered 91 degrees F. Gulls seabasked in the shade of the gunwhale.

Proud as a Viking, the spaniel surveyed it all from his own corner of the quarter-deck; that is, perched in the praam which snuggled alongside like a foal clinging to the mare. Being in no hurry to do anything nor to go anywhere, I decided not to shatter the stillness by cranking the engine. Instead, I hoisted a square yard of canvas which in *Noah's Ark* was called the sail. Thus pro-pelled, the boat lolled leisurely to the St Anthony lighthouse.

Having rounded the point, I came under the lee of some cliffs, and so lost the breeze, but held on, more or less maintaining steerage way, until the village hove in sight on the far side of the creek, creating an English *côte d'or*; the houses rising in terraces among palm trees—whitewashed, pinkwashed, emerald, ame-thyst—with here and there an ebony door, a primrose shutter, a rose-red roof. By this time several motorists had appeared, careening their speedboats as Jehu flogged his chariot. Exactly as though he were at the wheel ashore, one of the maniacs cut across my bows, and demanded to know what the hell I thought I was playing at. However, I weathered the storm of petrol, received a seamanly berth from the Percuil ferry, and drifted slowly toward a reef, on which an old man was fishing. An amphibious duologue ensued, across twenty yards of water.

"Admiral, you'm heading for disaster."

"She'll tack."

"Then her'll have to look sharp 'cause this puff o' wind is the last till sundown. Strikes me you'd best nip over the side and *blow* her along. Sturdy old craft, though."

"Board of Trade A.1."

"Way back in 1940 I was adrift in one o' they, somewhere off Ushant. Only for six hours, mind, but to me it seemed six centuries. How close to the wind does she sail?"

"About twenty points."

"Twent . . . ah, you'm pulling my leg. That old tub could sail round the world."

"I doubt it."

" 'Course she could. Stands to reason. Her was built t'old thirty castaways in latitude God-knows-what."

At that moment the breeze uttered its last gasp. Spinning the wheel, and nudging the mizzen, I just managed to tack within a yard of the reef.

"I will," I called to the old man, "bring you back a parrot."

Half-an-hour later I made-fast to an enormous buoy which loomed above the gunwhale, like something out of Jules Verne; and there I lay, too hot to move. The only way to keep cool was to dive overboard every five minutes, that being the time taken by the sun to dry the skin. It was all delightful, memorable, important . . . the tang of brine, the mewing gulls, the glimpse for'ard of a boundless blue horizon, and—through the cabin door —the occasional tremor of a lamp in its gimbal, the only visible sign that the sea was not a mirror. Though a haze of heat and silence I heard Falmouth chiming four. Then silence returned. Even the dockyard welders had downed tools. But I could hear some sheep in the hills, and once the clop of rowlocks as a small boy performed imaginary feats of lifeboatmanship outward bound from St Just.

At five o'clock, when I was about to brew tea, the Customs launch sighted me. Although we were good friends, I thought it advisable to grab a spanner, and pretend to repair the engine; a ruse at which the Customs connived with Nelsonic eye: "Don't 'ee bide there too long, Noah's Ark. Costs a hundred quid a minute to tie-up alongside that buoy."

At six o'clock I heard the distant throb of a frigate chasing her own bow-wave. Soon the roar dwindled to the countable heartbeats of "Slow Ahead Both". Very cautiously the frigate drew nearer, graceful and grey. Just before she came abeam I dipped my pennant, and stood to attention, and saluted, precisely as I had been taught long ago. And that was that, or so I assumed. But *Noah's Ark* and her dog-in-the-praam must have caused some amusement, because the Captain of the frigate stared hard and then returned my salute. There are times when I rate that exchange of courtesies as the proudest moment of my life; not personal pride, but the pride of service to something greater than self-interest.

Two hours later a breeze confirmed the prophetic fisherman. Little lollops began to slap the clinker hull. The praam pitched daintily. The pennant perked up, like a flower after rain. Peering above the cabin roof, I felt cool for the first time since breakfast. Up went the square yard of canvas, away came the bow rope, and at two knots we headed homeward up the creek. One small anchor was enough in such calm weather and such rockfree waters. Away it went, resonant as an oarsman's "puddle," soap-sudding the surface. Slow as a yawn, *Noah's Ark* swung bowfirst to the tide. Another voyage had been completed, into the uncloying waters of familiarity.

When the light was already failing, a retired coastguard hauled his outboard dinghy to the water. That done, he paced up and down for a long time, glancing at his watch and then at his cottage in the trees. At last his wife appeared, clutching her handbag. Across the water I heard the coastguard say: "Lord save us, woman! What have 'ee been doing all this while? We'm only going to the pub."

"We'm not going anywhere. Not until you wipe that seat for me."

"That seat . . ."

"That seat's still wet, and I'm not leaning up against the bar with a tattoo on my torso."

Away they went, disturbing a mile of serenity. But distance at last swallowed them, and once again I could hear the tide rippling against the hull.

Then the stars began to shine, and patterns of seaweed glided past, like silver lace. While making the rounds before turning in, I glanced down-stream at the frigate, ablaze now with her own portlights. And for a second time I saluted, not with my hand, but by remembering some words which every member of the Service bears in mind: "a security for such as pass on the seas upon their lawful occasions . . ."

9

Down Blackberry Lane

To us the lane seemed infinite because we had only lately learned to ride bicycles, and a mile felt even longer than a month. We called it Blackberry Lane, a name which stuck so fast that, on returning after nearly half a century, I found it still intact; not on the arm of a signpost, but on the lips of a ploughman who had not been born when our grandfather led my sister and myself in search of blackberries for the pot.

One end of the lane branched eastward from what was then rated a busy main road, though the traffic would now appear rather a trickle than a spate. After a few yards the lane passed under a railway bridge which really did carry a spate . . . ponderous freight trains, with smoke rising snugly from the guards van . . . sedate local trains, keeping death and diesel off the roads . . . and expresses racing to Scotland or from Wales, flattening their white smoke by day, and at night shedding sparks above the fairy-lamp coaches. How many hours have I stood on that bridge, sedulously recording the name or number of every locomotive, as though they might one day be needed by the General Manager. The other end of the lane humped its way across a canal bridge overlooking a house whose lawns sloped to the water, and were graced by some willows which formed a boathouse for the green-painted punt. Having crossed the bridge, the lane joined one of those minor roads that were the true arteries of England, bearing an occasional cart, a cycling shepherd, and—perhaps twice each week—the duke's Daimler or a yeoman's Ford, neither of which exceeded twenty miles an hour: the former, on principle; the latter, because

it carried rather more poultry than had been envisaged by Mr Ford's blueprint.

Midway along the lane stood a farmhouse and nothing else except fields, far as the eye could see, their gentle undulation heightened by a range of distant hills. The lane's surface was dusty and full of flints that flew upwards with a pinging sound. Pot-holes were plentiful, punctures not rare, and the only mechanised traffic a horse-drawn reaper. Long tracts of the hedgerows were intertwined with brambles whose fruit blossomed on an air so deserted that there was no need to seek the berries nor make-do with those which other pickers had overlooked. Sometimes there was no need even to pick them; we simply held our tin under a spray, and then shook the stem, wherefrom the fruit fell lusciously. Engrossed by the task, and eager to be the first to fill a tin, we worked in silence, interrupted only by the sound of a distant train, or a shrill "Ow!" whenever a thorn pricked our fingers. After a while, however, topography mated with ontology, and begat a question.

"Grandpa, what's this lane called?"

"Nothing, my child."

"Then oughtn't we to call it something?"

"I see no reason why we ought."

"But . . ."

"But equally I see no reason why we ought not."

"You're a clergyman. So you must christen it. I know . . . we'll call it Blackberry Lane."

With a glance at our juice-stained fingers, grandfather nodded, though I do not recollect that he uttered anything more liturgical than: "If you wish." So, when next a neighbouring cleric called, we told him: "Grandpa took us to Blackberry Lane."

"Which lane?"

"Don't you know? It crosses the canal at Simpson."

"Indeed? How very interesting. I've often wondered whether that lane possessed a name."

"Do you know who did name it?"

"Some wise old man, my dear, many years ago."

At that point grandfather coughed, our courage failed, the subject switched. The visitor himself, no doubt, passed the news to his son, who shared it with the sexton, from whom it spread to the publican, the policeman, and every child in half-a-dozen hamlets.

The name "blackberry" is an Old English word, coined to describe ripened fruit, whereas botanists refer to the red or unripe berry, *Rubus fruiticosus*. Organised blackberrying—with tin in hand, and a pudding in mind—ought to be a self-denying ordinance whose contributions are gratefully received and honourably pooled. Never once did grandfather pop a plump one into his mouth. Every berry entered the tin, shaming our own daubed lips. Casual tasters, by contrast, are free to feed as they please, untroubled by the conflict between immediate gratification and postponed pleasure. Blackberries have sustained many a country-man who by mischance or miscalculation has found himself foodless at tea time. Now I come to think of it, blackberries have considerably reduced my own cost of living, for when I first set up home I had only to step over the flowerbed in order to enter a meadow whose hedges teemed with the fruit; and at my present home the brambles are so rife that I am obliged to wage perennial war against them. If you examine the tip of a trailing bramble you will notice that, when it touches the ground, it takes root there, propagating a prickly species. I doubt, however, that you will discover why the redbreasted brambling or bramble bird was so named, for blackberries are not an important item of its diet, neither does the bird nest among brambles (only once has a brambling's nest been seen in Britain, and that was in 1920, among the hills of Sutherland). True, the German *brama* does mean bramble, but that merely transfers the mystery overseas.

The farmer whose fields adjoin my own keeps a pair of working horses. Ambling along the lane, sampling its blackberries, I hear the plod of those horses homeward from the last journey across the final field. I hear the jingle of their harness and the farmer's "Hoop . . . hoop" as man and beast share an ancient Esperanto. Midges meander like leisurely atoms caught in a shaft of the sun; somewhere a robin sings, autumn's hedgerow herald; and a warm haze dims the distance. It makes a placid scene, mellow and mellifluous, for the land and its people are never so relaxed as when corn has been gathered, pears become pickable, and firelogs stand by the door.

Lulled into forgetful remembrance, I half-expect to see grand-father beside me, wearing a black straw hat; his eyes blue as a benign sea; his cheeks ripe as apples. Nor would I feel surprised by the face—the fruity face—of a little girl, and a voice saying: "Grandpa, what's this lane called?"

A Local Gossip Column

It is quite untrue to say that men never gossip. In the past their gossip column was the village anvil, a fact which our Saxon forebearers acknowledged by regarding all smithy conversations as off-the-record and therefore not slanderous at law. Farriers having declined in number, and taverns being now partly feminine, the menfolk conduct their "he said" and "somebody saw" at the village barber's shop; not, indeed, that the talk is all tattle. The weather comes first, followed by farming and politics. Among the also rans are football, cricket, television, and that hopeful form of almsgiving which we call "backing the winner". The barber himself acts as mediator, audience, and informer; striving—if only for mercenary reasons—to be all things to all men. The best barber I ever met was an unmechanised craftsman whose shampoo bowl (*c.* 1905) contained water from a kettle (1919) which simmered permanently on an oil stove (1930). All four of them were at work until the 1960s.

But no village barber earns his living solely with scissors and razor. He sells tobacco and toothpaste and sometimes picture postcards of Tarr Steps or Melrose Abbey. More than once I have bought a box of matches flecked with shaving soap. Many sorts of good advice can be taken at such shops. During Hitler's war, for example, I visited a Devon barber, an old sailor and proud of it: "I used," he told me, "to trim a Commander in a battlewagon. Commander X he was called, though he's been promoted now, and flies his own flag. Fiery but fair, that's how I'd describe him. And there was always one way of coming alongside safely. No matter what the weather—even if the ship were sinking—you'd only to say, 'It's a bonnie morning, Sir,' and you was in his good books." Some weeks later it fell me to brief a Flag Officer while he inspected a contingent of Sea Cadets. The officer, I discovered, was X himself. Remembering the barber—and despite the rain—I remarked: "It's a bonnie morning, Sir." The Vice-Admiral looked at me, said nothing, and that was that. But when the inspection ended he beckoned me aside: "You briefed me very nicely," he observed, adding as an afterthought: "And somebody briefed *you* very nicely."

The barber's red-and-white pole is not an invitation to come and be gashed. It is a reminder that his mediaeval ancestors were also chirurgeons or medical practitioners: *Finget se medicum rasor* (every barber fancies himself a doctor). The breed was still propagating when George Crabbe, himself a physician, depicted an eighteenth-century specimen in Suffolk:

> A patent quack, long versed in human ills,
> Who first insults the victim whom he kills . . .

Our racial consciousness was so harrowed by its surgical trauma that not even Harley Street could obliterate the memory: "The sixth commandment," said Sydney Smith, "is suspended if you have a medical diploma."

In the years when threepence was worth a shilling nobody grudged the farmhand who on Saturday evening sat back like a lord while his lackey shaved him. One needs not be a Keynes in order to perceive that the present cost of a haircut is caused largely by the number of adolescent cavaliers who can afford to pay it. Myself, I demand to know the price beforehand, and if it exceeds three old English shillings, I depart unshorn despite the shearer's plea of 'overheads'. Thomas Hardy must have gleaned many small harvests whenever he visited Edwin Pitfield's shaving saloon at High West Street in Dorchester. He may even have met, or heard about, the Mayor of Casterbridge, Clym Yeobright, Gabriel Oak, Tess, Eustacia, Jude. According to Pitfield's assistant, Hardy seldom spoke. "Sometimes," the assistant remembered, "he could be induced to talk of the weather or local gossip matters, but never politics." Although Hardy patronised Pitfield's for many years, he never once tipped nor gave the staff a Christmas Box.

Profound indeed are the maxims to be heard at a village barber's shop. Even the badinage can achieve a sublime silliness, as when a ploughman expresses his disapproval of unruly students: "My old dad used to say books wasn't meant to be read." Up in Westmorland a creditor confronts his debtor in the chair: "Shave him reet close, Barber. Happen he'll not come here again till he's paid me for owd ram." On a commuting escarpment of the

Chilterns a retired builder recalls the cost of living while the barber trims his eyebrows: "Twelve thousand they were asking. The house agent said it was a great opportunity. 'Oh,' I told him, 'I lost my opportunity fifty years ago when I built the place, and charged 'em six hundred.' " In County Down a milkman recounts his escape from a tourist's gin-and-Jaguar: "The speed he came round that bend made the lightning o' God seem slower than a horse and cart. Anyway, I picked myself up, and got on the bike again. I was just passing the hotel when I noticed the car outside, and himself in the bar. So I stopped a minute and then I went inside and said to him: 'Are you in a hurry at all?' He shook his head: 'Not in the least,' he said. 'Then I'm glad to hear it,' I told him, 'because I've just let the air from your tyres. ' "

There are still some splendidly uncontemporary barbers' shops in Britain, many of which seem likely to flourish when the up-to-date saloons have disappeared. No matter what his vintage, a true country barber retains a forthright chairside manner. I remember especially the barber at Beauly in Scotland who glanced at my hair and then asked me how I would like it. "I leave it to you," I replied. Again he glanced at the few wisps: "That's no' leaving me much choice." In mountainous districts a barber may combine his skill with other forms of livelihood. Customers make an appointment *viva voce* through the postman, and are cropped at the smithy or above a fish-and-chip shop. Some customers prefer to be waited on in their own home (a useful arrangement for private schools and mothers of eight). One or two elderly farmers shear themselves, disregarding any fashion other than 'short back and sides'. The effect of such do-it-yourself can be startling. Thus, on Friday morning the farmer is a curly Cavalier, but on Saturday night he has become a close-cropped Cromwellian. In Wales, I remember, the barber would sometimes deputise when the vet was not available. One evening, while he was shaving a customer, the telephone rang. The barber disappeared and soon afterwards returned, wearing gumboots: "Ifor Gwyneth," he explained, "I have been called away. But you will understand, being a farmer. That was Dai from Pont-y-rhydd. His mare has the colic. Lying on her side she is. Dai said he'd write her off already, except she can still hiccup."

The Heart of England

There was no sound anywhere; not a bird, not a bee, nor even a breeze; only the Shirescape stretching through a heat-haze of stubble interspersed with pasture and a few fields that had yet to be reaped. This was Copston Magna, a Warwickshire hamlet of five or six cottages, a Victorian schoolhouse, and a small church overlooking a silent farm. Here, they assured me, lay the heart or centre of England. I doubted, however, that even Malinowski's geometry could pin-point the middle of a kingdom so uncircular as England. At least three other Warwickshire villages claimed to be the hub of things: Meriden, Lillington, Minworth. Minworth, indeed, claimed to be the centre both of England and of gravity, because the boys of King Edward's School at Birmingham once drew forty cardboard maps of England, thereafter weighing them to discover their centre of gravity, which each map revealed as Minworth. Undaunted, Lillington staked its own claim, and marked it with an oak. At Meriden they counter-claimed in stone.

Careless of such transient squabbles, the day followed the typical September cycle, beginning as a mist, out of which the sun at mid-morning arose like Venus from the water, gradually and as it were limb by limb. At noon the sun surmounted the mist, and by its light all things were burnished. The barkless bole of a wood-pecked elm shone brighter than parquet flooring. The lip of a chalk pit, from which a beech sapling grew, resembled the foyer of a floodlit restaurant. Not August itself had so blazoned the asters and roses and dahlias. Berries on a mountain ash seemed too red to be real. Caught by the sun, a segment of grass through a glade seemed likewise artificial, a fibre-grass carpet in a bargain basement for campers. And beyond them all, cornfields bleached a blue horizon, beneficent as Crabbe's granary:

> It was a fair and mild autumnal sky
> And earth's ripe treasures met th'admiring eye . . .

Bemused by that munificence, I learned against a rick, and must have dozed, because I was aroused by a tremendous roar as from an aircraft about to land on the back of my neck. The dog, too, was startled. Nor were we the only disturbed creatures, for sparrows and robins—dumb since dinnertime—flew from their roosts in the hedgerow, followed by a brace of pheasants. Unlike conventional aircraft, however, this one neither advanced nor retreated, but appeared to hover above a fixed point. Several moments elapsed before the mystery solved itself. On the far side of the rick (unnoticed when I arrived there) stood a combine harvester whose crew—awakened from their own siesta—had set the Juggernaut in motion; and away it went, flailing and floundering like an amphibious paddle-steamer designed by the late Heath-Robinson. While the scarlet apparition trundled to a far corner of the field, I remembered those older and quieter reapers whom I had seen in Perthshire long ago, sickling the swathes as they went. Although nostalgia mourned their passing, the sickle and the horse-drawn reaper could no longer feed a superfluity of infertile factories. So there the harvesters crouched, coughing and spitting among dust and diesel, helpless as a spider caught in the fumes of its own making.

By mid-afternoon the sun was really fierce. Left and right the fields were criss-crossed with bales of straw miming the ruins of a perished civilisation. As though to heighten that impression, one of the bales collapsed, suddenly and without a sound. The Juggernaut, too, was silent; its slaves having retired to take tea in the shade of a linney. They were, I discovered, amiable men and wise also, insofar as they appeared reasonably content with their destiny. Even a brief conversation proved that none of them was either willing or able to assume the role of his employer: "Come five o'clock I'm homealong, and that's the end of it. I let th'old bugger do his own worrying. So long as I gits paid, that's all I care about. I watch the telly, and when I'm stuffed with that I goes down the pub."

Half-an-hour's stroll took me to a crossroads, anciently the most important in Britain, where the Roman Watling Street met the Roman Foss Way. The former was almost too dangerous to cross; by their speed alone the motorists proved that they would not and could not give way to pedestrians. Foss, by contrast, still observed the courtesy of the road, being a country lane whose westward arm led to Devon and the sea. In 1712 the Earl of Denbigh subscribed with other landowners to erect a monument in the middle of the crossing, as a "perpetual remembrance of peace at last restored by Queen Anne". Celia Fiennes, that

L

intrepid Jacobean traveller, paid her *devoir* to the crossroads: "I came," she wrote, "to High Crosse which is esteemed the middle off England, where the two great Roads meete that divides the kingdom in the Saxons tyme in 4 parts . . ." Ten years later another antiquary, William Stukeley, drew a sketch of the monument, showing four Doric columns, each facing one of the crossroads, supported by four Tuscan pillars, each bearing a sundial. When David Defoe saw the monument he pronounced it "a cross of handsome design, but of mouldering stone, a deceit of the architect." In Defoe's day the traffic allowed him to commune with Clio, the Muse of History: "It is a most pleasant curiosity to observe the course of these famous old highways . . . the Watling Street, and the Foss, in which one sees so lively a representation of the ancient British, Roman and Saxon governments, that one cannot help realizing those terms to the imagination." Part of The inscription mentions *Venonae,* a small Roman settlement near the two roads: "If, traveller, you search for the footsteps of the ancient Romans, here you may behold them; for here their most celebrated ways, crossing each other, extend to the utmost boundaries of Britain. Here the Venones had their quarters and at the distance of one mile from hence Claudius, a certain Commander of a Cohort, seems to have had a camp towards the street, and towards the Fosse a tombe." In 1791 the monument was damaged by lightning, and the remnants were re-erected in what is now the garden of High Cross Farm, formerly an inn, where the famous cross remains, falling to bits, flanked by the jetsam of cars.

Like Celia Fiennes, I followed the Foss westward, finding it, as she had found it, "a road very commodious" . . . not wide nor busy, but a true country road, differing from others of the sort only because long tracts of it kept to the original straight course. As the sun sank lower, taking the warmth with it, the western sky resembled a golden bowl which has been so beaten and purified that it lacks everything except the power to shine. The last ray of it caught the upper windows of a farm, setting them on fire, or so it seemed.

The end came swiftly, for darkness walked faster than feet. Whenever I halted, I saw mist above the stubble, like a tentacle from October, tingling the finger tips.

Return of a Native

Some people suppose that a countryman's life is a perpetual holiday. One doubts, however, that the harvester would agree, toiling under a September sun. One doubts that the ploughman would agree, seared by a March wind. One doubts that the shepherd would agree, awakened at midnight to dig his ewes from a January blizzard. One doubts that the housewife would agree, or the postman, or the doctor, or any others who earn their living in the country. Nevertheless, it is easy to see why some people do misinterpret country life as a series of *dies non*. Every morning the countryman awakes to green fields, thatched roofs, quiet lanes, Tudor inns, Caroline cottages, Georgian manors . . . a background which the townsman regards as part of his annual holiday, a corruption of 'holy day', the day chosen by the Church for worship, rest, and recreation. The number of those holy days far exceeded the number of days in an average modern holiday. For example, only the bare necessities of agriculture were performed during the week before Christmas and after; and to that respite were added not only the other great Christian festivals but also a litany of local observances throughout the kingdom, as when the people of Tissington in Derbyshire dressed their wells with petals; when the people of Allendale in Northumberland lit their New Year torches; when the people of Helston in Cornwall held their Celtic Furry Dance; when the people of Spaunton in Yorkshire took two days' leave in order to beat their parish boundaries.

Those holy days were a blend of worship and whoopee; the latter predominant. All save the infirm and the unrepentant went to Mass, and thereafter observed whatever ceremonies were appropriate to the occasion. That done, they either went dancing, or played games, or got drunk, or committed adultery, or practised archery, or risked poaching, or fell asleep. Either way they enjoyed themselves despite the rumour of plague, the cost of living, and anything else that was not to their liking. Such were the men and women whom Piers Plowman beheld in his vision of mediaeval England:

> Watt the warner and his wife both,
> Tim the tinker and twain of his prentices,
> Hick the hackneyman and Hugh the needler . . .

After the Reformation the holy days became holidays, which is to say Sundays and almost no other days except Christmas (and even that was quashed by Cromwell). The principal causes of the change were Mammon and Puritanism, which in those years shared many common factors. Thus, in 1583 John Stubbe's *Anatomie of Abuses* demanded to know "Why should they (the workpeople) abstaine from bodely labour, peradventure the whole week . . .?" In 1671 James Janeway's *A Token for Children* posed another question: "Do you dare to run up and downe on the Lord's Day?" In theory, of course, a mediaeval cottager was bound by service to his lord's estate, but in practice he sometimes ventured beyond the manor, as itinerant mason, carter, drover, or servant accompanying his lord. Nevertheless, England's holy days were at-home days, and remained so within living memory. A farmhand of the 1930s might take his family by charabanc to the seaside, yet they all returned at nightfall, having much to do in the garden, on the allotment, about the house, among their friends.

Many minds are so shallow that not even a trip to the Moon could broaden them. Arriving at Lunar Airport, such persons would at once ask the way to the cinema, the casino, the fish-and-chippery. And if en route the speed of their vehicle were hindered by an Ancient Monument, they would complain to the Council for Uncivil Liberties, adding (quite untruthfully): "We didn't come all this way just for fun." Other minds are enriched by holidays abroad. They return with a deeper understanding of foreign nations and with a more informed awareness of the merits and defects of their own. Yet one wonders what will happen when the tourist trade has so standardised the Earth that there seems little point in wandering from one commercial site to another. When Greenland's icy mountains are littered with centrally-heated chairlifts . . . when the queues for the Pyramids stretch halfway to Cairo . . . when Ben Nevis is crowned with a Bingo Bar, and Cader Idris with a cabaret . . . then, like Horace, the wise man will shun the crowd (*Vulgus et arceo*), and some of the crowd itself will discover that their own tastes can be satisfied more easily and less expensively at Margate.

Perhaps there will always be the villager for whom the best part of his holiday is the end of it. Having basked in the sun, and trudged through the ruins; having scaled Mont Blanc, and envied the Bedouins; having savoured every nuance of novelty, he will suddenly feel as Thomas Bewick felt when, from a strange city, his thoughts turned homeward to Northumberland: "The country of my old friends—the manners of the people—the scenery of Tyneside—seemed altogether to me a paradise, and I longed to see it again." So, having dumped the last suitcase at the foot of the stairs, the returning native goes out to greet his home. First, no doubt, he will survey the lawn, now weedily overgrown, and then the flowers, autumnally fading. But his home does not end there. It includes every hill and field that are part of his daily round. Therefore he strolls down the lane, to an accustomed bridge beside a familiar stream, where he fancies that the stream is pleased to see him again, and that its babblings really are a welcome. From the stream he can just see the top of the church tower, and beyond it a white gate leading into the woods. Gladly he relinquishes his passport as a citizen of the world, and, like John Clare, once more resides where he belongs:

> The crows upon the swelling hills,
> The cows upon the lea,
> Sheep feeding by the pasture rills,
> Are ever dear to me.

When he has reunited himself with the horizon, he returns uplane, eager to greet his favourite chair, his books, his tool-shed, and all the treasury of privacies that we call his bits-and-pieces. And when at last he lays his head on his own pillow, serenaded by an owl, he accepts John Keble's verdict:

> Sweet is the smile of home. . .

Britain's Common Market

It is one of those autumn days that cause you to exclaim: "If only the weather had been like this in June." The shops and houses of the little country town gleam white and yellow and pink and blue. The guildhall's gilt cupola shimmers against a brilliant sky. Nearby stands a Victorian market house whose covered and cobbled yard was designed to receive sheep, cattle, horses, corn, vegetables, fruit, and other Devon commodities. Old men can remember market days when the town was crammed with Exmoor farmers who prodded the fleece, thumbed the grain, bit the apple, quizzed the pony. But there are no livestock on sale today, for the agricultural market is dead, and Thomas Hardy wrote the obituary:

> And every flock long since had bled
> And all the dripping buyers have sped,
> And the hoarse auctioneer is dead.

On Thursdays, however, the market house still resounds, albeit to a more domesticated commerce, while hawkers and well-to-do farmwives commend their wares to your notice; the former, by shouting; the latter, by means of neatly-printed cards, saying (of honey) *Home Made,* and (of flowers) *Cut This Morning.* Sometimes a card gets misplaced, so that marrows become *Guaranteed Waterproof*, and gumboots are *New Laid.* Despite—and also because of—its regional idiosyncrasies, our weekly market is one of many that remain common throughout Britain. Several of them are nearly as old as the Celtic pedlars who pioneered the Icknield Way from Cambridgeshire to Wessex; others were first held beside a conspicuous natural feature which the tribesmen acknowledged as a site where they might safely meet to parley. Matthew Arnold described the foreign buyers as "Iberian traffickers", adding that they were "sly". Some of the British salesmen were certainly shy, for they would set their wares (tin, corn, jewellery) on the beach, and then retire from sight while the Iberians sampled the goods, chose what they required, set down their own idea of fair barter, and themselves withdrew; whereupon the British crept from their hiding place, examined the offer, and either clinched or rejected it.

The right to hold a mediaeval market was granted by the King or by a local magnate. Near Penzance, for example, the hamlet of Marazion was anciently called *Marchas bichan*, two Cornish words, meaning 'a small market'. Some historians believe that the original market was granted to the monks of St Michael's Mount, a few hundred yards offshore. Place-names prove that markets were held throughout England: Market Harborough, Market Drayton, Market Deeping, Stowe Market, High Wycombe (formerly Chipping or Cheaping Wycombe), Chipping Norton, Chipping Campden, Chipping Sodbury, Eastcheap. Every sizeable market imposed a levy on traders from other parts, and was jealous of its

privileges. Thus, the Wiltshire towns of Cricklade, which gave
shelter to the Empress Matilda during her feud with King Stephen,
was rewarded when Matilda's son, having become Henry I,
exempted Cricklade traders from levy at all markets in the
kingdom; a right which they still exercise. In many small towns
the market house is the most impressive building after the church;
and some of them are relatively modern, like that at Helston,
which was built in 1839. Even more impressive is Barnstaple's
pannier market, the largest in the West Country. If a mediaeval

town lacked a market, the people usually bought and sold at the
church gate, and sometimes in the church porch; a scandal which
the Bishops rebuked in vain. Perhaps because he had spent much
of his own life in commerce, an eighteenth-century ship's purser—
John Waller of Kirkby Stephen in Westmorland—built at his own
cost a handsome stone facade, known as the Cloisters, to separate
the peace of the church from the hubbub of the market at its gate.
      Meanwhile, our little country town offers a replica of larger
markets. Like Sam Weller's knowledge of London, its wares are
both peculiar and extensive: crockery, flowers, eggs, pasties,
nylons, cream, tomatoes, bedsteads, cosmetics, clocks, jewellery,
frying-pans, soap, shrubs, mats, brooms, pins, potatoes, raincoats,

anti-macassars, weed-killer, aspirins, cups of tea, hot sausage rolls, cold cream, socks, and what the Romans called *cetera,* including a bookstall offering copies of *King Solomon's Mines, Algebra for Beginners, Lorna Doone, With Allenby in Palestine, Austin Seven Handbook, Lives of the Popes, How to Win at Whist, Guide to Lynton and Lynmouth* (1903).

The market's earliest arrivals appear before breakfast, in good time to erect their stall and to quiz the sky. The forecast is not always hopeful: 'Fair pissing, eh?" Today, however, the glass stands steady and high: "My old woman said to wear a weskit, but damme I was sweating afore I'd laced my boots." Although most of the buyers and sellers are Exmoor folk, we are sometimes visited by traders who claim to have travelled vast distances in order to offer bargains at a loss to themselves (and therefore never to be repeated): "Nar take a look at this. You ain't never seen such a carpet in all yer life. In London you could offer fifty quid for that carpet, and they'd himpolitely tell you what to do wiv it. But me ... I'll take thirty quid. In fact, I'll take twenty-nine ... 'ow much, Sir? A fiver? Luvvus, it corst more than that to unwrap it." The Cockney's stable mate relies on repartee: "This 'ere cup'n saucer was made in the Black or Pot Country as it is sometimes called. I guarantee ... what's that, lady? Got Japan written on the back? Of course it 'as. Bound to by law. J. Pan and Co. manufacturers." He brandishes a plate: "The Queen of England would be prard to eat orf this, especially if she knew that everyone wot buys 'alf-a-dozen will receive a free picture of 'Arold Wilson and Jack the Ripper." Country people enjoy those comic interludes, but only in small doses, for the patois is often strange to them, and not always intelligible. Moreover, they buy and sell with an inborn gravity, and are not wholly at ease when entrusting their money to strangers. They know that a local trader dares not cheat them, because news of the misdeed would very soon banish him to some market which had not yet suffered his depredations.

One or two of the traders have evidently come rather for pleasure than for profit. The ladies especially enjoy meeting people, and hearing their own products praised. Why else has that housewife arrived in a Land Rover, to sell home-made jam at a price which will scarcely pay the cost of petrol from West Buckland or Heasley Mill? One thing is certain; not the Artful Dodger himself could pull the wool over the eyes of farmfolk who finger a chintz as cannily as they handle a horse. When at last you have bought, or decided not to buy, you still linger awhile, listening to the voice of Britain's common market: "I told 'en straight, if that's a purebred Exmoor, then I'm a studbook Friesian" . . . "So the doctor took one look at her nose and said, 'That's not acne . . . 'tis alcohol."

The Fruits of the Earth

The church was so hard to find that I feared I had misread the map or perhaps followed a wrong footpath. Not a single house showed itself anywhere; only an ocean of amber stubble surging to a skyline crowned by beechwoods. So on I went, hoping for the best, through copses and over stiles; crackling the straw, rustling the leaves, and at length joining a lane.

Presently I sighted a cyclist full-speeding downhill, with a haversack on the handlebars, and a scythe under his arm.

"Church?" I called, as the farmhand flashed by.

With a perilous wobble he jerked a thumb over his shoulder; so once again I went on, into the sunlight, the stubble, the silence. But still no building appeared. When I had almost reached the summit, I noticed a white gate and beyond it a house, the unoccupied vicarage; but of church and village I saw nothing (the former, I discovered, lay a mile from the latter). A well-kept avenue led from the house to a mansion; and between them, hidden among trees, I found at last the elusive church, the centre of a trinity—God's House, Manor House, Priest's House—that had been set down without reference to the convenience of the congregation. When England was a Christian kingdom the villagers took that mile in their stride; but who nowadays would visit a place so isolated? The churchyard was tidy, and the church exterior in good condition; yet I anticipated the worst when I opened the creaking door, for on similar occasions I had too often been greeted by musty obsolescence. I entered, and was dazzled because the walls were lit by the fruits of the earth; grapes, carrots, marrows, pears. A rainbow of dahlias outshone the mediaeval glass; apples stood like rubies at the foot of the font, interlaced with loaves that had been baked in the shape of stooks. Posies of marigolds, plucked by loving fingers, were beacons on the choir stalls; the lectern rose like a golden eagle from an eyrie of white chrysanthemums; immense potatoes and terrestrial melons made an appetising Alp beside the organ. Here indeed was the meaning of the words 'colourful' and 'fragrant'.

Our modern harvest festival was devised by R. S. Hawker, vicar of Morwenstow, Cornwall's most northerly parish, perching on a cliff above the Atlantic. In 1843 Hawker told his flock that the bread for the next Holy Communion would be baked from corn which they themselves had reaped. Many clerics disapproved, regarding the innovation as Popery; but Hawker so stirred the parish imaginations that, thirty years later, another parson, Sabine Baring-Gould, wrote: "There is scarcely a church in England in which a Harvest Festival Thanksgiving is not held." It seems unlikely that Hawker's first Harvest Festival was so fertile as our own. Neither melons nor peaches were common in Victorian Cornwall. Nevertheless, the wayside flowers and the homebaked bread did encourage the womenfolk to practise their skill as interior decorators. Nonconformists soon copied the Anglican fashion. Even Strict Zion countenanced an horticultural Gaudy. But, of course, some form of Grace after Harvest was co-aeval with man's earliest religion. The Old Testament declared: "Thou shalt observe the feast . . . after that thou hast gathered in thy corn. . . and thou shalt rejoice in the feast, thou, and thy son, and thy daughter, and thy manservant, and thy maidservant, and the Levite, the stranger, and the fatherless, and the widow, that are within thy gates . . ." The phrases "harvest-home" (first recorded in 1573) and "harvest-queen" (first recorded in 1579) recall the secular festivals that were held throughout rural Britain, but have now disappeared from a mechanised landscape. When I was a child, living in the Fens, casual or extra harvesters were still called Patsies, that is to say Paddies or Irishmen, a reminder that in Victorian times many Irish labourers had roamed the British countryside, seeking work. Until 1930 one Cambridgeshire farmer gave each of his harvesters an extra shilling and enough malt to make three barrels of beer.

A slight sound disturbed my reverie. Glancing up, I saw that an elderly woman had emerged from the vestry, carrying an armful of red roses.

"Do you like our Church, Sir?"

"It's one of the most beautiful I've ever entered."

"People are so kind. The baker made them loaves special. Her ladyship gave the fruit and vegetables. And my grand-daughter . . . where is she, by the way? O, you naughty little thing! I said *not* to eat 'em. That fruit's for the hospital and old folks like grandpa and me." We were both smiling: "This little sprite, Sir, she arranged all them marigolds herself."

The sprite, who was aged about six, looked as guilty as Eve, but could not hide the apple because it was larger than the hand that held it.

"Do many people come to worship?" I asked.

"In wintertime there's seldom more than six at Evensong. And the vicar nowadays lives a dozen miles away. But we do our best." Then, as though she feared that I would not understand, she glanced through a window, to the wider world: "When so many men are being so wicked, the best thing we can do is just to get on with the day's work, and have faith in the power of ordinary decent people."

"You have that faith?"

"We all have it, or ought to. 'Tis the light that lighteth every little child as cometh into the world." She gazed at the roses in her arms, as though they might answer a question: "But bless me if I can understand why so many folks lose the light, or throw it away, or pretend that it doesn't exist."

When I slipped a coin into the offertory box, it struck the wood, but never another coin. The woman herself was what we might now call a simple soul, because, when I said goodbye, she gave me a rose, and asked God to bless me. So I went out, into the wide and wicked world; a silent place except for two robins; yet loud with headlines that would have sounded hilarious had they not harrowed the heart and bewildered the brain.

Although it is grounded in Christianity, my experience at that church transcends dogma. By its own example it withers the cynic who smirks at sentimentality, and the sceptic who scoffs at superstition. It is the recipe—the only recipe—wherewith men and nations achieve greatness; and for lack of which they decline and fall. It is the spirit that led Noah and his circus into the Ark, sustaining them until a rainbow and a dove appeared. No nation holds a monopoly of that spirit, though some have sold it for a mess of prosperity. In Britain it flourishes most strongly among country folk; a fact that is proven by the village churches which at this season shed colour and fragrance from Land's End to John o' Groat's.

IO

Over the Hills and Far Away

All day a brilliant sky had lit even the deepest combe, but when at length the sun sank below the woodland track, the warmth went with it, and for the first time since April I remembered what the winter would be like.

Presently the track entered a coppice and then bisected a billowing ploughscape with more woods on the summit. The trees shared an autumnal resemblance with men, for while some of them were already fading, others seemed from a distance to be as green as in July. Squirrels scurried through last year's fallen leaves, grubbing for acorns and beechmast, flitting from treetop to treetop, on twigs that bent without ever breaking. The birds were silent except for a brace of rooks indulging a domestic squabble whose wing-flapping grew so violent that it sent the leaves tumbling before their time. When the dispute had ended, stillness returned until—surprising at such a late hour—I heard what Mary Webb observed among the Shropshire hills:

> Memoried deep in Hybla, the wild bee
> Sings in the purple-fruited damson tree.

On went the track, climbing a knoll above a combe where rabbits were such strangers to mankind that they stared at me, unable to believe their own nostrils. But the truth dawned at last, and the rabbits were away before it became the dog's turn to sniff and then belatedly to understand. In the chase that ensued, the dog had no chance at all, partly because he is an elderly Lakeland, and

partly because he handicapped himself en route by yapping so loudly that every rabbit in England must have heard and heeded. The hubbub reverberated throughout the combe, which, though girt by beechwoods, was too spacious to seem oppressive. The track itself skirted the rim of the combe; and on top of that rim stood an ancient farmhouse, proud as a monarch surveying his own. For thirty years the place had been a favourite haunt of mine. An old man lived there with his wife and grandson, in glorious isolation, nearly an hour's walk from the village, which they reached via a footpath through the woods.

On a previous visit—made after several months' absence—I was told that the old man had died, that his wife soon followed him, and that the house stood empty because no tenant would lease such a remote place. Nevertheless, I now followed the track for old times' sake, in order to pay my last respects to three countryfolk whose talk and tales had enriched my own. When I arrived, I found that the old woman's flower beds were choked with weeds. Bent by their fruit, the plum trees could not console me for the loss of friends and for the decay of their home. A broken windowpane and several loose tiles had already admitted the weather. Two cups and a saucer stood on the kitchen table, alongside some rusty shears and a pile of farming magazines. Ash from the last fire created a forlorn Alp whose summit had been eroded by wind through the broken window. I saw also a bottle of milk, its lower half solidified into green fungus; and on the mantelshelf one of the old man's briar pipes, with amber mouthpiece and metal band. Wind through the broken pane uttered a spasmodic elegy, and I turned away, heavy with many memories.

A later visit verified the triumph of time, for the roof had collapsed, the doors had gone, and rats nested in crevices. Once more I turned away, knowing that I would never return. Halfway down the track I met a ploughman, a former Italian prisoner-of-war, who, although he had been a British subject for twenty years, continued to break his English.

"All gone," he sighed, nodding toward the derelict house. "Verra sad. When I first come here they treat me like I was their own son. She cooka my bacon special when I get gack from Mass. He teacha me English so good you wouldn't never guess I wasn't not born here. I lika the boy, too. One night he drink sixa pints of cider. Sixa pints. And then he turns to me and says, 'Tonio,' he says, 'I feel thirsty. Let'sa have a drink.' "

Again the ploughman sighed: "We come. We go. But I tell you something. Every time I plough thisa field I say, 'Hail, Mary,' I say, 'and do what you can for them because the old one he teacha me English so good, and the young one he drink like a whale, and dear mama she cooka my bacon special.' " He crossed himself, like a good Catholic, and then spat, and said, "Thisa damned field it get bigger every time I plough the bastard." Then he offered to roll me a cigarette, which I felt obliged to decline.

"You knew mama?" he asked.

"I knew them all."

"Then how come we never met? Or maybe you arrive when I was courting, eh?"

"It is possible."

"She was lovely, mama. She look good, she cook good, she do good, and by golly she speak nearly so good as what I do. I remember one day I write to my own mama in Italia: 'Dear mama, I used to think there was only one like you in all the world. But I was wrong. There is two.' " He paused, lighting his cigarette. "And what do you think mama said to that?"

"Well?"

"She writa to this mama, and she say, 'God bless you because you are good to my Tonio.' " He beamed. "Now wasn't that nice?"

As I came within sight of the farm, I remembered that meeting with Tonio, and wondered whether he would appear for a second time, but this was Sunday, and his plough enjoyed a siesta in the sunset. Suddenly I halted. Was there any good purpose in proceeding? Would it not be morbid to re-examine the progress of decay and the blurring of memories? Since self-analysis tends toward inaction, I decided that it would be wiser—or at any rate warmer—to step briskly up the remaining yards of the hill, bracing myself against a melancholy prospect. You may therefore imagine my surprise when, instead of seeing the skeleton joists, I beheld a brand-new roof, and under it some new window frames, and over the doorless porch a patch of new wall, built in the old style, with brick-and-flint. A phoenix was arising from the ashes.

No one in the village knew the identity of the prospective occupants, but the nature and extent of their renovation convinced me that they were people of means and of taste. So, although I shall never again sit in the stone-floored kitchen, listening to country talk, I can at least reflect that a home has been reborn, in ways which would have pleased my three old friends who once lived there.

A Feature of the Village

"With Norman font, Perp. tower, and traces of Saxon herring-bone work, the church," said the guidebook, "is a feature of the village." It is indeed, though nowadays neglected except by sightseers and a few worshippers. The Church Commissioners have already closed or sold many redundant churches, and hundreds more will soon go the same way. Yet even an atheist would preserve some of them, if only as subjects for a secular quiz. Where, for example, is England's smallest complete church? Cumbrians may say: "At Wasdale Head, where the chancel-cum-nave measures forty feet long by seventeen feet wide; and one side of the roof is only six feet high." Yorkists may counter-claim with the elder of two churches at Upleatham, which is seventeen feet long and thirteen feet wide. The Isle of Wight may advance St Lawrence's Church at Ventnor. Buckinghamshire may reply with the mediaeval church at Little Hampden. Small though they are, none of those claimants takes the prize, because each is either a part of an older church, or only a chapelry. The true claimant is Culbone church in Somerset, cupped deep in an Exmoor combe beside the Severn Sea. Its nave is only three-and-a-half yards wide; the chancel arch, only two-and-a-half feet wide; the number of seats, about thirty-eight. The village which that church once served has disappeared except for a house and a cottage; (the latter is occupied by the sexton and his wife, both of whom are past eighty years old). When Wordsworth was staying at Alfoxton he visited Culbone church, and noted its likeness to the church of his friend, Rev. Robert Walker, vicar of Seathwaite in Lancashire. All such places, said Wordsworth, "exhibit a well-proportioned oblong, with suitable porch, in some instances a steeple tower, and in others nothing more than a small belfry . . . how small must be the congregation there assembled, as it were,

M

like one family; and proclaiming . . . the depth of that seclusion in which the people live, that has rendered necessary the building of a separate place of worship for so few."

I believe it correct to say that at Staunton Harold in Leicester-shire is the only complete survivor of the handful of churches which were built during Cromwell's Republic, not by the Dictator himself, but by one of his opponents, whose family have held the manor since they acquired it by marriage in 1423. A plaque states: "When all things sacred were throughout ye nation Either demollisht or profaned Sir Richard Shirley Barronet founded this church whose singular praise is to have done yet best things in ye worst times and hoped them in ye most cala-mittous." Building began in 1653, and ended in 1665, a year before the Restoration. Sir John Summerson described the church as "an almost incredible salient of the Laudian ideal into the anti-Laudian Commonwealth."

Curious indeed are some of our consecrated buildings. At Ravenstonedale near the source of the River Lune in Westmorland the Georgian church contains a three-decker pulpit, crowned with a seat for the vicar's wife. Evidently the carpenter had disregarded John Knox's anathema: "God hath revealed to some in our age that it is more than a monster in nature that a woman should reign and bear empire above a man." At Keld in the same county the sixteenth-century monks of Shap Abbey built a small chapel which, after the Dissolution, served first as a house and then as a barn. When a local antiquary, Rev. J. Whiteside, discovered the barn's time identity he bought and restored it; and in 1918 Sir S. H. Scott, Bt. gave it to the National Trust.

Part of the parish church at Mapledurham beside the Oxford-shire Thames belongs to a Roman Catholic family. The paradox began when a lord of the manor, Sir Robert Bardolf, enclosed a section of the aisle which, since 1490, has been used as a family bur-ial place by the Blounts and their heirs and successors through the female line. The last burial—that of Michael Henry Mary Blount—was conducted in 1874 by the vicar, Edward Coleridge, nephew of the poet. A Victorian incumbent did dispute the anomaly, but the Chancellor of the Diocese of Oxford upheld the Blounts' claim because they possessed the only key to the crypt, and had main-tained exclusive use for centuries. In one respect the church is unique, for among its vicars was a King's illegitimate son, Lord

Augustus Fitz-Clarence, one of ten children born to Mrs Jordan (an actress) and the Duke of Clarence (who became King William IV). Like the Duke, the son had been trained as a naval officer, but quit the sea, and entered the Church, in order to please his father. We do not know why he chose Mapledurham (perhaps for its beauty and seclusion), but we do know that the vicar thereof had to be bribed to resign the living (the King appointing him Bishop of Chester and ultimately Archbishop of Canterbury). Nothing could be simpler than the inscription on the royal grave: "Augustus Fitz-Clarence, vicar of Mapledurham."

Most people know the story of St Piran's Oratory, the sixth-century church which sank into the Cornish sands, and was replaced by an eleventh-century church which likewise sank; but few people know of the Wiltshire church which may be said to have arisen after centuries of submersion. The story began in 1858 when Canon William Henry Rich-Jones, vicar of Bradford-on-Avon, happening to look down upon the town from a high terrace, noticed something curious in the shape of three roofs far below, which suggested that they concealed an older building. The Canon's researches confirmed that William of Malmesbury had mentioned a church at Bradford-on-Avon, founded by St Adhelm, and dedicated to St Lawrence. To cut a long story short, the chancel of the church had become a cottage; the nave was a school; next to it the master had built his home; and against the west wall stood a wool factory. Not until 1870 did all the premises fall vacant, whereupon the task of discovery began, revealing what Professor Freeman described as a small Saxon church of the sixth century. Freeman was mistaken about the date of foundation, for most experts now agree that the church was built *c* 900. One wonders which was the greater . . . the rejoicing over a lost lamb that was found, or the bewilderment of shepherds who for so long had remained unaware of its absence.

The Horse Before the Cart

At the far end of the village, in a cul-de-sac near the church, an old warehouse still bears traces of its trademark: *Liza Somesuch, carrier to all parts*. The claim was not larger than the claimant's ingenuity, for if a cottager had asked Liza to transport a crate of hens to Zanzibar, she would probably have complied; but her speciality was local rather than terrestrial, and she performed it by means of a horse-and-carter who once called at the house where I then lived, to deliver some articles of furniture and after-wards a homily on horses. "Oi aren't agoing to say as 'orses is faster," he admitted, "but oi do this . . . you ain't never seen a 'orse git a puncture. You ain't never seen a 'orse run out o' petrol. Ah, and you ain't never seen one as 'ad trouble with 'is gearbox."

I confessed that I had not.

"Now young Joe Varney . . . him as owns a lorry . . . if you was to harsk 'im to quote for carting them chairs to Bix Bottom, he'd tack-on wart the lawyers call a cav-eeat, but instead o' tacking it in small print he'd announce it in wart the lawyers call viva-vivoce. In other words he'd say, 'Weather and crankshaft per-mitting.' " As though by way of emphasis, the carter glanced at his horse and then at the steep landscape. "Now afore you come to live here . . . about the toime as Joe bought 'is first Ford . . . one day 'oi 'eard 'im charging hup this 'ill with a load o' book-shelves for The Bield. Droiving loike a marn possessed he were. Twenty moile an hour oi shouldn't wonder. And then wart? Oi'll tell you. Joe got as far as Roop's Farm . . . you can just see the roof through them trees . . . and suddenly thart Ford she blew her big ends and little ends and middle ends and . . . Lord, you never saw such a mess. Oi come up soon arterwards, leading my mare Polly with two hundred-weight o' coal for the Major . . . and when oi turned the corner thart old Ford she were steaming loike a bloody kettle."

"As you say, this is a very steep hill."

"Oi said more nor thart to Joe Varney. 'Boy,' oi said, 'my Polly gits in a lather sometimes, specially up this one, but damme,' oi said, 'she don't never hexplode.' Joe didn't loike thart. He just looked at Polly and then he muttered something about dog's meat and cart's meat. 'Cart or dog,' oi told him, 'if you warnt thart kettle shifted you'd best ask Polly. Either thart or ring up the Hay-Hay.' "

"Did you manage to shift it?"

"No trouble at all. Polly got the Ford up loike it were a paper-weight, and then we come down and loaded the bookshelves. Oi couldn't 'elp but laugh though, seeing young Joe steer a car he couldn't even sit in. He fair scowled when oi said to him, 'Is this lump o' tinware a twelve 'orsepower or only ten?' "

One country carter has become immortal, though not for reasons that are likely to have commended him to heaven. In 1799, you remember, William and Dorothy Wordsworth set up home at what is now called Dove Cottage in Grasmere, but not until they had camouflaged its history by halving its name:

> There, where the Dove and Olive-Bough
> Once hung, a poet harbours now,
> A water-drinking bard . . .

In its less abstemious days the cottage had been a tavern, much frequented by a carter who too often partook too deeply. Wordsworth told the story in *The Waggoner,* which he dedicated to Charles Lamb "in acknowledgement of the pleasure I have derived from your writings . . ." One night, alas, the alcohol of Westmorland led the waggoner into the waters of oblivion, for he and his vehicle came to such tipsy grief that they were compelled to retire from business:

> Two losses had we to sustain,
> We lost both Waggoner and Wain!

As recently as the 1930s many cottages regarded the carter as a link with the wider world. They either travelled with him to market or employed him to do their shopping when he got there. If a purchase seemed too personal, the carter sent his wife to make it: "T'ain't a marn's job to queue for a pair o' bloomers." Although the carter was an obliging man, he did expect to receive the co-operation of his customers: "Missus, if you warnts paraffin you'll 'ave to fetch it yourself in future. Either thart or git a bottle with a proper stopper." It was useless for the woman to protest. "Oi aren't agoing to argue, Missus. If you warnts a hexplanation, you'll git it from old Roop's woife. No doubt she'll tell you wart she's just told me. 'Carter,' she said, 'thart lump o' cheese you delivered last week . . . I'm 'aving to use it as a foireloighter.' "

The journey to market took longer than it does now, and the waggon's bare-board seats were less comfortable, being quite unshielded from the elements; yet the leisurely jolting had its compensations, for it allowed you to see the fields, to hear the birds, to smell the hay, to share the news. And the price of a return journey was less than one-quarter of the current single fare. Between the Age of Steam and the Era of Accidents a horse-and-carter plied a brisk trade, especially if he lived near to a railway station. During the 1940's, for example, the Great Central Railway employed a horse and cart to collect and deliver mixed cargo at the Chiltern villages and farms. Although the vehicle never exceeded walking pace, no one questioned the validity of its placard: *Express Delivery*. It was pleasant to sit beside the carter, ambling uphill and down, while saucepans rattled, hens cackled, pigs grunted, sofas swayed, and a large cheese mingled its aroma with honeysuckle trailing across the lane. In summer the carter received a cup of tea or a glass of homemade wine; in winter he rested by the fire, and was sometimes known to remain there: "T'ain't no use going any further, Missus. Oi'd need a snowplough to git up to Ballinger, and a pair o' snow-shoes to git down to Missenden. So if oi *am* going to be stuck, oi moight as well choose a bit o' comfort." The carter himself held the key to many cupboards. His *obiter dicta* were textbooks of topography, genealogy, politics, psychology; all emphasised by a flick of the whip as we sighted a manor or passed a farm: "Thart farmer wouldn't even give you a glass of water not unless you offered to pay." Sometimes we called at a cottage that was notorious for its hospitality: "They say she's married, but they don't tell you how many husbands she's got." Once or twice we delivered to the clergy: "You won't never warnt for a meal at thart rectory. Oi've delivered there afore breakfast and arter supper, and th'old parson always says, 'Come in and have a boite o' summat.' " Even the nobility were waited on, though not always to their satisfaction: "Her ladyship said to me, 'Thomas,' she said, 'you can take it bark where it come from 'cause them pheasants is so 'igh not even a heagle could catch 'em.' "

Hunter's Moon

On a shining night the Lincolnshire poacher delighted to play the role of Autolycus, that snapper-up of other men's considerable trifles, who worked best in the dark and among byways: "gallows," he admitted, "are too powerful on the highway . . ." Adapting the poacher's ditty to their own lawful occasions, the Lincolnshire Regiment chose it as a marching song. But no county holds a monopoly of theft. The Border Ballads long ago extended an invitation from Ettrick Forest:

> There's hart and hind, and roe and doe,
> And of wild beasts a great plenty.

Countryfolk still name the moons of early autumn. The first or Harvest Moon waxes full within a fortnight of the September equinox; the second or Hunter's Moon is the next full moon after October. By the light of it the poacher trod warily lest a trap ensnared him, or a twig told the keeper where to aim. Starvation, revenge, profit, idleness . . . those were among the poachers' chief motives. Many of the predators belonged to a class of persons (not yet extinct) whom Daniel Defoe noticed at Tiverton: "Such," he called them, "as need not be unemploy'd, but were so from mere sloth . . ." Others were indeed employed, but so miserably paid that only by stealing food could they save their wives and children from hunger. Merrie England spread its *meum et teum* too unevenly. From time immemorial the poacher has been known to turn gamekeeper, and vice-versa. Chaucer himself remarked on the custom of setting a reformed "theef of venisoun" to catch one who was still impenitent:

> A theef of venisoun, that hath forlaft
> His likerousnesse, and al his aolde craft,
> Can kepe a forest best of any man.

William Gilpin, a Hampshire parson, described "a forest verderer who had formerly been a noted deer-stalker". During his pre-regenerate days the man "carried with him a gun which he screwed into three parts and which he could easily conceal in the lining of his coat. Thus armed he would drink with the under-keepers, without suspicion; and when he knew them engaged would securely take his stand in some distant part and mark his buck."
  As Charles Kingsley said:

> The forest laws were sharp and stern,
> The forest blood was keen . . .

Death became the penalty, and might be inflicted without trial.

In 1293 King John ordered his keepers to arrest all poachers, no matter at what cost: "If any forester do kill any such offender, he shall not be impeached for his felony." Even dogs were maimed lest they worried the deer. During the sixteenth century it was made illegal for any man to take game, even from his own estate, unless his annual income were at least £100, in those years a considerable sum. Two centuries later Sir Roger de Coverley mentioned "a yeoman of about one hundred pounds a year . . . just within the Game Act."

Throughout most of the eighteenth and nineteenth centuries the poachers roamed in gangs, waging war against the land-owners, who were compelled to defend themselves. Lord Berkeley, for instance, employed eight head keepers, twenty underkeepers, and thirty nightwatchmen; but Lord Suffield relied on man-traps and spring-guns. In 1781 several poachers raided the Duke of Cumberlands' deer coverts in Windsor Park. After a fierce battle they ran short of ammunition, whereupon the keepers charged with drawn cutlasses, and arrested the robbers. In 1800 Parliament enacted that members of poaching gangs be sentenced to hard labour; for a second offence they might be drafted into the Army. In 1803 the Ellenborough Act made armed resistance to game-keepers a capital offence. In 1817 the penalty for night poaching was increased to seven years' transportation; a sentence which Sydney Smith disapproved: "the preposterous punishment of transportation," he declared, "makes the poacher desperate, not timid." It must also have made the undesperate poacher think twice before breaking the law. In any event, Smith felt no sympathy with professional thieves, whom he arraigned as "thoroughly bad and corrupted". How did the thieves sell their swag? That question was answered when W. B. Daniels published *Rural Sports,* which exposed the traffic in stolen goods. Higglers, as they were called, acted as middlemen who bribed passengers and guards on the Royal Mail to smuggle the stolen game to London, where unquestioning shopkeepers "paid four (and sometimes as high as eight) shillings for a brace of Partridges".

By the middle of the nineteenth century the violence had so waned that poaching became rather a sport than a profession. Richard Jefferies met one of those amateurs, lying drunk in a Wiltshire lane. At a second and more sober meeting the rogue told him: "I've been before the bench, at one place and t'other, heaps of times ... Last time the chairman said to I, 'So you be here again, Oby; we hear a good deal about you.' I says, 'Yes, my lard, I be here agen, but people don't hear nothing about *you.*' That shut the old duffer up." Oby was a thief, but not a murderer. His species is hardily perennial. Not long ago a self-confessed Scottish poacher, Ian Niall, published *The New Poacher's Handbook,* sub-titled *For the man with the hare pocket and the boy with the snare.* It was an amusing piece of work. Nevertheless, stealing is theft, and law is order. To despise a thief is wiser than to admire his ability to steal.

Looking back at the eighteenth-century rural scene, Jefferies remarked: "Let us not wish for the good old times of Gilbert White. They are gone; but his fields and hedges remain to us more peaceful now than ever." The modern British countryside may justly repeat that claim. Cottagers have no need to steal food; their wives go shopping by car. The handful of poaching gangsters have no need to murder keepers; they are away before their crime has been detected. In short, autumn's frosty nights can be relished without reference either to crime or to hunger. In the far north the last harvesters are working overtime, their combines and tractors pin-pricked like assiduous glow-worms. Elsewhere the stillness is heightened by myriad small sounds. Fieldmice rustle crisp meadows. Heifers peer over hedges, their breath smoking when it meets the air. Moonlight casts metal bars across the footpath. When a vixen barks, the whole world seems to echo; and the brook is as a nightingale that sings throughout the year.

The Road to Autumn

The mist was so thick that I stopped the car, and walked a few yards uplane, hoping to find a gate where I could reverse and then return to Horncastle. The trees dripped above grassblades that were already bent, and beads of moisture speckled my jacket, like miniature silver buttons. Although I found no gate, I did reach a signpost to Ashby Puerorum, a blend of Latin and Old English names, meaning a village or homestead, set among ash trees, belonging to *pueri* or boys. Having travelled several miles in order to revisit another Lincolnshire village, and feeling reluctant to be thwarted by the weather, I drove into Ashby of the Boys, at an average speed of twelve miles an hour, trusting that Keats's autumnal mist would yield to fruitful mellowness. Ashby, I discovered, contained a mediaeval church, a few cottages, and a man who told me that Ashby became Puerorum during the Middle Ages when a local landowner bequeathed an estate for maintaining the choirboys at Lincoln Cathedral.

Faith has not yet moved mountains, but I can testify that hope did coincide with a lifting of the mist; not an immediate and complete dispersal, yet enough to allow me to reach Somersby, birthplace of Tennyson, high in the Wolds; a situation worth emphasising because Lincolnshire is commonly dismissed as a flat country despite the fact that Bassingthorpe Hill near Grantham marks the highest point of the railway line between King's Cross and Edinburgh. The scenery was admirably described in Hugh l'Anson Fausset's study of Tennyson: "The Lincolnshire countryside, from Somersby to the sea, is unusually varied. It has three distinct characteristics, of wold, marsh and fen, and the native can choose whether he turn to upland or lowland. . . ."

Now Somersby is such a quiet place that I do not care to disturb it by making a noise, so I left the car outside the village, and proceeded on foot; a courtesy which the sun approved, for I had walked scarcely a hundred yards when a patch of clear sky pierced the veil. Within three minutes the grey became white, and was swept away by a sea of surging blue. Trees that had mimed mournful wraiths arose from the light of their own gay garments. Grass came alive again, flaunting the dew like diamonds. Far below, a vast plain sparkled with stubble and sheep. Farm windows winked at the sun. Pools outshone the maps that paint them. Damp opacity became warm lucidity. Such transformations are common in October. Gilbert White experienced the same thing two centuries ago: "As the morning advanced," he wrote, "the sun became bright and warm, and the day turned out to be one of those most lovely ones which no season but autumn produces; cloudless, calm, serene, and worthy of the South of France itself."

As for Somersby, it looked the same as ever I could remember it; a hilltop place with a church on a knoll; a farmhouse attributed to Vanbrugh; and the former rectory where Tennyson was born, the fourth of the rector's twelve children. The house is nowadays a private residence, not open to the public; but I have been privileged to see over it and to discover that it has not greatly changed since the poet played there. Time, however, has superannuated Cadney's village school, where Tennyson received the elements of education before proceeding to Louth Grammar School and thence to Trinity College, Cambridge. Gone, too, are

> The seven elms, the poplars four,
> That stand beside my father's door.

The oldest section of the house contains a Georgian staircase; parts of the south side were designed by George Tennyson, and built chiefly by his coachman, Howlings.

The Tennysons left Somersby in 1837, six years after their father's death, when Alfred was twenty-eight years old. His sorrow at leaving is distilled from *In Memoriam*:

> I turn to go: my feet are set
> To leave the pleasant fields and farms;
> They mix in one another's arms
> To one pure image of regret.

> We leave the well-beloved place
> Where first we gazed upon the sky;
> The roofs, that heard our earliest cry,
> Will shelter one of stranger race.

True; yet the strangers maintain Somersby House in a manner he would have approved.

As on my previous visits, Somersby appeared to be uninhabited except by *flora* and *fauna*. Two cats sunbasked in the middle of the lane. Robins pecked dung heaps in a farmyard. Nasturtia crept like slow fire at the foot of stone walls. And that was all ... until I saw an old man scything a patch of grass, as though he were the very one who had cheered Tennyson:

> O sound to rout the brood of cares,
> The sweep of scythe in morning dew ...

A stream flows near the old rectory, turgid with twigs and mud. I once met an excessively refined lady who, having spied the stream, called to her companion that she had found Tennyson's brook: "The one, my dear, that babbles over nooks and crannies." Happening to be only a few yards away, I ventured to suggest that the lady was mistaken.

"Indeed," she replied, slowly inclining her neck toward me. "And where, pray, *is* the brook?"

"In Kent, Madam."

"Kent? What on earth was he doing down there?"

"Staying with his brother-in-law, the Vicar of Boxley. And the six springs in the Vicarage garden led him to compose *The Brook,* which, as you so nearly remarked, babbles on the pebbles."

But all that had been long ago. The present was indeed now, these moments of sunlight through fiery leaves, of late bees among last flowers, of far-away sheep, and then silence and the old scythes-man swishing his swathes.

The Thankful Villages

Passing one day from Wales to Herefordshire, I entered Lingen, a hamlet so peaceful that the call of a calf created a disturbance. Outside the church door I noticed a memorial to parishioners who died on active service during the 1914 war. I had just read the names—there were four—when the church clock struck four. The coincidence went so deep that its impression has lasted twenty years.

There is, we are told, no love greater than that of the man who lays down his life for his friends. Nearly every British village sent men to the Great War, but few indeed received back all whom they gave. Those fortunate few are still called Thankful Villages. The first of them in alphabetical precedence is Arkholme on the River Lune in Lancashire, which sent and received back fifty-nine men in both World wars, eight of whom had emigrated, and were serving with New Zealand forces.

Simplicity is the motif of the war memorials that stretch like milestones from Cornwall to Caithness. The most northerly of them—near John o' Groat's, along a road overlooking the Pentland Firth—is a statue of a Scottish soldier, alone in what seems to be an uninhabited land. South of the border, in the Yorkshire village of Arncliffe (where Charles Kingsley wrote part of *The Water-babies*), one of the three war memorials in the riverside church commemorates the men who in 1513 marched to meet the invading Scots; the other memorials commemorate the men who in 1914 and 1939 marched to meet the invading Germans. At Chollerton near Hadrian's Wall in Northumberland

the men who died defending their homes invite us not to forget:

> Ye that live on, in English pastures green,
> Remember us and think what might have been.

"What might have been" . . . there sounds the challenge which is ignored by those who speak always of the horrors of war, never of the just cause for whose sake the horrors are endured. If a man has lived through two world wars he may be excused for not wishing to perish in a third. Unlike most of the pacifists, he knows (because he has experienced) what they are shouting about. But he knows also that they are free to shout because in 1939 this kingdom said to itself what King George V said to the American Ambassador in 1914: "My God, Mr Page, what else *could* we do?" Many non-Christians cite Christ as an example of the man who will watch his children being killed, and his country over-run, without taking up arms to defend them. But Christ told the soldier: "Do your duty," and to men of military age he said: "Render unto Caesar the things that are Caesar's . . ." The commandment of Yaweh, "Thou shalt not kill," was a ban on blood feuds and territorial aggrandisement. It did not require Gideon to submit passively while an enemy scorched the earth of his native land.

Near the Atlantic coast in north Cornwall lies St Juliot, a parish without a village, whose church bestrides a hill among hills. On one of its walls is a framed drawing which Thomas Hardy made when, as a young architect, he restored the building, and there met his future wife. On another wall you will see a memorial which says: "Erected by a Grateful Parish in remembrance of William Henry Martin, Edward Spry, Edwin Philip who gave their lives for their country in the Great War 1914-1918."

Those memorials are more than milestones; they are signposts. One of them will name a dozen men from the Durham Light Infantry; another, a quartet from the Sherwood Foresters; a third, men from the South Wales Borderers or from a local RAF station. The sea speaks for itself via a necklace of names all around the coast. We need no unilateral disarmers to compute the irreparable loss. Milton counted it nobly:

> For Lycidas is dead, dead ere his prime
> Young Lycidas . . .

Nor need we disturb the dead by raising our voices. The eye alone will settle the matter, gazing at China, Hungary, Czechoslovakia, the Berlin Wall . . . sights sedulously overlooked by those who cannot see beyond Rhodesia, Portugal, Spain.

The towns are as mindful as the villages. Not long ago, while I was being conducted around Hughes wheel factory in Birmingham, I noticed a memorial to the fallen of both wars. The inscription said all that needed to be said, and said it superbly: "To the glorious and ever sacred memory of our fellow shopmates who nobly gave their lives for our liberty . . ." When you have unmixed (if you can) the motives which lead men to war; when you have indulged (if you must) your fill of cynicism; still you confront the fact that the overwhelming majority of names on those memorials were borne by men who dared to die because they loved their land as Rudyard Kipling loved it:

> Land of our birth, our faith, our pride,
> For whose dear sake our fathers died.

What a tragedy, that men who have served their country in time of war, so often become and beget the saboteurs of its peace.

Sometimes the memorials take what we call a practical form, as at Great Hampden in Buckinghamshire, where the 1914 memorial is a road which the villagers built to link outlying farms and cottages; the 1939 memorial is an extension and improvement of the village cricket pavilion. Many memorials enshrine a private grief, like the lych-gate at North Walsham church in Norfolk, which the rector gave in memory of his son, a lance-corporal in the Norfolk Regiment: "He fought at Mons, Le Câteau, The Marne, The Aisne, The First Battle of Ypres, and at Hill 60, and went down in the torpedoed Transport *Royal Edward* in the Aegean Sea, 13th August 1915." With what care did the father select the epitaph: *Mediterraneis sepultus sub undis . . . ante diem periit, sed miles, sed pro patria*: "Buried beneath the waters of the Mediterranean . . . dead before his time, yet as a soldier, and for his country." No matter what their style, the village war memorials remind us that in 1918 and again in 1945 we said: "Their sacrifice was not in vain." But it *will* have been in vain if, like an ostrich, we once more plunge our head into the sand of unreality, trusting that a world of sophisticated savages will refrain from attacking us in the rear. No new weapon has in any way at all changed the basic issue:

> We must be free or die, who speak the tongue
> That Shakespeare spake.

All those things come to mind on Remembrance Sunday. In some minds they always are remembered, though the face and the voice have faded after fifty years. It is necessary to speak of such things as simply as language allows. Neither the living nor the dead demand an orotund requiem. They ask only that all people of goodwill shall keep their powder dry, and thereafter give thanks to the goodwill of all people who did not fold their passive hands, but went out, and drove back the aggressor.

When you have asked for whom the bell tolls, recollect that it peals for posterity.

Light on a Dark Subject

Marooned in the miasma of a London fog, Stephen Mallarmé praised its sooty particles, calling them dear (*les chers brouillards*) even although they did fuddle his brain (*emmitouflant nos cervelles*). It may seem archaic to cite poetical opinions of scientific problems, yet verse is not *per se* incompatible with veracity. Two centuries ago James Thomson understood that fog is an amalgam of moisture and season:

> Now, by the cool declining year condensed,
> Descend the copious exhalations . . .

Has any Briton ever relished a fog? It seems unlikely. Will any Briton ever again suffer a pea-souper? That, too, seems unlikely, because pea soup is another name for coal dust, which has been banned from many parts of Britain. Fog there must be; but legislation has dispelled most of the murk from *Bleak House*: "Fog everywhere. Fog up the river, where it flows among green aits and meadows; fog down the river, where it rolls defiled among the tiers of shipping . . . fog in the Essex marshes, fog on the Kentish hills . . ."

Peering through a windscreen darkly, the average motorist curses he knoweth not what, for the nature of fog remains swathed in mystification. Most people assume that it is intrinsically different from mist. Fog, they say, is an urban blight, created by dust in the atmosphere; mist, on the other hand, is a rural event and therefore less pernicious. That antithesis over-simplifies the equation. Both mist and fog are formed when air reaches a point—we call it the dew point—beyond which it can contain no more moisture; but whereas dew may be described as water that has been deposited on grass-blades, fog is water that has been deposited on particles of salt, sulphuric acid, calcium chloride. Earth's atmosphere always contains some of those particles, and since it can never be freed from them over a wide area, it follows that fog can never be widely eradicated.

There is a hoary legend that Britain remains perennially fog-bound. Tacitus had the news second-hand from his father-in-law, governor of Britain: "The British climate," he reported, "is made repellent by much rain and many fogs." During the sixth century, in a book called *History of the Wars,* which he wrote at Byzantium, Procopius announced that the climate north of Hadrian's Wall was so vile that only serpents could live in it. Procopius, too, received the news at second-hand, from some Englishmen (southrons, by the sound of it) who had attached themselves to the Frankish embassy. More than a thousand years later, Dumas was peddling the same libel, declaring that in England the sun is a synonym for the moon: *"L'Angleterre c'est un pays où le soleil ressemble à la lune."* The debate, however, is not simply an ethnic feud between two sorts of subjectivity. Statistics prove that Britain is less misty than many other lands, and less foggy than some. Thus, our atlas describes as foggy any area in which the stuff persists for more than ten days in a year. Britain contains only two such areas (London and parts of the industrial North), yet in California the sun-tanned playfolk will discover places where fog persists for more than sixty-five days in a year. If they are really adventurous, the playfolk will discover a light-house that is hidden by mist for weeks at a time. Nevertheless, the air in some parts of Britain remains so foul that its fumes may affect an area sixty miles down-wind from Marble Arch.

Fog being formed by condensation, the clouds exert a dramatic influence on visibility. In the south-west, for example, the pre-vailing warm winds are often cooled by their passage over land surfaces, whence the sea mists along the coasts of Devon and Cornwall, and also the wetness of those mists (only an oilskin will protect you when Bodmin Moor is hidden). Gilbert White knew that trees can be both umbrellas and shower-baths: "In heavy fogs, on elevated situations especially, trees are perfect alembics: and no one that has not attended to such matters can imagine how much water one tree will distil in a night's time, by condensing the vapour, which trickles down the twigs and boughs, so as to make the ground below quite in a float . . ." Along our north-western seaboard the mists are called Scotch, heavy-laden with Atlantic moisture. But the east coast, too, can disappear, as it did when,on reaching St Andrews, I was greeted by headlamps through the midday murk. An hour later the city basked in sunshine. All such sea mist implies motion or turbulence above the surface of the water; therefore the pockets of moist air may rise and fall. While living in a boat in Cornish waters I used sometimes to steer by the masts of yachts whose hulls were invisible . . . a form of navigation not to be recommended unless the helmsman has a radarlike remembrance of every object in the fairway.

In *Bleak House* a visitor was told: "This is a London particular . . . a fog, Miss." But you need not visit London in order to lose the way. Many a countryman has gone adrift within fifty yards of his own home. I did it myself once, after dark, fumbling and stumbling to a point where the lane bisected itself. Tapping with my stick, I must have touched the wrong side of the grass triangle at the crossing, because I soon noticed that I was on level ground instead of on a hill. I managed to reach the grass again, and once more to tap the wrong side of it. A car travelling too fast then caused me to seek shelter in a ditch, where I waited for the madman to lighten my darkness. Unobligingly he halted, reversed into a gate, and went back the way he had come. By this time completely lost, I spent an eerie five minutes, tapping like a blind man, veering like a tippler. Then I heard old Farmer Clarke cursing his own dilemma: "The gate must be somewhere 'cause 'tis only yesterday I mended the damned thing." A muffled consultation ensued.

"Is that Clarke?"

"Just about. Is that you?"

"More or less."

"Heading north, mister, or south?"

"Becalmed."

"I've never known nothing like it, not in seventy-three years I haven't."

"We still seem to be in the parish."

"Maybe we are. But where's the pillarbox? Oh . . . I damned near walked into it. Now all we got to do is follow the hedge."

Clarke went north, I turned south, wondering whether, after all, the twain of us *would* meet. Having at last found the track which really did lead home, I decided that Mallarmé had been sitting by the fire when he praised his "beloved fogs".

Straight from the Horse's Mouth

He even looks like a horse. Mind you, a closer inspection does reveal certain differences between man and beast. For one thing, the man has only two legs. Nevertheless, his lifelong devotion to horses has so marked him that, as I say, he achieves a visible empathy with them. Indeed, the psycho-somatic bond is so potent that it attracts not only horses but also their straw. The stuff gets in his hair. It clings to his breeches. I have seen it protruding from his nostrils (they are of the snorting or equine sort, more vehement than words). In short, he is a stud groom. One might almost say that he was predestined to the trade because he was born bandy, curved as it were aforethought to fit a rounded girth. Having learned to walk, the child soon taught himself to ride. Like Shakespeare, he received no formal instruction in the mastery of his calling. Watching the practitioners, he one day went away and outshone them, for it was his good fortune to have arrived before horsepower became cubic centimetres. His Edwardian employer kept a carriage and pair, two hunters, and a brace of dogcarts. Moreover, the life of every farm and large estate was hauled by horses; the head carter being a type of rustic majordomo, to whose expertise the farmer himself would bow. Long journeys, of course, were made by rail, yet the trains were met by horse-drawn vehicles. It was a reversal of the story at sea, where the last of the sailing ships were met by the first of the steam tugs.

In 1914 the stud groom enlisted with the county yeomanry; and when his regiment was permanently unseated, he got himself posted as galloper to a Major-General, with whom, when the Armistice was signed, he rode home. He has been riding ever since.

And although the years now make a saddle seem higher than it is, they have not lessened his love of horses and of the world of horsemen. When summer wanes, and cubbing draws near, he plays his part in Dylan Thomas's vision of

> The spellbound horses walking warm
> Out of the whinnying green stable
> Onto the fields of praise.

In place of "He" I might well have written "They", for the breed flourishes from Land's End to John o' Groat's. That the horse itself has become a luxury instead of a necessity in no way alters the *camaraderie* among horsey folk. If an English farrier or a Welsh gipsy could be introduced to some American Indians of the last century, they would soon find themselves assessing withers, quizzing teeth, laying odds. Like poets, a true horseman cannot be manufactured. Only a miracle would have transformed Dr Johnson into a Newmarket man; he did well to cling astride while exploring the Hebrides with Boswell. Another clinger—though of a less sedate sort—was John Gilpin, who "grasped the mane with both his hands . . ." The result was predictable:

> His horse, who never in that sort
> Had handled been before,
> What thing upon his back had got
> Did wonder more and more.

My own seat (safe though never impeccable) was conditioned by the cavalry squadron of the Oxford University OTC, at a time when martial patriots fought for King and Country with sword and lance. Our instructor was a corporal of horse from the Household Brigade. His *ex officio* voice quivered with what I can only describe as menacing encouragement: "Any bad 'abits wot you young gents 'as acquired, Hi shall heliminate. Now, on the command one . . . steady, Sir, steady, or that bay will think you're going to bite 'im. Now, as we were. On the command one, place the left foot smartly in line with . . . no, no, sir . . . you over there wot's left your spurs orf . . . if you must 'ang on, please use the 'orse's 'ead and not its bloody tail."

Although he is less lethal than the man who dotes on his fast car, a bad equestrian can become so ambivalent that he strikes his horse, curses it, plays cruel tricks with its mouth. Like the car

fiend, he is arrogant, ignorant, boorish, blasphemous. You find
him in every hunt and among all classes of society. He is not a
horse-lover at all. He uses a horse as others use a car, in order
to exercise his own aggressive conceit. Some female members of
the horsey species are more remarkable even than the male. Every
countryman has met the veteran spinster who preferred horses to
humanity (perhaps because humanity preferred horses to herself).
I have met many such, and admire several, especially those who
have curbed their *animus* or Jungian masculinity. Is Miss Blank
still alive, I wonder . . . that last scion of a Devon family, who, in
order to maintain her hunter, sold what remained of the estate
and moved to a bed-sitter at the inn. What a pleasant face she had;
what a Pucklike sense of fun. Many a man who married a blonde,
now wishes that he had drawn a Blank.

Winter or summer, a stable exudes its own aroma, like a smithy,
a flour mill, an oasthouse, a hay barn. Saddles peer down from
their pegs; bridle and bit gleam silver and brown; bottles of
embrocation stand alongside switches and spurs; copies of *Horse
and Hound* form a cushion for *Days in the Saddle, Mr Jorrocks, The
Show Jumper's Manual, Stag-Hunting on Exmoor.* The sounds, too,
are evocative. Munching and champing improvise on a theme of
contentment. A hoof clops the cobbles. Cocked ears appear from a
loosebox, crowning a portrait of patience, affection, strength. Men
who live and work in such surroundings are sometimes blessed
with the gift of healing, like old Matthew, the farrier, whom Flora
Thompson sketched in *Candleford Green*: "Horses appeared to be
more to him than human beings; he understood and could cure so
many of their ailments that the veterinary surgeon had seldom to
be sent for by Candleford Green horse-owners." Nor were horses
his only patients: "If a cow had a difficult calving, or a pig went
off its food, or an infirm old dog had to be put away, Matthew was
sent for."

As with gardens and small boats, the man who works most
understands most. The MFH may be a noted steeplechaser; the
vet and the breeder will possess a scientific knowledge; but were I
about to buy a horse or break one, I would consult those curry-
comb men whom John Masefield collected under the name of
Huntsman Dawe:

> The horses in stable loved their straw.
> "Good-night, my beauties," Said Robin Dawe.

On Top of the World

"The mountains here are all accessible to the summit, and furnish prospects no less surprising and with more variety than the Alps themselves." Who made that claim? Was he a cameraman climbing the Andes? A hunter in Africa? A botanist in the Pyrenees? Not at all; the words are taken from Father West's *Guide to the Lakes,* which was published in 1778 and then re-published every three years until 1812, as though to prove the popularity of Westmorland and Cumberland among those whom Wordsworth described as "Persons of taste, and feeling for Landscape". Wordsworth's own *Guide to the Lakes* still out-tops all others in the same genre. It first appeared in 1810, as an anonymous preface to a guidebook by his friend, Rev. Joseph Wilkinson. In 1820 it was included among a selection of Wordsworth's poems. Two years later it appeared separately, and was hailed by the *Edinburgh Review* as "full of fine feeling and fine philosophy. He analyses the whole country, and shews all the sources of pleasure which it is peculiarly fitted to yield to enlightened and thoughtful minds" (motorways had not then accelerated Man's inhumanity to Nature). In 1835 the essay assumed its final form and title, *A Guide Through the District of the Lakes in the North of England, with A Descriptive of the Scenery, etc. For the Use of Tourists and Residents.* Despite Wordsworth's letters to the *Morning Post,* progress invaded Lakeland, disguised as the Kendal and Windermere Railway. As a result, the 1835 edition of the *Guide* was encumbered with tips for tourists, trips for tandems, hints for herbalists, and (to quote the publisher) "several new routes and approaches to the Lakes, by railway and steam communication . . ." Posterity has misinterpreted Wordsworth's demand that the Lake District be regarded as "a sort of national property, in which every man has a right and interest who has an eye to perceive and a heart to enjoy." Perceptive enjoyment is incompatible with heavy traffic and caravan sites. John Ruskin, who lived near to Coniston Water in Lancashire, was speaking to the wind when he said "the pursuit of science should constantly be stayed by the love of beauty . . ."

The word "Lakeland" was first recorded in 1829, but "Lakers" had been known since 1798. The spate of books about the district can be traced to William Hutchinson's *Excursion* of 1733, followed by the *Tours* of William Pennant and Arthur Young. The former did justice to England's highest mountain: "Skiddaw," he reported, "rises gently to a height that sinks the neighbouring hills . . ." Arthur Young, on the other hand, believed that only a painter could set the scene: "Would to heaven I could unite . . . the glowing brilliancy of Claud, with the romantic wildness of Salvator Rosa . . ." Not every Augustan traveller had a head for heights. Daniel

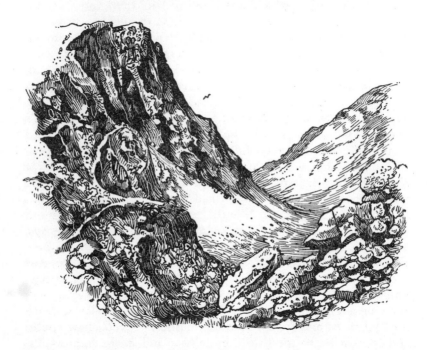

Defoe found a bone to pick with Rochdale: "the town," he complained, "is situate so remote, so out of the way, so at the very foot of mountains . . ." The older the century, the greater its aversion from mountains. In 1697 Celia Fiennes rated the Northumbrian fells precipitous: "as my man rode up that sort of precipice or steep his horses heeles cast up water at every step." In 1692 John Ray felt impelled to defend mountains "because they have been lookt by some as Warts and superfluous Excresences, of no use or benefit . . ." John Leyland, official antiquary to Henry

VIII, found the Caernarvonshire peaks "horrible with the sight of bare stones". William Camden found the Yorkshire dales "rough all over, and unpleasant to see". Michael Drayton found the Worcestershire Beacon "terrible and grim". As late as 1767 Thomas Gray found Borrowdale a terrifying place: "passing a brook called Barrow-beck, we entered Borrowdale; the crags named Lowdore-banks begin now to impend terribly over the way, and more terribly, when you learn that three years since an immense mass of rock tumbled at once from the brow . . ."

A clear day in autumn, before the blizzards descend, is a fine time for reaching the roof of Britain. The crowds have departed; the air is a spur; the summits wear enough snow to make you feel intrepid but not in trepidation. I have done some clambering in my time; once to the peak of Ben Nevis, and once to within a few hundred yards of it, where deep snow barred the way. Another favourite is Plynlimon, which I first scaled through mist and sleet, literally following in a shepherd's footsteps; but when I reached the top the sun came out to greet me, and I found a wooden signpost saying *Source of the Severn*.

A third favourite is Cross Fell in Cumberland, apex of the Pennine Way. But beware the Helm Wind. It may exceed ninety miles an hour, and will juggle a rick of hay as though it were a wisp of straw. On Cross Fell, as on any other summit, only a fool deliberately defies a falling glass. Wisdom watches the weather, and takes a fellow traveller. In Perthshire I scaled Ben Lawers, partly to see the remains of a cairn that had been built there in 1878, under the auspices of Malcolm Fergusson, a local patriot. The cairn once stood sixteen feet high, that being the distance by which Fergusson raised the summit of Ben Lawers from 3,984 to 4,000 feet: "A guid roon' number," as the gillie remarked.

Among my near-neighbours at home is Dunkery Beacon, the summit of Exmoor. In the old days we climbed it via a narrow path which did not invite callers. Nowadays motor vehicles deposit people and paper within a stone's throw of the pinnacle. In November, however, the moor knows them not. On a clear day Dunkery stands in glorious isolation, steadfastly answering the gaze of the Black Mountain near Llandovery in Wales. Sheer idleness dissuaded me from conquering the Black Mountain. Having crawled pretty well to the top, I sat back in the sun, and nearly went to sleep.

In some parts of the world climbing is a matter of life and death, but in Britain it ought to be light-hearted, a pastime of amateurs, not the penance of professionals. When you do reach the summit you are at liberty to commune with yourself and with whatever (if anything at all) you believe to be greater than yourself. Such a climber was Wordsworth, who, although he had been born their son, bestowed a father's blessing on

> ye mountains, and ye lakes
> And sounding cataracts, ye mists and winds
> That dwell among the hills where I was born.

A Gentleman of the Road

From a gap in the hedge he emerged backwards and on all fours, preceded by a saucepan. Having attached that utensil to a piece of string around his waist, he spat, lighted the stump of a cigarette, blew his nose between thumb and forefinger (which necessitated relighting the stump), and then rummaged among the wayside grass, as though he had lost something. That he had not lost it was proven by the unconcern with which, when he saw me, he stood upright and began to hum a cracked tune.

He was greyhaired, unshaven, slovenly. He wore a check cap; a naval officer's bridge coat which had been stripped of its buttons and braid; someone's evening dress trousers; and a non-pair of brown shoes. He introduced himself by asking whether I happened to have such a thing as a match. I shook my head.

"Or a lighter?"

"I'm afraid not."

"Non-smoker, eh?"

"A pipe now and again. But seldom out of doors. And never when it's raining."

"Don't much matter anyway," he muttered, balancing the fag-end on his left-thumbnail and then flicking it over the hedge, with as much gravity as though he were spinning a coin to decide choice of stations in the Boat Race. Since I had not the heart to shun his company, I was obliged to suffer it for the best part of a mile; an experience which might have proved informative had I not already encountered many of his kind; sly, whining, insolent. Although I had never seen him before, he insisted that his name was known in these parts: "People," he added, "pay a lot of attention to names. That's why I changed my own."

"Indeed?"

"Percy would only make 'em giggle. But Benjamin . . . that's something they can get their teeth into. 'Here's old Benje.' they say . . . and out comes the teapot. And when that happens you're halfway to getting a tanner."

"Only sixpence?" I queried, coining the old English currency.

"Coupla bob maybe. Or perhaps a pair o' trarziz." He resumed his theme: "Very important is names. Take Julius Caesar. Would he have been bumped orf if his Mum had christened him Percy? 'Course not. Nobody bothers to poison Percy."

"But Caesar wasn't . . ."

"Wasn't called Percy. That's exactly what I'm saying. It's the same wiv the other professions, guv. What does Bert Jones do if he wants to sing in hopra? Why, he calls hisself Roberto Spaghetti."

Despite his own profession, I noticed that the gentleman of the road walked slowly and without zest; so I asked how many miles he covered in a day.

"As few as possible," he boasted. "If I can find a nice dry barn, I stay just long enough to stop 'em shouting 'Git art of it.' " He drew a deep and wheezy breath: "Can't beat a life in the open hair. Nobody tells *me* what to do. I'm my own master I am."

I could not help feeling that the masterful vagabond was a poor argument in favour of freewill, for his sniffings and scratchings betrayed many compulsions, and I doubted that he was following the example of the vagabond in Yeats's poem:

> "Time to put off the world and go somewhere
> And find my health again in the sea air,"
> Beggar to beggar cried . . .

Nevertheless, he continued to praise his way of life.

"I love the country, I do."

"But you weren't born in it."

"I was, you know. At a circus in Bedford. Or was it Bradford? Anyway, when my old man got fed up wiv playing the donkey's hindlegs, he switched to the fish-and-chip business in Battersea."

"Hav you tried any regular employ . . ."

"Never, guy. Work don't come natural to me. Between ourselves, I've always regarded it as a shocking waste of time." He gave me a shifty glance: "I don't suppose your sort could even imagine what the working classes owe to the bloke as invented National Assistance. In the bad old times we had to work or starve. But nowadays . . ." He halted in the middle of the lane, and with a dramatic gesture whipped open his bridge coat: "Do I show any signs of wasting away?"

When he understood that I was not going to give him money he dropped his air of camaraderie: "This is where we part. There's a place under that rileway bridge. Cool in summer, dry in winter. Plenty o' wood for a fire. Water laid on from the stream. And a fieldful o' rabbits." He hitched up his saucepan: "So long, guv, and thanks for nothing."

With a tinkle of tinware he climbed the barbed wire, and headed toward a disused railway line, leaving me to reflect that a year or two of deep analysis might have uncovered the reasons why he had shirked the responsibilities of maturity in favour of a mean and sterile dream world. Dorothy Wordsworth's *Journal* describes some very different tramps, victims of a society which neglected the needy as flagrantly as we now penalise those whose skill and labour achieve prosperity: "we met a woman with two little girls, one in her arms, the other, about four years old, walking by her side, a pretty thing, but half-starved. The mother, when we accosted her, told us that her husband had left her, and gone off with another woman . . . Then her fury kindled, and her eyes rolled about. I was moved, and gave her a shilling . . ."

Charles Lamb maintained that charity ought to take beggars on trust: "When a poor creature come before thee," he urged, "do not stay to enquire whether the 'seven small children' in whose name he implores thy assistance, have a veritable existence. Rake not the bowels of unwelcome truth, to save a half-penny. It is good to believe him." Compassion can never be misguided, but it does often mislead. Would Lamb really have us believe that the tramp wandered for the sake of fresh air and fine views? Edward Thomas wandered far more widely, and with an incomparably greater interest in what he saw, yet he supported a wife and children, often by undertaking hackwork. Even in the remotest countryside he washed, pared his nails, and abstained from pilfering. He cared somewhat for mankind, and did not brood solely on his own misfortunes. Above all, he was spared the delusion which hopes that a shaggy beard will conceal a mediocre mind. In Lamb's day the state of the market drove many industrious souls to beg for their bread, but in our day a tramp is the victim rather of his temperament than of society's disregard. If only for his own sake we must cease to clothe him in the raiment of romance.

An Evening at Home

We are strange creatures, all of us, and often amazed by our own inconstancy. Two weeks ago I stood on a hill, mourning the end of the mellow autumn; this evening I sit by a fire, savouring the approach of hoary winter. Purists may protest that, so far from savouring winter, I am eluding it behind a barricade of beech logs, crumpets, candlelight, and the shrill sounds which a dog utters when, in his dreams, he outstrips the hare. Winter, however, cannot be wholly eluded. You may raise the temperature, but you cannot quell the storm. Outside, the wind is as shrill as Cathy's voice when she called to Heathcliff through the snow. It thumps the four walls of the house, and, finding the door locked, plunges down the chimney, preceded by a fanfare of smoke. If I draw aside the curtains, and peer at the distant hill, the lights of the only visible house seem to wink; yet they burn steadily enough; the illusion is created by treetops swaying across the window.

How, I wonder, are the birds faring? Even while they sleep, their feathers must be ruffled by an east wind rasping the naked hedgerows. With inward vision I follow a path over the hills to a moorland tavern whose signboard creaks on its rusty hinge, eerie as a robber hanging in chains. I know, too, the ruts along the green track beyond that tavern; brimmed now with rain, their waves beat against red earth, swirling the fallen leaves. And the mountains? There is no rain atop Ben Nevis tonight. Any moisture that does fall thereon is snow. A man might climb so far as the bend which takes a last look at the hostel far below; but all beyond is hip-high and hazardous. And the moors? You will need to be strong indeed en route for the summit of Dunkery

Beacon. You must stoop as though entering a low tunnel; and in order to breathe freely you must turn you head sideways from the gale. No lights dimple the Severn Sea this evening; only blackness and the dark rods of rain. And the Fens? If anyone is walking to Crowland, he will be wet as well as weary, blistered by a wind straight from the Steppes. Unless he finds a dyke or maybe the lee of a barn, he has no shelter from anything at all. And if he ever does reach Crowland, he will see the rain gushing in three directions because the bridge there has three roads over it.

Still shivering from those armchair journeys, I re-open my eyes, and see firelight daubing rafters, walls, books. Although the gale holds its course, and the rain its frenzy, each beat in vain against the sanctuary, the hearth, which the Romans venerated as a symbol of domestic peace and power. Entering the kitchen, I hear rainwater scalding from gutters and thence on to the drive that leads to the lane, and so downhill to a farm in the coombe. Returning to the hearth, I share William Cowper's snug reflection:

> 'Tis pleasant through the loopholes of retreat
> To peep at such a world . . .

April will be welcome when it arrives; May will be missed when it departs; but tonight the countryfolk hug their fireside *con amore*; and when in June they mow the lawn, who shall say that their content is deeper than on this wintry evening while firelight paints rainbows on books tiptoe from floor to ceiling, each book waiting patiently on our mood, never reserving to itself any kind of right; all inscribed with our own biography in so far as they were read or re-read during this or that crisis, this or that interlude of endeavour, laughter, peace. It is pleasant to share such warm security with as many other firesides as we remember or care to imagine; pleasant also to visualise the travellers who have reached home, and are at this very moment crossing their own threshold . . . windswept, mudmucked, dripping like a tree. If any should knock at our own door, seeking shelter, there they will find it, for that is the least we can do by way of warming the outcasts, who, like Lear's jester, cry: "Here's a night pities neither wise man nor fool."

They tell me that most of the average fireside talk is now uttered by television. I take their word for it. I have no television. My own *soirées* are shared with persons who prefer their friendship *viva voce*. Whenever I invite or am invited, I expect to receive or to be received. I do not expect to be greeted with a sidelong glance: "Ah, you're just in time for Sex on Sunday. It's in colour, by the way."

Nothing excels the power of firelight to evoke good talk and times past and things to come. Starting with a dissertation on roast pig, you find that you have ended by confirming Cato, or confuting Keynes, or recalling the rector who twice trumped your ace. Sometimes, indeed, the soul's antennae both span and plumb their own solitude, so that firelight induces the intimacy of a confessional and the nakedness of a surgery. By losing ourselves we discover one another. But when the time comes to switch on the light, we blink at its brightness, and are apt to suppose that reality is a matter of voltage.

Having taken his fill of reverie, a truly convivial countryman offers his fireside—or accepts another's—for the sake of good companionship. In summer, no doubt, he and his cronies will lean on a gate, talking till the cows come home; but there are not many midnights which invite an out-of-doors discussion, nor many whose hearth would not look better for a fire. And when at last the guests have gone home, or we have returned to our own hearth, how pleasant it is to end the day with a glass or a cup of something cordial, and those evanescent shadows polishing the floor, the silver, the brass, the beams, the books. So, after all, my evening at home was less egocentric than at first appeared, for it fulfilled a large part of Hilaire Belloc's hospitable ambition:

> I will hold my house in the high wood
> Within a walk of the sea,
> And the men who were boys when I was a boy
> Shall sit and drink with me.

12

The Shape of Winter

If you visit the ruins of Top Withens, which was incorporated into the house called Wuthering Heights, you will notice a number of thorn trees; and having noticed, you will admire the skill with which Emily Brontë used them as barometers: "gaunt thorns," she wrote, "all stretching their limbs one way, as if craving alms of the sun." Such were the power and prevalence of the north wind on a Yorkshire moor. Similar contortions are performed by trees on any land that is both high and exposed; especially on land overlooking the sea. Many examples can be found among the thorns on Exmoor, 1,600 feet above the Severn Sea. When wind and frost have done their work, those thorns resemble rather a besom than a tree, for their trunks incline at an angle of forty-five degrees, and the branches extend parallel with the ground. Ruskin diagnosed the arboreal arthritis: "The whole bough bends together," he observed, "affected throughout with curvature in each of its parts and joints . . . You will find it difficult to bend the angles out of the youngest sapling . . . and absolutely impossible, with a strong bough."

Trees cannot grow unless the temperature reaches at least fifty-one degrees Fahrenheit for at least eight weeks of each year. Since the mean temperature in the north falls by about one degree with every 270 feet, it follows that no British tree will take root above 2,200 feet (and experience has shown that such trees must be protected from the wind). On the east coast of Scotland, at

1,200 feet, only the hardiest species survive. They are bent, gnarled, and salty (a strong gale may drive the spray fifty miles inland). The highest trees I ever saw are near Ashgill in Cumberland where Scots firs at 1,600 feet stand as high as a house; but at 2,000 feet the stragglers are scarcely as tall as a man.

England contains some classic trees. Among them, in Shropshire, is the Boscobel Oak whose hollow trunk concealed Charles II and Colonel Careless when they eluded the rebels after the Battle of Worcester. I was once shown an oak near Boscobel House, with a plaque stating that it "had the honour of sheltering from his foes His Majesty King Charles the Second". Those loyal sentiments are less than accurate because the hollow tree had long since disappeared. Prompted by her Germanic entourage, Queen Victoria deleted from the Prayer Book a form of thanksgiving for Oak Apple Day, 29th May, the anniversary of the birth and also of the Restoration of Charles II. Throughout the Hanoverian dynasty many parish priests had observed the day. In 1768, for example, the Rev. James Woodforde of Somerset noted in his diary: "I read Prayers this morning . . . being 29 of May the Restoration of King Charles II." A century later the Rev. Francis Kilvert of Herefordshire noted: "Oak-apple day and the children all came to school wearing breast-knots of oak leaves." At Chelsea Hospital, which was founded by Charles II, the redcoated veterans celebrate Oak Apple Day by parading before the King's statue, wearing a sprig of oak leaves. A comparable ceremony is observed at another haven for ex-servicemen, the Lord Leycester Hospital at Warwick.

Few English trees have been so revered as the ash which forced its way through the floor of a cottage at Tunstead in Derbyshire, the home of James Brindley, builder of canals. When I visited the site I was shown an ash that is still called Brindley's Tree. In North Devon the mediaeval Forest of Exmoor was said to have contained only two trees, Hoar Oak and Kite Oak. The former collapsed in 1658; its successor lived from 1662 till 1916, and was replaced by a sapling which soon became stunted.

During November the trees assume an austere grandeur which led Dorothy Wordsworth to exclaim: "what a beautiful thing God made winter to be, by stripping the trees, and letting us see their shapes and forms." George Meredith had an ear for the wind on the heath:

And round the oak a solemn roll
Of organ harmony ascends,
And in the upper foliage sounds
A symphony of distant seas.

The winter grass withers, and we do not care; flowers fade, and we soon forget; but the death of a tree disturbs us because it mimes too vividly our own decease: "Cut down," we say, "in his prime." Walking one day through the parish of Eversley, Charles Kingsley noticed a newly-felled tree lying beside the lane. His curate, who was with him at the time, recalled the incident: "He stopped, and looked for a moment or so, and then, bursting into tears, exclaimed, 'I have known that tree ever since I came into the parish.' " Even when a tree *must* go—for our own safety or for another's convenience—still we are oppressed by the foreboding which affected Gerald Gould:

In the green quiet wood, where I was used,
In summer, to a welcome calm and dark,
I found the threat of murder introduced
By scars of white paint on the wrinkled bark.

Few people are so realistic that they consciously and perpetually marvel at the Universe. The majority seldom emerge from their cocoon of cash-and-carry. We have built our house upon a vortex of superficial ingenuity. Darwin in his age lost all taste for poetry and music: "My mind," he complained, "seems to have become a kind of machine for grinding general laws out of a large collection of facts." Yet Darwin in his youth had relished what he called "one of the most glorious spectacles in the world, the first bursting into full foliage of the leafless tree." Thoreau—a practical man who built his own house—went to the other extreme by communing with the forest: "I have," he would tell his friends, "an appointment with a tree" . . . and forthwith he strode off to keep it. Another mystic, Edward Carpenter, came close to the root of the matter: "The day was still," he wrote, "and there was no movement in the branches, yet in that moment the tree was no longer a separate or separable organism, but a vast being ramifying far into space, sharing and uniting the life of Earth and Sky, and full of most amazing activity." William Blake expressed it more briefly: "A fool sees not the same tree that a wise man does."

In Time for Christmas

As I approached the barn I heard the farmer say to his man:
"He drove down this hill . . . and 'twasn't more than five minutes
ago, mind 'ee . . . drove that fast I said to myself, 'Davey's won
the pools at last!' "

"Oh?" exclaimed the ploughman, perking up.

"Anyway, he had to brake on account o' they old ewes was
crossing the lane. So when he pulled up I said to 'en, 'Have 'ee
won the treble chance?' "

"Had he?"

"Could be, 'cause he just grinned, and yelled 'Seven'."

"Seven, eh?" The ploughman scratched his nape. "Hundreds,
did he mean, or thousands?"

"Whatever it was . . . thousands or hundreds . . . 'twill come in
handy. Real Santa Clause stuff, eh? Just in time for Christmas."

And with that they parted, the farmer into his barn, the ploughman into a meadow; leaving me to puzzle over Davey's swift
descent of a hazardous hill. Even if he had won a million, I
thought, it was unlike him to emulate Jehu's crazy chariot. He was
a steady man; a bell-ringer, a book-reader, three years married
to a girl from Somerset. Davey was more likely to lean on his
spade, admiring the view, than to step on the gas, screeching the
tyres.

Where four lanes meet, in the middle of nowhere, stands my
nearest post-box. I had just thrust some Christmas cards into it
when a lorry-load of heifers drew up; quite an event at such a
spot. We got talking, and presently the driver asked whether I
had seen Davey.

"I believe he passed here about twenty minutes ago" I replied.

"Ah, I thought 'twas Davey. Does he always drive so fast?"

"On the contrary."

"Or drink?"

"Two pints on Saturday, they say."

"Drunk or sober, he grazed my rear mudguard that close I
heard the paintwork complain. Ah, *and* he swore."

"Davey did?"

"Sounded to me like a swear. 'Heaven!' he shouted."

"Are you sure it wasn't *seven*?"

"Seven? Seven what?"

"That's something I don't quite know. For his sake, though, I hope it's thousands."

"Oh, so that's it." The driver switched on his engine. "A great one for the pools, is young Davey. Says he'll buy a farm one day, and send his eldest t'Oxford."

For a second time two men parted, neither of them any the wiser about Davey's roistering arithmetic.

There is a small village hereabouts—three or four miles from the house—containing one shop, which, when I entered it, caused me to feel as though I were following the instalments of an exciting play.

"Didn't he say," a customer was asking, "anything at all?"

"Never a word," replied the shopman. "He just poked his head round the door, and held up seven fingers. I tell 'ee, 'tis the strangest order I've ever received. Did he mean seven apples, seven loaves, or seven pound o' dog biscuit?"

"Doesn't sound like young Davey."

"That's exactly what I said. In fact, if I hadn't known the fella, I'd ha' smelt beer."

"I do truly hope there's nothing wrong with 'en. Nor with his wife neither. They were both all right, last we heard. Everything going according to plan."

Once again I departed amid deepening mystery. The more I thought about it, the less credible it appeared. I seemed to be treading in the tyre marks of fantasy. Yet it is difficult to doubt the evidence of your own senses. Were not the shopman and his customer alive and real and audibly discussing the enigma?

I seldom walk into the little town, for it lies six miles away, up-and-down-and-round-about a maze of hairpin bends, of winter-filled fords, of one-in-three gradients. However, this time I did walk, chiefly because I was still wrapt in the unsolved mystery of pools and Davey and seven and sterling. Even so, few meditations become so profound that they remain oblivious of a steep hill. Halting, therefore, on the summit, to scan the view and to refill my lungs, I forgot about young Davey, and thought instead of the old year which, though it was visibly dying, looked so hale that the blue sky and a mild air would have seemed seasonable in April. Northward and just out of sight, the Severn Sea met the

Atlantic, each glinting as vividly as the other. Southward the moor rose and, as it were, heaved without moving. Hazel catkins hung like wayside decorations for Christmas. Red as the holly berries, a robin staked his staccato claim while a thrush looked on, confident as an athlete who is reserving his own solo for a more auspicious moment. The hilltop woods gleamed like black eyebrows; how difficult it was to visualise them as they would soon become, green and fulsome and flowering: as difficult as to surround the shaggy ewes with lambs, or to people the meadow with reapers. Willy-nilly a countryman lives chiefly in the present, so that summer will dim his remembrance of bare boughs and dumb birds.

Almost before I knew it, I had joined the highway, and after another mile or so I sighted the little town, perching breezily on a hill. And the first townsfolk I met were discussing Davey.

"He's been going the rounds this morning all right."

"So I've 'eard. Even told the police station."

"Seems he can't get it off his chest quick enough. He come in yere just now, with a grin that wide it would have swallowed a Cheshire cat. But he wasn't expecting it, mind. Not yetawhile. 'January,' he used to say, 'that'll be my lucky month.' " For a fourth time I went my way, marooned in the mystery of Davey . . . his fullspeed descent of a hazardous hill, his voiceless request for seven unspecified commodities, his loud proclamation through the town.

The denouement occurred while I was buying a loaf. In dashed young Davey himself, his features alight with happiness. Turning to his cousin—who was in the bread queue—he cried: "My wife . . . our first . . . a boy . . . seven pounds!"

All Aboard

Once each week an omnibus waits at the crossroads, to collect and deliver passengers for market day in the town twelve miles away. Some people call the crossroads a hamlet. Others deny it, saying the place is only a cluster of five cottages. Probably the prohamleteers are justified because a church lies somewhere near, facing two farms. Certainly the cottagers rate themselves a hamlet in need of public transport. At least four of the elderly residents are without a car; and if the entire hamlet travelled to market by omnibus, they would decrease the congestion in the town itself. Meantime, the motor trade boasts that every Englishman will eventually own two cars; a prospect which would enable me to contemplate my own demise with an equanimity bordering on impatience, were it not that the lanes hereabouts are so car-free that some of them imperil a motorist by amazing him when he does meet another. This safe quietude is due partly to the fact that our omnibus still does ply for hire. Indeed, its once-weekly arrival causes quite a stir, not least on winter nights when a tipsy reveller, thinking that he has reached his destination, stumbles into the darkness, and discovers that he has not.

"You never heard such language," one woman complained to her neighbour. "He kept on saying, 'Am I at bloody Barnstaple?' So my old man—he used to be a petty officer, and they'm never short o' hepithets—my old man said to 'en, 'No, you'm bloody well *not* at Barnstaple. And by the course you'm steering you never will be.' "

"So what happened?"

"So the fella asked when the next bus was due. I couldn't help but laugh, you know, 'cause my old man said to him, 'In seven days' time.' Of course, I put it down to the wages they earn. I mean, he can't ha' been above seventeen. Where does a boy his age find the money to get drunk? And 'twasn't beer, you understand. Even from where we stood he had gin written all over 'en. Anyhow, the last we saw he was being sick in the phone box. Normally we give anyone a lift, but my husband said to me afterwards, 'If we'd took that creature in the car his curls would ha' clogged the gearbox.' "

Such an inebriate castaway is, of course, rare. Most of the market passengers are matrons; bonneted, basketed, buxom, beaming. Some of them do have a car, but on weekdays their husbands take it to lay a hedge or to plough a field. Others never did have a car, and never will: "It costs twenty-five quid afore you can drive 'en. Then there's the insurance. And first of all you've to buy the damned thing. I told my husband straight: 'You please yourself,' I said. 'It's your money. But if you *do* buy a car you won't find me getting into it.' So after a while he said, 'Oh, in that case . . .' I never interfere, mind. A man must do as he likes. I just say what I feel, and leave it at that."

The most eventful omnibus I ever boarded was Scottish, outward bound to John o' Groat's. After two days on the train, I had reached Wick, the terminus, in time to be greeted by a blizzard. One pessimistic passenger said to the driver: "Willie, we'll no' make it." "We must make it," Willie replied, glancing at a little girl who sat beside him. "You's my wee grand-daughter, and if she's no' in bed by seven o'clock I'll ne'er hear the end of it." As we bumped and slithered along that wild coast, with the wind howling, and the snow slashing, I overheard several private lives: "The doctor," one woman was saying, "told me no' to worry. 'If we canna cure your husband,' he promised, 'we'll kill him. And either way you'll be better off than you are at present.' Aye, he's a rare comic is Dr Sinclair." A greyhaired minister remarked to a trawlerman: "So the dominie picked himself up and said to young Fergus, 'What a coincidence. I can see the rest o' that banana skin in your hand . . .' " A mother whispered to her son: "I'm thinking you'll no' be able to travel half-price much longer. It's three years since you were nearly twelve." An old woman lamented the folly of youth: "What could I tell the lass that we hadn'a told her afore she married him?"

In wildest Wales, where they sing like nightingales, and play Rugby like Machiavelli, you will hear the bus conductor saying to the churchwarden: "He put the ball in the scrum and then he whisked it out before the referee could . . . well, man, even the Bishop of Builth would have said tut-tut."

En route from Barbon to Kirkby Lonsdale, a passenger in the bi-weekly bus announces that an elderly farmer has lately married his housekeeper: 'Owd James Douthwaite mun soon regret eet. Three pun a week he paid yon woman. Happen she'll be asking six now she's wed. 'Jamie,' I told him, 'at thine age there's nowt she'll gie for six pun as she wasna' gieing for three.' "

When my friends in Ulster and Eire have ended their uncivil war, I hope once again to be jolted merrily while Finn the fisherman tells the passengers how his film-star daughter climbed from Hibernia to Hollywood: "When she was seventeen she was earning twenty pounds a week. When she was eighteen she was earning forty pounds a week. When she was nineteen she was earning sixty pounds a week. And today, my friends, at the advanced age of twenty, she's only to open her mouth, and it costs someone a thousand dollars. Ah, and she never forgets her old father's birthday. The first year she was away she sent me some bedsocks. Fitted like a glove, they did. In fact I still wear one of 'em as a nightcap. And on my last birthday . . . the priest wrongfully announced it as my seventieth on account of his arithmetic was mental . . . what do you think she sent me for that?"

"Pigs?" suggests a fellow-passenger.

"It's a common fella you are, Patrick Murphy, steeped in the swill o' your own sty. But I'll tell you what she did send, having first paused to let you recover from your astonishment before you do hear it. She sent me . . . express mail and prepaid, remember . . . that daughter o' mine, dwelling in the celestial penthouse o' stardom . . . she sent me a blank cheque for five hundred guineas. And if that's not a miracle, then this is . . . the cheque didn't bounce!"

The horse has gone, and the wagon with it; most of the rural railways have gone, and with them a century of grapevine gossip; but the rural omnibus abides, bearing in up-to-date fashion a mixed cargo whose talk is often timeless because it concerns the climate, the crops, the price of bread, the pains of rheumatism, the new rector, the old squire, and the woman next door.

Gale Force

Soon after teatime, when the gale was at its height, I lit a hurricane lamp, donned an oilskin, and walked to the woodshed, which is a derelict cottage in a hilltop paddock. Seldom had I seen the rain so violent, and the trees in such anguish. Within six seconds my oilskin was a head-to-heel cataract. Stumbling up the narrow path, I reached the shed, where I hung the lamp on a nail, and then looked around.

Although the building lacked a door or any windowpane, it seemed as snug as a haven and as sturdy as a light-house, for the walls—nearly two feet thick—repelled the rain, and subdued the roar. In some places those walls retained their plaster; in others the bare stone was lichened. The ceiling had long since disappeared, but the roof remained sound. Glancing up at it, I seemed to have entered a church; an illusion that was heightened by the bedroom windows, which might have been clerestoreys. Built two centuries ago, the cottage had spent the last twenty years as a hen-house. Indeed, when I first took possession the floor was covered with a foot of chicken dung. This I gave to the garden, thereby exposing the flagstones in the cottage.

Forgetful that I had come to saw wood, I sat on an upturned wheelbarrow, listening to the gale as it tumbled the leaves in and out of a doorless doorway. Then a gust jerked the lantern, so that the illusory church became an imaginary ship whose oil lamps swayed while the sea surged against the side. But when I noticed the axe and a length of chain hanging from the stone wall, the maritime makebelieve gave way to a mediaeval castle. I was about to get on with the job, when the logs themselves—stacked high against one wall—suggested a fourth change of scene, this time transforming the castle into a wine cellar. After that, I caught sight of a besom broom, and would have felt only half-surprised if a Welsh-hatted witch had commandeered it en route to join the Valkyrie. Before the spade and the shovel and the pickaxe and the sledge hammer could evoke any more flights of fancy, I removed my oilskin, placed a bough across the barrow, and began to saw.

For the felling of timber a mechanised saw is, as we say, the answer; but when it comes to sawing small logs I find the answer too shrill. And not only too shrill but also too lazy. Machines mow timber as monotonously as they mow grass, without sharing their exertions with the mechanic. But a strong right arm and a well-sharpened blade may be likened to a horse and rider, each testing the other's hardihood. It is the difference between playing Rugby and watching a Cup Final. Some people, seeing my pile of hand-sawn logs, would exclaim: "What a waste of time." It is true, of course, that the hours which are spent in sawing wood cannot be passed in reading Pindar nor even in scanning the Dow Jones Industrial Index. A second truism is this: the years which are given to watching television are taken away from exercising the body in fresh air. Meanwhile, my own exercise proved so agreeable that it quite obliterated the gale outside. Indeed, half a hundred logs had been cut before I noticed that the lantern, instead of flickering, now burned as steadily as a nursery night-

light. The leaves, which had scampered in and out like irresolute
mice, lay still. And the rain had ceased.

I peered through the doorway. The trees were calm: stars shone
where clouds had raced; and among them the moon presided. Far
below, the stream through the valley was in spate and just audible,
soft as a contented sigh. In short, the gale had spent itself.
Presently a sheep bleated, and was followed by two owls from the
paddock, a most friendly sound, not at all eerie, except to Gothick
imaginations. Returning to my task, I disposed of one more bough,
and then stacked the night's work. No longer accompanied by the
music of a saw, the present stillness became more noticeable
than the past shrillness. Very loud were the logs as I chucked
them into the barrow. Even the stacking of them was loud, like
the click of billiard balls many times amplified. When a log toppled
from its perch the effect was far more startling than the owls. The
task completed, I gazed complacently at the wood pile, enough
to warm the winter and to thaw the spring, with a firm foundation for next autumn's wind and rain. Connoisseurs, no doubt,
would separate their various woods, but since my own trees are
chiefly ash and beech from overgrown hedgerows, I lump them
together. After all, anyone can identify cherry and apple and oak,
and then select them for special occasions, such as Christmas,
birthdays, and the visits of townsfolk who regard log fires as an
eccentric luxury, on a par with mulled ale and this morning's eggs.

The felling of a hale tree is always sad. Sometimes, however, a
tree impedes the true wellbeing of mankind, and then it must go.
Several of mine went in order to reveal the vista and to admit air
among damp places. But one impediment was spared—a gnarled
veteran, bent by the wind that blows from the sea—and there he
stands, like the survivor in Muriel Stuart's winterscape:

> When swerving seagulls scream and strive
> O'er the brown furrows driven by men,
> His dole of berries keep alive
> A yellowhammer and a wren.

Foresters plant for a future which they will never witness. Even
the sawyer takes a chance when, in a corner of his shed, he stacks
the elm that needs three years to ripen. Intent upon less distant
prospects, I loaded the barrow with some apple and cherry that

had been felled two summers ago, and would therefore burn merrily without ado.

An hour later the logs blazed, the candles glowed, and the first of the guests, standing on the threshold, exclaimed: "You certainly know how to make yourself comfortable."

Time and Tide

Some villagers dislike the way in which others celebrate Christmas. "I can cope with the shopping," one housewife remarks, "but not with the religious business." Other villagers express a different sort of disapproval. They feel that Mammon has become over-zealous in its jubilation at the birth of Jesus. They wish that the uncommitted revellers would transfer their December spree to New Year's Day (calling it, perhaps, Turkeytime), thereby allowing the faithful to observe Christmas fittingly and in quietness. One's first reaction is to dismiss that wish as Puritanism pulling a long face. Is it really sinful to relish the holly, the ivy, the crackers, the pudding? Would not the Founder of Christianity approve the ancient custom of sharing goodwill by exchanging gifts? He would certainly approve the pleasure which Santa Claus gives to children. But what of the Christmas Eve cabaret and the Boxing Day booze? Such jovial interludes seem an inappropriate way of accepting an Incarnation which many of the celebrants reject. It is as though the Cornish were to use the Passover as an excuse for demonstrating in favour of Home Rule for Truro.

"To every thing there is a season," says the Bible, "and a time to every purpose under the sun . . . a time to weep, and a time to laugh; a time to mourn, and a time to dance." Among those whom it truly concerns, Christmas is indeed a time of rejoicing. But it is also a solemn season, when thoughtful youth tries to imagine the nature of time, and when older people try to imagine the nature of timelessness. For my own part, since I live near the sea, I make a Christmas pilgrimage to a certain small cove, knowing that I shall be the only visitor. There is no road to the cove. You must either sail or walk. The walk itself follows a stream through a ravine. On one side the land is covered with bracken and ling; the other side is shale, so steep that not even the ewes dare trust their nimbleness. After about a mile the two summits draw close together, hiding a large segment of sky, and then the stream enters the sea; not at a sandy beach, but over pebbles and boulders. Northward in clear weather you can sight the Welsh hills; westward the Atlantic leads to solitude.

Except for some clifftop holly bushes, the cove lacks any Christmas decorations. No cardboard angels trumpet the glad tidings that Lunch Is Now Being Served. No placards exhort you to buy

the Christmas spirit. Robert Bridges echoed the sea's disregard of man-made calendars:

> The sea keeps not the Sabbath day,
> His waves come rolling evermore;
> His noisy toil grindeth the shore,
> And all the cliff is drencht with spray.

Nunquam minus solus quam cum solus: least alone when most alone. Counting them from a distance, you bless those whom you love. You examine your attitude toward those whom you do not love. You compute the extent to which mankind is outnumbered by its fellow creatures, the birds, the fishes, the animals, insects, reptiles, plants, trees. You ponder the trustful ignorance of Sir Thomas Browne, a staunch upholder of the Church of England: "The whole Creation is a mystery, and especially that of Man." Or you may prefer Schweitzer's more eclectic submission: "All thought which thinks itself out to the end must find that end in mysticism."

On some days the cove is cold, grey, shrill; on others it becomes mild, colourful, quiet. During calm weather the ebb tide sounds no louder than a lapping sigh, but during a storm the waves climb the cliff, or try to, until they collapse halfway, and are swallowed by the next mountaineer. Nothing on such days is distinctly audible, because all things—waves, rocks, gulls, wind—submerge their identity in a single quivering roar. Generally, however, the cove lies midway between those extremes, as though to reflect a typical day in an average life, neither tempestuous nor idyllic. This morning, for example, a mist hides the Welsh hills, yet two ships are visible, and the gulls mount up like eagles to an eyrie out of sight. A baulk of timber prods the foot of the cliff, causing you to wonder whether it rose from a wreck or fell from a farm. Then a curlew calls, insistently announcing that its nickname ought to be "Coor-lie" . . . "Coor-lie." Somewhere in the bracken a red stag may lurk, waiting to destroy a field of root crops. Above the bracken a kestral hovers, so astutely endowed that it knows to fly forward at exactly the same speed as the wind which blows it back. Our Jacobean forefathers named the bird well, "wind-hover."

Presently the mist clears, revealing Wales, and posing a question: why do the Calvinist Welsh emphasise Christmas while the Calvinist Scots tend to pass it by? A few Welsh farmers still observe *Plygain* or First Light, a rustic carol-singing which they inherited from the Celts. *Plygain* seems to have originated as a service that was held immediately after Midnight Mass on Christmas Eve, but during the later Middle Ages it was commonly held at dawn on Christmas Day, whereafter the younger singers, instead of seeking their beds, assembled at a farmhouse to eat *cyflaith* or treacle toffee.

"The sea," said Euripides, "washes away the ills of man." It certainly cuts him down to size, urging him to consider whence he came, whither he goes, and for what purpose, if any at all, his troubled voyage was undertaken. Such considerations heighten the fellowship which men of goodwill share by means of Christmas cards, Christmas gifts, Christmas carols, and those resonant New Year bells whose peal led Tennyson to hope that they would one day

> Ring in redress to all mankind.